TRUTH, HOPE, AND POWER

DOUGLAS E. WILLIAMS

Truth, Hope, and Power: The Thought of Karl Popper

UNIVERSITY OF TORONTO PRESS
Toronto Buffalo London

© University of Toronto Press 1989
Toronto Buffalo London
Printed in Canada

ISBN 0-8020-2643-5

Printed on acid-free paper

Canadian Cataloguing in Publication Data

Williams, Douglas E., 1949–
Truth, hope, and power

Bibliography: p.
Includes index.
ISBN 0-8020-2643-5

1. Popper, Karl Raimund, Sir, 1902–
– Political and social views. I. Title.

B1649.P64W5 1989   192   c88-094886-8

This book has been published with the help of a grant from the Social Science
Federation of Canada, using funds provided by the Social Sciences and
Humanities Research Council of Canada.

Contents

Preface

There seems little purpose in recording hits on a
target that has no existence outside our own minds.
John Dunn

This study is an interpretation of the social and political thought of Karl
Popper, one of the most heralded yet controversial philosophers of our
time. I hope to present a more coherent, accurate, and systematic account
of Popper's thought and of its relevance to students of politics and society
than is currently available. Anyone familiar with the vast commentary
on his thought might reasonably ask, 'Will the real Karl Popper please
stand up?' So radically disparate and, by and large, misleading are the
accounts currently in vogue.[1]

I see few scholarly values, present or future, being served by allowing
Popper's commentators to score 'hits' against a 'Popper' (or an alleged
part of a 'Popper') that simply does not exist.[2] And the same is even
more true of those who enlist Popper's ideas in support of causes that
he detests – scepticism, relativism, and historicism, for example.[3] I have
tried to remedy these confusions about Popper's thought by, first, emphasizing certain historical and contextual factors in the structure and
development of Popper's ideas and, second, allowing Popper's own formulations to take precedence over those of his commentators. The unity
of Popper's philosophy lies in its moral dimension, his life-long determination to conserve in a distinctively Kantian fashion the intellectual
foundations of hope and progress that human autonomy requires, the
belief that mind can and should be decisive in practical affairs no less
than in the struggle with nature – the twin pillars of the Enlightenment
and modern liberalism alike. Given the nature of our times – a century

of 'total' war, endless crises, and one intellectual revolution after another – such an endeavour is no small achievement. Indeed, few thinkers in our century have possessed the intellectual powers, the courage, and the faith in humanity necessary to sustain such a project. Bertrand Russell is perhaps the last that comes to mind. If a thinker like Popper can also find hope in the prospects for the orderly growth of mind and society alike, then we certainly owe it to ourselves to pay very special attention to the structure of Popper's vision and to the source of the light he seeks to provide. Only then will its shadows, or limits, be evident.

I tried to capture the essence of my interpretation of Popper in the title of this study. Without the belief in the possibility of objective *truth* – knowledge that exists regardless of whether we acknowledge its existence or not – there is little *hope* for the 'open societies' of the Western world; liberalism has always underestimated the need to institutionalize its best interests against the threat of many forms of illiberal *power*, particularly of the 'unintended' variety. Popper's vision is a combat-toughened conception of reality, and of the corresponding rationality necessary to survive, let alone live well – the desideratum of Western political theory.

At several stages in this study, I presuppose three levels of analysis: texts, commentaries, and my judgment about Popper's legacy. I have approached Popper's works using methods from the *history* of ideas and political thought, largely because of the state of the critical debate. This literature is deeply polarized and excessively specialized and tends to neglect or severely misrepresent the unifying themes and underlying unity of Popper's philosophy. Because so many 'Poppers' have emerged within the commentary I embraced certain guide-lines from recent work in the history of political thought, where such problems are regularly encountered.

Quentin Skinner, John Dunn, and J.G.A. Pocock, among others, have disabused us of a number of anachronisms and other methodological errors in the study of political theory.[4] In his important study of Locke, for example, Dunn begins by noting: 'The claim that the account given here of Locke's argument ... is "historical" implies that its status depends upon the adequacy of its identification of Locke's own meaning ... By "historical" then, is meant an account of what Locke was talking about, not a doctrine written (perhaps unconsciously) by him in a sort of invisible ink which becomes apparent only when held up to the light (or heat) of the twentieth-century mind.'[5] And, in his now-seminal article, 'Meaning and Understanding in the History of Ideas,' Skinner similarly warns us against succumbing to 'mythologies' that belie the general danger of 'the priority of paradigms' – of our preconceptions determining our perceptions.[6]

I can see no compelling reasons for limiting the force and application of such criteria of adequacy and interpretation to texts of the past. In the first instance, they should apply equally to the study of our contemporaries, particularly in the absence of scholarly consensus on the individual's contribution. Only then, I believe, can criticism claim to be well informed, the product of scholarly concerns rather than some ulterior motive.

As a fierce gladiator in the realm of ideas, Popper himself has contributed to the proliferation of polarized and one-sided interpretations of his thought. Ironically, given Popper's hostility to his philosophy, Hegel observed that different philosophical systems typically evolve in such a 'one-sided' fashion, since 'they owe their origins to a reaction against what has gone before.'[7] Popper would surely agree, for 'enemies' have played a prominent role in his treatment of other thinkers and ideas. In chapter 3, I argue that the positive ideals Popper seeks to defend are essentially those of the Enlightenment and that the metaphysical structure (and limitations) of his assault on their putative 'enemies' are profoundly Kantian in inspiration and design. As far as I know, virtually nothing has been written about Popper's defence of the cultural ideals and supports of Western society. If I can amplify the sustaining unity and power of Popper's vision, then one of the primary aims of this study will have been achieved.

I assume that other related studies in the still-evolving debate between Kantianism and Hegelianism – between transcendentalists and formalists, on the one hand, and historicists and contextualists, on the other – would enlarge our understanding and appreciation of Popper's philosophy in ways other than those pursued here. This has certainly been true of the debate concerning the liberal and equally Kantian 'deontological' philosophy of John Rawls.[8] I am sure that future studies of Popper's 'consequentialism' and 'modification of utilitarianism' will prove equally illuminating in ways far beyond the scope and design of the present interpretation.

I also believe, based on research that has not found its way directly into this study, that further inquiries into the socio-political and intellectual milieu in which Popper was raised would deepen, rather than contradict, the preliminary references to such factors in chapters 1, 2, and 8. Seldom have the cultural and institutional supports necessary for genuine liberalism been as weak and vulnerable to subversion from within and without as in the Vienna of Popper's youth. By the same token, seldom has a milieu been as conducive to the sort of intellectual ferment, creativity, indeed 'revolutions,' so typical of our age. Popper's ability to discern and forge the foundations of orderly growth in mind and society amid such chaos is perhaps all the more remarkable. Fuller recognition of his context and achievement might enrich our understanding of yet-to-be-explored expanses of intellectual history and contemporary social theory – for example, contrasts and convergences between Popper's work and that of liberal compatriots such as Joseph Schumpeter, Hans Kelsen, Paul Lazarsfeld, and, above all, Friedrich Hayek.

The fact that 'enemies' have played such a large role in Popper's philosophy is certainly not an unmixed blessing, tending as it does toward a Manichean-like 'good guys, bad guys' frame of mind. Ironically, this approach tends toward precisely the sort of anachronism from which I have tried to rescue Popper's thought. But, except in chapter 6, little is said here about the obvious limitations and inadequacies of Popper's approach to earlier philosophers and ideas; the secondary literature exposes these problems at great length.[9]

What follows is primarily a constructive interpretation of Popper's attempt to conserve the intellectual and moral foundations of the liberal way of life in an essentially hostile environment. That, even within the constraints of such a positive and constructive design, there is ample need and room for criticism will be clear, particularly in chapters 6, 7, and 8 when the larger task of 'lighting the way' is behind me.

Acknowledgments

Over a number of years, research for this study received generous financial assistance from the University of British Columbia, the Canada Council, the Social Science and Humanities Research Council of Canada, the Canadian Federation of the Humanities, and the Canadian Political Science Association, which allowed me to attend the European Consortium of Political Research at the University of Essex. I would also like gratefully to acknowledge a research fellowship from Dr R.D. Fraser, dean of arts and sciences, Queen's University, Kingston, as well as a research grant from the Advisory Research Committee of Queen's University.

Gratitude of a more personal variety is due to Professors Alan C. Cairns and Robert H. Jackson, friends and teachers of mine who jointly supervised this study in its original form, as my doctoral dissertation at the University of British Columbia. I also appreciate and have learned a great deal from comments on an earlier draft of this work by Professors George A. Feaver, J.A. Laponce, and E.J. Hundert, University of British Columbia, and Robert Orr, London School of Economics and Political Science. Professor David Kettler, Trent University, was kind enough to share his vast knowledge of Karl Mannheim's thought in an extended response to chapter 6, which also had the benefit of thoughtful reactions from Professors A.P. Fell and J.W. Grove, Queen's University. And J.A.W. Gunn brought his critical care and enormous erudition to bear on the entire study in ways for which I will always be grateful. The manuscript also has benefited a great deal from the comments of several anonymous referees at the University of Toronto Press and the Canadian Federation of the Humanities.

Thanks are due also to Jan Carrick, Bernice Gallagher, Shirley Fraser,

Leisa Macdonald, and Andy Fong for their expert typing and word-processing. R.I.K. Davidson and John Parry have been extraordinarily sympathetic editors at the University of Toronto Press, making the publication of my first book at once a pleasure and an education in the best sense of the word. And, finally, I cannot begin to express my indebtedness to my wife, Cynthia. Her love, understanding, patience, and scepticism were essential to the completion of my labours; her own fine capacities as a scholar were undoubtedly also at play.

Abbreviations

The following abbreviations in the text refer to these works by Karl Popper:

CKP 'Conversation with Karl Popper,' in Bryan Magee, ed, *Modern British Philosophy* (London: Paladin 1973) 88–107

CR *Conjectures and Refutations* revised edition (New York and Evanston: Harper and Row 1964)

HSP 'How I See Philosophy,' in J. Bontempo and S.J. Odell, eds, *The Owl of Minerva* (New York: McGraw-Hill 1975) 41–55

IA 'Intellectual Autobiography,' in P.A. Schilpp, ed, *The Philosophy of Karl Popper* I (La Salle: Open Court 1974) 3–181

LP 'What Can Logic Do for Philosophy?' *Proceedings of the Aristotelian Society* supplementary volume, 22 (1948) 141–54

LSD *The Logic of Scientific Discovery* revised edition (New York and Evanston: Harper and Row 1964)

LSS 'The Logic of the Social Sciences,' in T.W. Adorno et al, *The Positivist Dispute in German Sociology* trans Glen Adey and David Frisby (London: Heineman 1976) 87–104

NSD 'Normal Science and Its Dangers,' in Imre Lakatos and Alan Musgrave, eds, *Criticism and the Growth of Knowledge* (Cambridge: Cambridge University Press 1970) 51–8

OK *Objective Knowledge: An Evolutionary Approach* (Oxford: Oxford University Press 1972)

OS I *The Open Society and Its Enemies* revised edition, vol I and II
OS II (Princeton: Princeton University Press 1971)

P I *The Postscript to the Logic of Scientific Discovery* ed W.W. Bartley III,
P II vol I, II, and III (New Jersey: Rowman and Littlefield 1982)
P III

PH   *The Poverty of Historicism* revised edition (New York and Evanston: Harper and Row 1964)

RPE   'Some Remarks on Panpsychism and Epiphenomenalism,' *Dialectica* 31 (1977) 177–86

RR   'Reason or Revolution?' *European Journal of Sociology* 11 (1970) 252–62

RSR   'The Rationality of Scientific Revolutions,' in R. Harré, ed, *Problems of Scientific Revolution* (Oxford: Oxford University Press 1975) 72–101

SB   *The Self and Its Brain* with John Eccles (Berlin, Heidelberg, London, and New York: Springer Verlag 1977)

TRUTH, HOPE, AND POWER

1

Introduction

Our political ideas and what we call the rest of our
ideas are not in fact two independent worlds, ...
Though they may come to us as separate text and
context, the meaning lies, as it always must lie, in a
unity in which the separate existence of text and
context is resolved.

Michael Oakeshott

When we begin to study the immediate historical
background of contemporary philosophy we encounter a curious fact: one of the most important
parts of this background is precisely the disappear-
ance of this background from our field of vision.[1]

W.W. Bartley III

Since time immemorial, fundamental crises of intellectual and political
orientation have set the stage for our most enduring visions of man and
society. Plato's *Republic*, the first great paradigm of Western political
analysis, was a direct response to the institutional breakdown of the
Athenian polis. As Plato recounts in his Seventh Epistle, 'Our city was
no longer administered according to the standards and practices of our
fathers ... The written law and the customs were being corrupted at an
astounding rate, [and] I, who at first had been full of eagerness for a
public career, as I gazed upon the whirlpool of public life and saw the
incessant movement of shifting currents, at last felt dizzy.'[2] Similarly, an
equally profound sense that their 'world had become deranged' moti-

vated the thought of men as diverse as Marsilius of Padua, Machiavelli, Bodin, Hobbes, Locke, Tocqueville, and Marx.[3]

As is well known by now, during the closing decades of the last century, an equally disturbing rift began to develop between what Lionel Trilling has characterized as 'the master idea of the modern age' and the dominant institutions through which it originally was expected to find expression. If it had become a commonplace since the Renaissance that 'what the mind might encompass of knowledge of the physical universe has a direct bearing upon the quality of human existence, and ... that mind can, and should be decisive in political life,'[4] by the 1870s and 1880s, few but the most naïve of thinkers could escape the radical doubt beginning to surround these claims. As 'emancipated science' pushed Western society's apparently irreversible rationalization to new heights, its most sensitive students began to decry the disruptive effect of such 'progress' on all authority, religious, philosophical, or political.[5] Nietzsche observed, with characteristic insight, 'It is the disorganizing principles that give our age its character.[6]

Amid what Arnold Haultain recalled as the 'rather smug' and 'myopic' assumptions of the late nineteenth century, with its veritable cult of material progress and nearly universal worship of a mechanistic and uncritical positivism, it became increasingly more difficult 'to assume that in any large degree men were free to choose, were conscious of their own motives, were susceptible to rational argument.'[7] The masses seemed content to reap the benefits of and continue the struggle for the material gains and improvements in their standard of living brought on by the march of industrial capitalism. But, in one intellectual community after another, a 'growing sensitivity to [the] dissolving certainties' of the two preceding centuries 'displaced the axis of social thought,' and even the soberly courageous Max Weber had to confess: 'Not summer's bloom lies ahead of us, but rather a polar night of icy darkness and hardness, no matter which group may triumph externally now.'[8] Caught in the disillusioning grip of the newly discovered worlds of Darwin, Nietzsche, Marx, Durkheim, and Freud, embatterd reason stood 'shivering timorously at the brink' and was 'obliged to walk a razor's edge' between the discredited naïvetés and confident optimism of the eighteenth century (Carlyle's 'mechanical spirit') and the irrational forces of destruction that seemed to lie in the immediate future.[9]

Doubts that the worst fears had been exaggerated were quickly dispelled as one European power after another was battered by the unparalleled social disorder, economic crisis, and institutional decay of the

1880s and 1890s. Whether one's barometer was fixed on the moral and political crisis accompanying the Dreyfus affair in France, or on the radical disorientation of traditional political ideologies and (particularly in the late-developing economies of central and southern Europe following the great depression of 1873–96),[10] or on the artificially contrived (and hence vulnerable) regimes that national unification had endowed upon Germany, Italy, and the Habsburg Empire, the 'icy darkness' seemed inescapable. Indeed, it was at hand. Thus, although scholars and intellectuals may have hoped to provide a firmer foundation for a science of society than their eighteenth- and nineteenth-century predecessors had achieved, their searching discussions and learned disputations were rudely cut short as 'forces prepared to raze rather than refurbish the Enlightenment's house of intellect'[11] transformed politics from debate and public dialogue into unbridled aggression and crude chauvinism.

Having witnessed mass destruction and a concomitant blunting of conscience on an unprecedented scale during the so-called Great War, by the 1930s 'an increasing number of European intellectuals were concluding that an attitude of political commitment was the only possible choice'[12] and basis for bringing the best in the tradition of the *philosophes* to bear upon the political turmoil of the age. This study examines the social and political thought and methodology of one of the most prolific and controversial twentieth-century champions of such Enlightenment ideals, Sir Karl R. Popper.

During the last four decades, and spanning a seemingly endless number of fields of inquiry, Popper has established himself as one of the most significant thinkers of our century. He has already been hailed as 'the John Locke of our time,' and another has argued that 'nobody can do serious work' in the fields touched by his ideas without coming to terms with his work (epistemology, metaphysics, philosophies of science, social science, and history, logic, ancient philosophy, social and political philosophy, quantum mechanics, evolutionary theory, and mathematics).[13] If one considers more practical, applied areas of endeavour (such as medicine, neurophysiology, biology, and geography), the list of tributes from noted authorities grows all the more impressive.[14] Sir Peter Medawar, Nobel laureate for medicine and keen student of scientific thought and practice, writes, 'I think Popper is incomparably the greatest philosopher of science that has ever been.' Sir John Eccles, Nobel laureate in neurophysiology, testifies to the immense impact of Popper's writings on his research: 'My scientific life owes so much to my conversion in 1945 ... to Popper's teaching on the conduct of investigations ... I have endeavoured to follow Popper in the formulation and in the investigation of fundamental problems in neurobiology.' Yet another Nobel prize-winner, noted mathematician and theoretical astronomer Sir Herman Bondi, has exclaimed: 'There is no more to science than its method, and there is no more to its method than Popper has said.'[15] Summing up the range of Popper's influence on contemporary thought and culture, and noting that this extends even to art historians (such as E.H. Gombrich) and leading politicians (the late Anthony Crosland and Sir Edward Boyle), Bryan Magee states simply that his impact is 'unapproached by that of any English-speaking philosopher now living.'[16]

For those of us who are primarily students of politics and society, Popper's writings have been equally significant, though less the object of systematic study than other facts of this thought.[17] In his biography of Karl Marx, Sir Isaiah Berlin has described one of Popper's two self-proclaimed 'war efforts,' *The Open Society and Its Enemies* (1945), as 'a work of exceptional originality and power ... provid[ing] the most scrupulous and formidable criticism of the philosophical and historical doctrines of Marxism by any living writer.'[18] Writing in the Introduction to the First Series of the *Philosophy, Politics and Society* essays, Peter Laslett describes Popper as 'perhaps the most influential of contemporary philosophers who have addressed themselves to politics.'[19] Upon its publication in 1957, Popper's other major work in social theory, *The Poverty of Historicism*, was proclaimed by Arthur Koestler 'probably the only book published this year which will outlive this century,' and it has become the object of two recent books consolidating this claim.[20] His views concerning the unity of scientific method and the role of so-called hypo-thetico-deductive explanations in the social as well as the natural sciences have become staples to considerable numbers of economists, sociologists, political scientists, and even anthropologists wishing to place their disciplines on a more credible and sophisticated scientific foundation.[21] And his methodological conception of liberalism as an 'open society' predicated upon the adoption of a fallibilist view of human nature and knowledge, to be institutionalized as a 'piece-meal social technology,' has been referred to on more than one occasion as 'the ideally appropriate metaphysical perspective' and 'most formidable' defence of liberal values yet advanced – a vast improvement, so these commentators claim, upon John Stuart Mill's philosophy.[22]

Popper's work has always been controversial, particularly his studies in the history of political thought and the logic of the social sciences. Among philosophers, it has frequently been said that one may philos-

ophize for or against Kant, but not without him. There are growing
signs that future generations of scholars will say much the same, and
for many of the same reasons, of Popper's ideas. In addition to the substance of his thought (some of which will be explored shortly), aspects
of Popper's intellectual style appear to have greatly contributed to this
effect and lend credence to the comparison with Kant. As had been the
case with Kant and so many other Enlightenment figures, in Popper's
hands the history of ideas and questions of method become veritable
battlefields where the forces of reason and passion, fallibilism and jus-
tificationism, historicism and indeterminism, and so on clash at every
conceivable turn. As one political theorist succinctly observed, 'Popper
is the sort of writer who produces hot or cold responses in his readers,
for his is self-admittedly a combative prose.'[23] Thus, in the second of his
three major volumes of essays on epistemology and methodology, *Conjectures and Refutations: The Growth of Scientific Knowledge* (1963), Popper
frankly admits that 'like many other philosophers I am at times inclined
to classify philosophers as belonging to two main groups – those with
whom I disagree and those who agree with me.'[24] Small wonder, then,
that, while some have hailed Popper as 'this century's Locke,' and as
propounding the 'ideal metaphysics' of a liberal society, others have been
most impressed by diametrically opposed implications and habits of his
thought.

One well-known student of political thought, for example, has com-
plained of 'the arbitrariness of Popper's fundamental principles,' that
'the use of "we" employed throughout [*The Open Society*] takes on an
insidious tone for all who are out of the charmed community' of critical
rationalism and that his liberal meliorism 'sanctions a dangerous extension of the interventionist state.'[25] From a radically different perspective,
several social theorists have charged that Popper has provided a 'justification for the cult of empiricism and pragmatic conservatism' and a
'comprehensive defense of the administrative technologists – indeed a
manifesto for them, no less effective for being unread by many who
most profit from it.'[26] In short, it appears that, precisely as Kant had
done, Popper has polarized the thought of his contemporaries and that
of at least the next generation on the most pressing questions of modern
life: What can I know? What ought I to do? and What may I hope for?
Not coincidentally, these happen to be Kant's three great questions, each
the subject of one of his monumental *Critiques*.

In the final chapter of *Politics and Vision*, Sheldon Wolin notes that
'to describe adequately recent and contemporary conceptions of what is

political is a risky undertaking full of the pitfalls that come from standing so close to events and interpretations of events.'[27] In the case of a thinker as influential and controversial as Popper, such risks must be not only acknowledged but specifically addressed. Perhaps the most notable risk stems from the tendency of a considerable body of commentary to lapse into a type of 'whiggish presentism,'[28] simply mirroring his current success and today's most fashionable criteria of evaluation. Increasing numbers of observers have noted this tendency when they lament Popper's having become a 'cult figure' whose disciples have vied for the master's mantle and whose doctrines have been scrutinized as much for heresy as for error.'[29] Similarly, a well-known philosopher otherwise quite favourably disposed toward Popper's thought writes: 'All too many of the contributors [to the Library of Living Philosophers volumes] come uncomfortably close to grovelling.'[30] Henry Veatch observers: 'Time was when only a pope was deemed a fit officer to draw a line of demarcation [between different modes of experience]; but nowadays this one-time papal function would appear to have devolved upon a unblushing and ever ready Sir Karl.'[31] Whatever the appropriate explanation for these uncritical, triumphalist responses, I believe they do his ideas, ourselves, and our posterity a great disservice – as do those who caricature his thought and portray it as something that neither Popper nor a careful student of his work would recognize.

One means (admittedly imperfect and difficult to execute) of avoiding these pitfalls is to conduct our discussion as an immanent critique, taking Popper's premises and ideas as our own and submitting them to the facts of experience and the tribunal of reason. The fact that our conclusions are not always 'Popperian' constitutes a gain in the overall appreciation of his thought and the future of liberal society which is his overriding concern. And, happily, we find considerable support for such a belief in Popper's own work. He is particularly fond of quoting Einstein's view that 'there could be no fairer destiny for any ... theory than it should point the way to a more comprehensive theory in which it lives on, as a limiting case' (*CR* 32). I take it that whatever the complexion of 'more comprehensive' theories of political liberalism in the future, Popper's ideas and arguments will indeed constitute a 'limiting case.' As we shall see in chapter 3, the entire structure of his thought, essentially Kantian in nature, is ideally suited to this task of securing orderly growth.

Ultimately, it will be argued that a good deal of Popper's work (including his epistemology and philosophy of science) is best understood as an attempt to conserve liberalism in the face of tremendous challenges

to the traditional bases of its intellectual confidence and political optimism. His early life in Vienna during the 1920s and early 1930s was
pivotal in the formation of his thought, and it is with this period that I
begin the analysis in chapter 2. The air of paradox contained in the title
of chapter 7 and one of the unifying themes of this study inheres in
contemporary liberal discourse itself – historically and philosophically
so far removed from (and, hence, ignorant of) its beginnings, frequently
the victim of its own success, and increasingly surrounded by hostile,
illiberal social forces and ideas. Popper has sharpened our perception
of these problems 'from within' our Enlightenment heritage – interro-
gating liberalism's own utilitarian vocabulary of desiring by reasserting
ture historians of political thought may thus discern in Popper's work a
sustained and systematic effort to save liberal society from itself, as much
as from its enemies – from expecting and asking too much of politics,
from embracing erroneous ideas and false idols, and, above all, from
asking such questions and believing what we believe in the 'wrong,' or
methodologically mistaken manner. An exploration of these themes is
pursued in chapters 5 and 7 of this study. That Popper's own faith in
the powers and progress of scientific reason may be at odds with the
maintenance of the individual freedom and autonomy he so much cherishes will be one of the principal paradoxes raised in my conclusion in
connection with his methodological liberalism.

2

Portrait of a critical individualist

From the criticism of a text to the criticism of a
society, the way is shorter than it seems.[1]
Joseph Schumpeter

Karl Raimund Popper was born in July 1902 in the Ober St Veit district
of Vienna. The only son and youngest of three children of Dr Simon
Siegmund Carl and Jenny (née Schiff) Popper, he recalls having been
greatly influenced by his father's intellectual achievements as well as his
mother's cultural interests. His mother is remembered as being very
musical, having heard Brahms, Liszt, and Bulow perform in their prime
and having 'played Mozart and Beethoven very simply and beautifully'
on the Bösendorfer concert grand in their dining-room.[2] Given his mother's family background and extensive interests in classical music, Popper
notes, 'For a time – between the autumn of 1920 and perhaps 1922 – I
myself thought quite seriously of becoming a musician. But as with so
many other things – mathematics, physics, and cabinet-making – I felt
in the end I was not really good enough.'[3] Hence, after a year's study
in Vienna's Konservatorium, Popper turned his attention and considerable energies to other pursuits. He credits the early influence of classical music and his 'unbounded admiration for the great composers of
old' for 'at least three ideas which influenced me for life': the contrast
between 'dogmatic' and 'critical thinking' and the significance of dogmas
and traditions, which stemmed from his early studies in educational
psychology; the immensely important difference between two kinds of
musical composition ('objective' and 'subjective'); and of 'the intellectual
poverty and destructive power of historicist ideas in music and in the
arts in general' (IA 42–3).

Popper's father was a professor of law but 'was really more of a scholar than a lawyer' (IA 6) – 'a poet, and excellent classical scholar and historian, particularly interested in the Hellenic period to which a considerable part of his library of ten thousand books was devoted.'⁴ 'There were books everywhere; the atmosphere in which I was brought up was decidedly bookish' (IA 5). His father had a capacity for long hours of hard work in both professional and leisurely activities, 'a light touch and strong sense of humour,' a keen interest in 'social problems,' and a studied reluctance to impose his own views on those around him (particularly his son) (IA 6–7). Like most Austrians, Popper's father 'respected the Emperor,' but politically he 'was a radical liberal of the school of J.S. Mill, and not at all a supporter of the government' (IA 5). Indeed, in 1904, he wrote 'a brilliant political satire, *Anno 1903*' under the pen-name of Siegmund Karl Pflung, which 'was seized by the police on its publication ... and remained on the index of prohibited books until 1918' (ibid). Although he apparently never discussed the matter with his son, he was very active in 'two committees which were running homes for the homeless,' whose numbers continued to swell as a result of severe agricultural depressions in the outlying provinces of the empire and as the lure of employment in Vienna continued to mount. As Popper learned later, one of those committees ran an (illegal) Free Masons lodge, of which his father was for many years the master and which ran a home for orphans, while the other built and administered a large institution for homeless adults and families (one of whose inmates was Adolf Hitler, during his early years in Vienna) (ibid). Ironically, the emperor knighted Popper's father for his contributions to such charitable causes.⁵

As for himself, Popper recalls, his philosophical development 'certainly started later than my emotional and moral development.' As a child, he notes, 'I was, I suspect, somewhat puritanical, even priggish, though this ... was perhaps tempered by the feeling that I had no right to sit in judgement of anybody except myself' (IA 4). He highlights 'frequent feelings of admiration for [his] elders and betters' as some of his 'earliest memories' and notes that he was 'what Americans might call a "softy", [with] compassion one of the strongest emotions I remember' (ibid). 'The sight of abject poverty in Vienna was one of the main problems which agitated me when I was still a very small child – so much so that it was almost always at the back of my mind ... 'Few people now living in one of the Western Democracies know what poverty meant at the beginning of this century; men, women, and children suffering from hunger, cold, and helplessness' (ibid). Popper was twelve years old when the First World War broke out, and, as he has frequently pointed out, 'the war and its aftermath were, in every respect, decisive for my intellectual development. They made me critical of accepted opinions, especially political opinions' (IA 8). Popper remembers having been 'staggered' at the sight of so many of his formerly and 'decidedly pacifist' friends swinging over to become supporters of the alliance between Austria and Germany and of Austria's expansionist policy in the Balkans (especially toward Serbia). Though he, too, had become 'a little infected by the general mood,' this lasted but a few weeks, after which time (i.e. during the winter of 1915–16) 'I became convinced – under the influence, no doubt, of prewar socialist propaganda – that the cause of Austria and Germany was a bad cause and that we deserved to lose the war (and therefore that we would lose it, as I naively argued)' (IA 9). Throughout the next three to four years, Popper points out, Vienna was besieged by rumours and a sense of imminent doom – rumours about the dissolution of the empire amid growing defections of Czechs, Slavs, and Italians from the Austrian army – 'and then we heard rumours about the death sentences for treason, and the terror directed by the Austrian authorities against people suspected of disloyalty' (IA 9–10). Karl Kraus, a leading literary figure of the period, observed that Austria 'served as a dress rehearsal for the apocalypse' – an opinion echoed by Robert Musil in *Man without Qualities*.[6] For those who cherished the traditional liberal ideals of peace, progress, and order, these indeed must have seemed like 'the last days of mankind.'[7] The forces that rose to challenge, and ultimately prevailed against, the belated ascendancy of Austrian liberalism 'could not fail to baffle an observer who viewed them through a liberal conceptual screen and with a liberal's expectations of history.'[8]

Late in 1917 Popper made one of the most significant decisions of his life. After being ill for over two months, he 'realized very clearly what I had felt in my bones for a considerable time: that in our famous Austrian secondary schools (called "*Gymnasium*" and horrible dictu – "*Realgymnasium*") we were wasting our time shockingly' (IA 23). That much of the teaching 'was boring in the extreme – hours and hours of hopeless torture' – was certainly 'not new to me,' but on his return from convalescence he 'found that my class had made hardly any progress, even in mathematics,' the one subject with 'an interesting and truly inspiring teacher.' 'That was the eye-opener: it made me eager to leave school' (IA 24). The following year brought defeat in the war and the imposed dissolution of the empire, the aftermath 'destroyed the world in which I had grown up' (ibid). This gave Popper the opportunity to leave school, and he eagerly seized it.

Popper notes: 'It was a time of upheavals, though not only political ones.' Runaway inflation, famine, and widespread hunger riots dominated, 'starving post-war Vienna.'[9] 'There was little to eat; and as for clothing, most of us could afford only discarded army uniforms, adapted for civilian use' (IA 24). Few thought 'seriously of careers – there were none' (except perhaps in commerce, which never interested him). Perhaps thinking of the marked contrast to our own times, he continues, 'We studied not for a career but for the sake of studying. We studied and we discussed politics' (ibid). 'If I thought of a future, I dreamt of one day founding a school in which young people could learn without boredom, and would be stimulated to pose problems and discuss them; a school in which no unwanted answer to unasked questions would have to be listened to; in which one did not study for the sake of passing examinations' (IA 31).

Popper recalls having been 'close enough to hear the bullets whistle when, on the occasion of the Declaration of the Austrian Republic, soldiers started shooting at members of the Provincial Government assembled at the top of the steps leading to the Parliament building' (IA 24). Soon thereafter, 'there began a period of cold and hot civil war which ended with Hitler's invasion of Austria, and led to the Second World War.' Against this background of nearly incessant political strife and economic ruin Popper decided in 1918 to 'stage my own private revolution' and leave school to study on his own as a non-matriculated student at the University of Vienna: 'The revolution ... incited me to stage my ... revolution' (IA 24). However, although the post-war settlement imposed by the Allies represented a change in constitutions and the overthrow of a dynasty, Austria's underlying social, political, and economic structure remained untouched.[10] And, as the next decade and a half demonstrated, the republican constitution, that 'foreign import,' clearly did not fit with the non-liberal traditions of the nation.[11]

Shortly after his 'private revolution' Popper resolved another issue crucial for his subsequent intellectual development – his 'encounter with Marxism.' 'Although the years after the First World War were grim for most of my friends and also for myself, it was an exhilarating time' (IA 29). As one would expect, 'there was an upsurge of ideals of the French Revolution, and of Marxism, and a hope of establishing a freer and better world, and to banish war and authoritarianism forever.'[12] Given the anti-liberal tendencies in Austria of both the German Nationals (later absorbed by the Nazis) and the Christian Socialists, the sole options were the relatively large Social Democratic party or the smaller communist party.

Initially, Popper recalls, it was virtually impossible to tell the latter two apart, since 'their Marxist beliefs were then very similar' and 'they both dwelt, rightly, on the horrors of war' (IA 24). The communists 'claimed they had proven their pacifism by ending the war, at Brest-Litovsk. Peace, they said, was what they primarily stood for; [and] ... not only for peace but, in their propaganda at least, against all "unnecessary" violence' (ibid). Thus Popper, as a member of 'the association of socialist pupils of secondary schools' (sozialistiche Mittelschuler) and at the meetings of socialist university students, listened to numerous speakers of both leanings, and 'for about two or three months I regarded myself as a communist' (IA 24–5). Then, shortly before his seventeenth birthday, Popper experienced 'one of the most important incidents in my life':

In Vienna, shooting broke out during a demonstration by unarmed socialists who, instigated by the communists, tried to help some communists to escape who were under arrest in the central police station in Vienna. Several young socialist and communist workers were killed. I was horrified and shocked at the police, but also at myself. For I felt that as a Marxist I bore part responsibility for the tragedy – at least in principle. Marxist theory demands that the class struggle be intensified, in order to speed up the coming of socialism. Its thesis is that although the revolution may claim some victims, capitalism is claiming more victims than the whole socialist revolution.

That was the Marxist theory – part of so-called 'scientific socialism'. I now asked myself whether such a calculation could ever be supported by 'science'. The whole experience, and especially this question, led to a life-long revulsion of feeling. (IA 25)

Though he still 'hoped for a better world, a less violent and a more just world,' Popper recalls, 'I questioned whether I really knew – whether what I had thought was knowledge was not perhaps mere pretense.' 'Had I examined it critically, as anybody should do before he accepts a creed which justified its means by some distant end?' (ibid). And, sadly, he was soon forced to admit, 'not only had I accepted a complex theory somewhat uncritically, but I had also actually noticed quite a bit that was wrong, in the theory as well as in the practice of communism, but had repressed this – partly out of loyalty to my friends, partly out of loyalty to "the cause", and partly because there is a mechanism for getting oneself more and more deeply involved: once one has sacrificed one's intellectual conscience over a minor point one does not wish to give up too easily' (ibid).

Though it was 'awfully depressing to have fallen into such a trap,' particularly 'for an intellectual, ... who can read and think' (ibid 26), Popper's subsequent career and interest would have been virtually inconceivable without his 'encounter with Marxism.' 'The experience enabled me to understand later things which otherwise I would not have understood,' and it 'taught me a number of lessons which I have never forgotten.' Above all, it taught him 'the wisdom of the Socratic saying, "I know that I do not know". It made me a fallibilist, and impressed on me the value of intellectual modesty. And it made me most conscious of the difference between dogmatic and critical thinking' (IA 27–8). These critical ideas with regard to Marxism 'led me to become interested in problems of the theory of knowledge and of the philosophy of science' and, in turn, 'their bearing on political problems.'[13]

Clearly, politics was a central focus of Popper's work from the beginning; he did not 'shift' his interests temporarily at 'mid-career' to problems in the social sciences and the threat of totalitarianism, thereafter returning happily to more basic concerns with logic, methodology, and epistemology.[14] The categorical structure of Popper's epistemology and the basis of his methodological prescriptions are inherently and distinctively political – he was dominated by a 'life-long revulsion of feeling' against the alleged causes and high costs of the war and its aftermath and determined to prevent their recurrence. Popper has always acted as if questions of knowledge have such practical, political consequences that to separate the two can lead only to further crises, if not disaster, for liberal democracies. And the major tenets of his philosophy have remained constant.

By the time he was seventeen, Popper had become an 'anti-Marxist,' though the decision to publish his views came only some sixteen years later, 'in an atmosphere poisoned by fascism and latent civil war' (IA 26). Popper notes that he remained a socialist for several years more but observes: 'If there could be such a thing as socialism combined with individual liberty, I would be a socialist still. For nothing could be better than living a modest, simple, and free life in an egalitarian society' (ibid 27). Unfortunately, Popper continues, this is 'no more than a beautiful dream.' Popper then distils the essence of his liberalism in the form of three axiom-like propositions: 'Freedom is more important than equality;' 'The attempt to realize equality endangers freedom'; and

'If freedom is lost, there will not even be equality among the unfree' (ibid 27).

Needless to say, the interpretation of 'the most relevant aspect' of Popper's political theory as its 'philosophy of social democracy' finds very little support in these remarks.[15] If one can find in Popper's writings any justification for 'a dangerous extension of the interventionist state,'[16] this must be traced to one of the critical, though unacknowledged, tensions in his thought – between his technological conception of rationality and his commitment to the maximization of individual liberty and autonomy. As he observed a decade ago, by the time he wrote the *Open Society*, he considered himself an 'individualist,' opposed in theory to such abstractions as 'class,' 'mankind,' and 'meaning in history,' and in practice to proposals (Marxist or social democratic) to nationalize the means of production.[17]

Popper passed his Matura (entrance examination) as a non-matriculated student at the University of Vienna in 1922, just one year later than if he had continued in secondary school. Although he took courses in a number of subjects (history, literature, psychology, philosophy, and even medicine), he recalls that he 'soon gave up going to lectures, with the exception of mathematics and theoretical physics' (IA 30). In 1923, he passed a second Matura at a teacher's training college, which qualified him to teach primary school. But there were no posts available for teachers, and so, having concluded an apprenticeship as a cabinet-maker, he became a social worker (Horterzieher) with neglected children. Early during this period, he further developed his ideas, initially prompted by his 'encounter with Marxism,' about the demarcation between scientific theories (like Einstein's) and pseudoscientific theories (like Marx's 'scientific socialism,' Alfred Adler's individual psychology, and Freud's psychoanalysis) (IA 31).

Having been 'brought up in an atmosphere in which Newton's mechanics and Maxwell's electrodynamics were accepted side by side as unquestionable truths,' and being therefore 'dazed' upon first hearing Einstein lecture in Vienna, 'what impressed me most was Einstein's own clear statement that he would regard his theory as untenable if it should fail in certain tests' (IA 28–9). Thus, Einstein observed, 'If the redshift of spectral lines due to gravitational potential should not exist, then the general theory of relativity will be untenable.'[18] In May 1919, Einstein's eclipse predictions were confirmed by two teams of British researchers, and Popper observes that 'a new theory of gravitation and a new cosmology suddenly appeared, not just as a mere possibility, but as a real improvement on Newton – a better approximation to the truth' (IA 28).

Einstein's method, Popper contends, led him to look for 'crucial experiments whose agreement with his predictions would by no means establish his theory' but whose disagreement 'would show his theory to be untenable.' In the work of Marx, Freud, Adler, and even more so that of their followers, an 'utterly different,' dogmatic attitude prevailed (ibid). Theirs was a world 'full of verifications ... It was precisely this fact – that they [i.e. their theories] always fitted, that they were always confirmed – which in the eyes of their admirers constituted the strongest argument in favour of these theories. It began to dawn on me that this apparent strength was in fact their weakness' (CR 35). Popper maintains that 'what made a theory, or a statement, scientific, was its power to rule out, or exclude the occurrence of these events: *the more a theory forbids, the more it tells us*' (IA 31).

In 1925, Vienna founded the Pedagogic Institute, inspired by the nation-wide educational reform movement of Otto Glöckel. Popper notes that the institute was linked loosely with the university and that, along with several social workers, he was admitted as a student. 'The purpose of the new Institute was to further and support the reform, then in progress, of the primary and seconday schools' that had been precipitated by the chaos of 1918 and after (IA 57).

Although the pre-war Austrian system of education compared quite well with the most progressive systems in Europe, it was 'hardly a paradigm of progressive thinking: instruction, largely in the hands of the Roman Catholic Church, was mechanical and as uniform as was practical.'[19] Reformers found that the major impediments to a thoroughly secular, liberal political culture – one that permitted a genuine clash of ideas and the development of each individual's capacities – were the writings of the German thinker Johann Friedrich Herbart (1776–1841). Herbart's philosophy was secured in Austria mainly by followers, such as Robert Zimmerman (1824–98), whose teachings dominated the University of Vienna's faculties of philosophy, psychology, and education until the 1920s.

Herbart sought to restore the classical harmony of Leibniz's monadology that had prevailed among eighteenth-century Austrian thinkers. 'It reaffirmed a modified realism against speculative idealism, and substituted for Hegel's dialectic a formal logic and a static ontology.'[20] Above all, his doctrine was easily accommodated by the Catholic authorities, 'for whom his very omissions became advantages.'[21] In particular, Herbart's metaphysically neutral view of theology was not self-consciously or critically Protestant, like Kant, Schelling, or Hegel had been. When read in connection with his life-long antipathy toward revolution and progressivist philosophies of history, Herbart's thought thus 'tended to train docile, law-abiding citizens, who relished work while despising unrest.'[22] Count Rottenham, a royal adviser, observed that the state's lower schools were 'to make thoroughly pious, good, tractable, and industrious men of the labouring classes of people.'[23] The constitution of the common schools, issued by the emperor himself, stated: 'The method of instruction ... must endeavour first and foremost to train the memory; then however, according to the pressure of the circumstances, the intellect and the heart. The trial schools will strictly refrain from any explanation other than those exactly prescribed in the "school and method" book.'[24] By encouraging students 'to understand what is already known, rather than to goad them into making discoveries,' Herbart and his followers thus tended to produce 'connoisseurs, not creators, just as in philosophy he fostered scholars of the subject, not creative geniuses.'[25]

According to Herbart's version of associationist psychology, the human mind was neutral and passive, totally lacking in innate faculties or structures for producing ideas from within itself.[26] Though ideas themselves might be active, Bartley notes that for Herbart and followers 'they lead their lives in passive storehouse minds.'[27] This theory of mind (and the obstacles it posed for school reform) came in for sustained attack at Vienna's Pedagogic Institute, led by the noted child psychologist Karl Bühler (1879–1963) and his wife, Charlotte, also a well-known Gestalt psychologist. And Herbart's doctrine resembles the view that Popper severely and early criticized as 'the bucket theory of the mind.'[28]

Against the associationist and empiricist tenets of Locke and Hume – contiguity and frequency – Bühler maintained that a basic and perhaps the most uniquely human function of the mind, theory-making, was independent of successive associations of sense impressions. For the Gestaltists, Bartley observes, 'Structural properties of the human mind gave priority to the organizing and theorizing activity of the mind, which in turn determined the kinds of wholes with which we would deal as "elements" of our thinking.'[29] Bühler also rejected the 'picture theory of language,' or 'logical atomism,' described by Bertrand Russel as follows: 'In a logically correct symbolism there will always be a certain fundamental identity of structure between a fact and the symbol for it; and ... the complexity of the symbol corresponds very closely with the complexity of the fact symbolized by it.'[30] Bühler dismissed such theories because of his deep, ultimately Kantian conviction that abstract words cannot be reduced to sense impressions. As we will see below and in the next two chapters, such a conviction is also at the heart of Popper's thought.

As one can imagine, the pedagogical implications of Bühler's ideas were profound and far-reaching vis-à-vis the method of the Herbartian educators and administrators of the Hapsburg era. The child was now to be seen as an active being 'whose mind was far more than a bucket to be filled with appropriate information.'[31] The reformers believed that emphasis on so-called unit ideas had produced an excessively compart-mentalized and 'atomistic' curriculum and teaching method. And we have Popper's own recollections as to just how boring and stultifying such an education actually was. Throughout the reform movement, par-ticularly at the institute, experiments accordingly were designed to pro-mote active participation in lessons, aimed ultimately at the development of the individual's capabilities or 'self-activity' (Selbsttatigkeit).[32]

During his sixteen years in Vienna, 1922–38, Bühler attracted a num-ber of students and disciples, many of whom attained great distinction – Paul Lazarsfeld, Egon Brunswik, Else Frenkel-Brunswik, Albert Wel-lek, Edward Tolman, Konrad Lorenz, Ludwig Wittgenstein, and the young ex–social worker, Karl Popper. Having 'had access to the psy-chological laboratory' at the institute, Popper conducted a few experi-ments of his own 'which convinced me that sense data, "simple" ideas or impressions, and other such things, did not exist: they were fictitious – inventions based on mistaken attempts to transfer atomism (or Aris-totelean logic ...) from physics to psychology' (IA 60). In this connection, Popper credits Bühler's *The Mental Development of the Child*[33] with having had far-reaching implications for his subsequent thought on the psy-chology of discovery and the growth of knowledge (IA 58). Most impor-tant was Bühler's theory of the three levels or functions of language: expressive (Kundgabefunktion), signal or release (Auslosefunktion), and, 'on a higher level,' descriptive (Darstellungsfunktion). Bühler 'explained that the two lower functions were common to human and animal lan-guages and were always present, while the third function was charac-teristic of human language alone, and sometime (as in exclamations) absent even from that' (ibid).

This theory confirmed Popper's earlier views concerning art, specif-ically that the conceptions of art as self-expression or as communication or 'release' were 'equally empty, since these two functions were trivially present in all languages, even animal languages' (ibid). More important,

·Popper credits Bühler's ideas, as well as his own discussions with Heinrich Gomperz (professor of philosophy at the university), with 'strengthening [his] "objectivist" approach' – that 'critical thinking or error elimination can be better characterized in logical than psychological terms' (IA 37) – and his realism – 'my conviction that there is a real world, and that the problem of knowledge is the problem of how to discover this world' (IA 59). Moreover, his searching logical critique of Bühler's (and Oswald Külpe's) conception of arguments eventually led Popper to posit a fourth, argumentative function of language – 'particularly important to me because I regarded it as the basis of all critical thought' (IA 58).

In 1928 Popper submitted a PhD thesis in which, he notes, 'I finally turned away from psychology.' 'On the Problem of Method in the Psychology of Thinking,' was 'a kind of hasty last minute affair originally intended only as a methodological introduction to my psychological work, though now indicative of my changeover to methodology' (ibid). Popper 'felt badly' about the thesis and, he notes, has 'never again even glanced at it.' He also felt badly about his two public oral examinations (or Rigorosum), in history of music and in philosophy and psychology. His examiners were Bühler and Moritz Schlick, founder of the Vienna Circle (or Wiener Kreis) of logical positivism. Popper remembers having done 'so badly on Leibniz that I thought I had failed. I could hardly believe my ears when I was told that I had passed with the highest grade, "*einstimming mit Auszeichnung*" ' (IA 62). The following year, Popper qualified as a teacher of mathematics and physical science in the (lower) secondary schools in Vienna, continuing in that capacity until he and his wife, also a teacher, emigrated to New Zealand in 1937.

Although the now well-known 'changeover to methodology' had already occurred by the time of his doctoral examinations, Popper observes that it was only afterward 'that I put two and two together, and my earlier ideas fell into place' (IA 62). To a large extent, this process was the product of Popper's effort to 'point out what seemed to me a number of fundamental mistakes' in the philosophies of the Machian positivists and Wittgensteinians of the Vienna Circle (IA 69; cf 63–6). Though never invited to attend any of the Thursday evening meetings of the Circle at Schlick's house, Popper became friends with several of its leading members (especially Herbert Feigel and Victor Kraft) and presented his criticisms of their views both privately and in a number of seminars or 'epicyclic' fringe groups that met regularly in one of their homes.[34]

The main bone of contention, Popper recalls, was the proper criterion for demarcating science from pseudoscience. Whereas Schlick's Circle was 'trying to find a criterion which made metaphysics meaningless non-sense, sheer gibberish,' Popper felt that this was 'bound to lead to trouble, since metaphysical ideas are often forerunners to scientific ones' (IA 63). Besides, such an approach 'merely shifted the problem,' since it presup-posed and required yet another criterion to distinguish between meaning and lack of meaning, which the Circle's notion of verifiability could not itself consistently provide.

More positively, Popper believed that now at last he understood why Schlick and his Circle had succumbed to his mistaken theory of science and could explain to them why he believed that he 'held in my hands for many years a better criterion of demarcation: testability or falsifia-bility' (IA 62). In essence, their error had been to confuse the Baconian method of induction with the laudable goal of finding a sound criterion of demarcation, compounded by their attempt to 'justify their theories by an appeal to the sources of knowledge comparable in reliability to the sources of religion' (ibid). But, according to Popper, 'a fairly com-monplace consequence of the Einsteinian revolution' was 'the hypo-thetical character of all scientific theories' (IA 64). When combined with his earlier interpretation of Bühler's psychology, particularly the view that 'theories are essentially argumentative systems ... [which] explain deductively,' Popper's ideas concerning the demarcation of science from pseudoscience, as well as the nature of scientific progress, had indeed fallen 'into place':

The falsification or refutation of theories through the falsification or refutation of their deductive consquences was, clearly, a deductive inference (*modus tollens*). This view implied that *scientific theories are either falsified or for ever remain hypotheses or conjectures*.

... Progress consisted in moving towards theories which tell us more and more – theories of ever greater content. But the more a theory says the more it excludes or forbids, and the greater are the opportunities for falsifying it. So a theory with greater content is one which can be more severely tested. This consideration led to a theory in which scientific progress turned out not to consist in the accumulation of observations but in the overthrow of less good theories and their replacement by better ones, in particular by theories of greater content. Thus there was competition between theories – a kind of Darwinian struggle for survival. (IA 62–3).

Popper notes that 'it had never occurred to me to write a book,' whether to air his criticisms of the Vienna Circle or to advance the positive views outlined above. But after a 'nightlong session' with Herbert Feigl, who 'told me not only that he found my ideas important, almost revolutionary, but also that I should publish them in book form' (IA 65), Popper set to work on *The Two Fundamental Problems in the Theory of Knowledge* – induction and deduction. Early in 1932, he completed what he then regarded as the first of two volumes. Much to his delight, in the following year, Schlick and Phillip Frank accepted the book for publication in their series Schriften zur wissenschaftlichen Weltanffassung (most volumes of which were written by members of the Circle). However, the publishers demanded that the volume be radically shortened, and by the time they accepted it Popper had written most of the second. With the agreement of Schlick and Frank, Popper then submitted a new manuscript consisting of extracts from both volumes, but this too was returned as too long. In the end, 'the final extract,' published late in 1934 as *Logik der Forschung*, was made by Popper's uncle, Walter Schiff (a professor of statistics and economics at Vienna). The *Logik* was not translated and published in English until 1959, appearing as *The Logic of Scientific Discovery*.[35]

Publication of *Logik der Forschung* brought Popper immediate acclaim. Indeed, the book 'was surprisingly successful, far beyond Vienna. There were more reviews, in more languages, than there were twenty-five years later of *The Logic of Scientific Discovery*, and fuller reviews even in English' (IA 85). Having decided as early as July 1927 that 'the democratic bastions of Central Europe would fall, and that a totalitarian Germany would start another world war' (IA 83), Popper accepted some of many invitations to lecture abroad in the hope of finding refuge. During 1935–6, he went on leave without pay for two long visits to England, where he lectured at a number of institutions on topics such as Alfred Tarski's semantics and theory of truth and on probability theory. In Friedrich Hayek's seminar at the London School of Economics (*LSE*) he read his controversial paper, 'The Poverty of Historicism,' delivered shortly before in German at the home of his friend Alfred Braunthal in Brussels.

In November 1936, Popper received an invitation from Dr A.C. Ewing, of the Moral Sciences Faculty of Cambridge University, together with a letter of support from the Academic Assistance Council, which was 'trying to help many refugee scientists from Germany, and had already begun to help some from Austria' (IA 88). On Christmas Eve 1936, however, Popper received a cable from Canterbury University College in Christchurch, New Zealand, offering him a lectureship in philosophy – a normal position, as opposed to the refugee status attached to the Cambridge offer. Though he and his wife would have preferred Cambridge, Popper thought that the 'offer of hospitality might be transferable to somebody else. So I accepted the invitation to New Zealand and asked ... Cambridge to invite Fritz Waismann, of the Vienna Circle, in my stead. They agreed to this request' (IA 88). Within a month, he and his wife had resigned their teaching positions and left for London. After five days in London, 'we sailed for New Zealand, arriving just in time for beginning the New Zealand academic year' (ibid).

During the next few years as Popper established his reputation as a leading political theorist with the publication of his two self-described 'war efforts,' *The Poverty of Historicism* and *The Open Society and Its Enemies*.[36] With the news in March 1938 of Hitler's occupation of Austria, he 'could no longer hold back whatever knowledge of political problems I had acquired since 1919' (IA 90). Both works 'grew out of the theory of knowledge of *Logik der Forschung* and out of my conviction that our often unconscious views on the theory of knowledge and its central problems ("What can we know?", "How certain is our knowledge?") are decisive for our attitudes towards ourselves and towards politics' (IA 91). Nothing could be clearer as to the target and context of Popper's polemics against the 'historicism' and 'essentialism' of Plato, Hegel, and Marx than the famous dedication to *The Poverty of Historicism*: 'In memory of the countless men and women of all creeds or races who fell victim to the fascist and Communist belief in Inexorable Laws of Historical Destiny.'

As with his earlier work on scientific inquiry, publication of *The Open Society* in 1945 brought Popper immediate success, albeit controversial. *The Poverty of Historicism* was rejected for publication by the editors of *Mind*, the leading journal of linguistic analysis at the time, and was published 1944–5 in instalments in *Economica*, the acting editor of which, Friedrich Hayek, sympathized with Popper's attack against all forms of collectivist thinking. In mid-1945, Hayek offered Popper a readership at the University of London, tenable at LSE (cf IA 96). Popper's gratitude ran deep, and his response was swift: 'I felt that Hayek had saved my life once more. From that moment I was impatient to leave New Zealand.'

From 1946 until his retirement from LSE in 1969, Popper enjoyed immense success as teacher, scholar, and leading public figure. He was knighted in 1965, has received honorary degrees from some of the world's leading universities, and has seen his works translated into more than twenty languages. These years also saw the long-awaited release of *The Poverty of Historicism* as a book in 1957. Two wide-ranging volumes of essays, *Conjectures and Refutations* (1963) and *Objective Knowledge* (1972), display his concern with the objectivity of knowledge, the increasingly 'Darwinian' dimension of his epistemology, and the problems of rationality.[37] Popper also regularly found himself embroiled in the major controversies of the day, whether in the philosophy of the natural science (perhaps best evidenced in his attack on the 'historicist' and 'psychologistic' views of Thomas S. Kuhn)[38] or in the logic of the social sciences (as in the so-called positivist dispute in German sociology, with his critique of the Frankfurt School).[39] More recently, Popper wrote a massive tome with his long-standing friend, Sir John Eccles, *The Self and Its Brain* (1977), in which he further develops his theory of evolutionism and its implications for the nature and objectivity of knowledge.[40] And, finally, recent years have witnessed release of his massive, three-volume *Postscript to the Logic of Scientific Discovery*, which probes a number of criticisms of the earlier work in great detail.[41]

A portrait is neither a thumb-nail sketch, a photograph from afar, nor an x-ray. Its intention is to capture certain detail and nuance that otherwise would be lost in presentation and refraction from other conceivable vantage points. And, in the history of ideas, portraiture more specifically helps us to appreciate the impact of certain phases and experiences of one's life on an author's style of thought, commitments, vocabulary, and the like. With regard to Popper's social and political thought, there can be no doubt as to the primacy of his experience in the war-torn Vienna of his youth. His own testimony should have established this point by now. Yet virtually nothing has been written about these events in connection with Popper's thought. This chapter has tried to reconstruct at least the rudiments of Popper's perception of this period and of its impact on his subsequent philosophy.

Implicit in such an approach is the belief that these early, formative influences have played a much more significant role in Popper's thinking about politics and society than later events in his life. In fact, Popper has said virtually nothing about the political crises and controversies of the last three decades; everything he has written on these subjects was cast against the background of Hitler's seizure of power and his eventual defeat. In this respect, to the extent that Popper's thought has developed or evolved in new directions, it has done so in terms of his epistemology and certain more or less technical areas of philosophy – logic, probability theory, and evolutionary theory. But (as we shall see), even in these areas of inquiry, Popper has not significantly altered the initial tenets of his thought, as found, for example, in *The Logic of Scientific Discovery*.

The next chapter also tries to draw attention to a hitherto neglected area of concern in connection with Popper's work: the crisis in the ideals of the Enlightenment and the profound effect that Kant's thought has had on Popper's life-long attempt to defend and conserve those ideals in an increasingly hostile environment. Then, in chapter 4, I outline the underlying unity and 'heat' of Popper's vision. Chapters 5 and 7 are concerned respectively with the implications for the conduct of social science that Popper draws from his reflections on the nature of the growth of knowledge and with the conservative tenor of his methodological and Neo-Kantian interpretation of liberalism. In chapter 6 I reconsider Popper's well-known critique of Karl Mannheim's approach to the sociology of knowledge, arguing that the latter actually is more consistent with Popper's own conception of objectivity, fallibilism, situational analysis, and the role of critical institutions and traditions in a free and open society than his own polemics to the contrary frequently suggest. And in chapter 8 I raise several criticisms that arise on even the most constructive and appreciative reading of his thought, such as I have tried to provide. Finally, in conclusion, I reiterate the significance and positive contribution of Popper's thought to the problems that our culture confronts.

3

Kant, Popper, and the crisis in Enlightenment ideals

> Science – the transformation of nature into concepts
> for the purpose of mastering nature – belongs
> under the rubric of 'means' ... But the purpose and
> will of man must grow in the same way, the inten-
> tion in regard to the whole.
>
> Friedrich Nietzsche

> The movements of the stars have become clearer;
> but to the mass of people the movements of their
> masters are still incalculable.[1]
>
> Bertolt Brecht

Popper's place in the tradition of Western thought should be seen against the rich historical background of the problems and intellectual crises his thought addresses. Modern philosophy has been persistently haunted by two problems: validation and enchantment. The problem of validation concerns how one – or, more accurately, one's culture – justifies holding certain beliefs to be true and, more specifically, a particular 'style of cognition amongst others.'[2] Since the late sixteenth century in the West, this has meant justifying scientific knowledge vis-à-vis other modes of thought and parts of intellectual culture. The problem of enchantment concerns the question of the meaningfulness of the universe and, above all, of human striving known as history. Not coincidentally, the question of meaning or enchantment has become increasingly acute in the West since the emergence and triumph of modern science, with its commitment to 'impartial subsumption [of phenomena] under symmetrical generalizations, ... treating all data as equal'[3] and its political counterpart, bureaucratic administration and rationalized production – in short, technocratic politics.

Ernst Cassirer, Leo Strauss, and Isaiah Berlin have taught us that modernity began with Machiavelli, the first critic of all varieties of transcendent philosophy.[4] The classical connection, so dear to Greek, Roman, and Christian thinkers alike, between statecraft and soulcraft was emphatically dissolved, and a penetrating justification was advanced for conceiving of reason as purely an instrument in the pursuit of worldly interests and goods. Knowledge thenceforth would progressively approximate Bacon's equation of theoretical knowledge with our power to manipulate and contrive the elements of nature as we see fit. And the underlying motivation of this vision of a distinctively modern philosophy was an unprecedented degree of optimism and radical self-confidence: what mind could encompass with its own power was sufficient to the task of making and remaking nature in the image of its own design.[5]

Although the apogee of this faith in the power of reason to secure practical and moral progress occurred during the Enlightenment, the metaphysical foundations of modernity's optimism and self-confidence were laid the century before, when thinkers such as Galileo, Descartes, Newton, and Hobbes systematically redefined the nature of philosophy. And the outward signs of modernity – its manifold technologies and the deep-seated faith in their progressive character – are testimonies to the longevity and promise of such intellectual self-confidence and optimism. Indeed, without this faith in these ideals and accomplishments, radical doubt or disenchantment has surfaced with regard to the very meaningfulness of modern life itself. Kant's great achievement during the twilight of the German Enlightenment was to rescue such optimism in our capacity to know and the all-important liberal corollary – that mind could be 'decisive' in political life – amid a growing chorus of scepticism and doubt. Like Kant, except during far more traumatic times, Popper has also proved an unrelenting advocate of the rational possibility of progress in mind and civil society alike. Theirs are philosophies of orderly growth – formal, methodical, dichotomous, and anthropologically transcendental and evolutionary in design. In light of the similarity of purpose of their respective philosophies, as well as the marked parallelism in the metaphysical structure and limitations of their thought, an initial overview of Kant's epistemology and the crisis to which it was a response will be helpful before we turn to Popper's critical rationalism.

Perhaps the greatest obstacle to natural science as we now 'know' it to have evolved was the influence of Aristotelianism on scholastic patterns of thought prior to the instrumentalization of reason in the seventeenth century. According to Aristotle's cosmology, the 'natural' state of a body was when at rest; a body at rest needed no further explanation, whereas bodies in motion were phenomena to be explained by discovering the relevant disturbing factors. And yet, Aristotle maintained, the movements of nature were also to be viewed as the actualization of potentiality (or *telos*): 'the fulfillment of what exists potentially, in so far as it exists, potentially, is motion.'[6] While both of these propositions accord nicely with a number of our commonsense experiences of motion, by the late fourteenth century persistent dissatisfaction with several applications of Aristotle's theory began to mount, particularly its inability to explain simple locomotion, like the behaviour of falling bodies and projectiles. Ultimately, such problems in Aristotle's physics were simply set aside, as subsequent thinkers such as Galileo and Descartes discovered the great benefits of abstracting from the sense manifestations of motion to its mathematical properties.

For his part, Galileo is most remembered for the 'marriage of the empiricism of technics with the rationalism of philosophy and mathematics' that has proved to be of such power and near limitless possibility in the struggle with nature.[7] Both Galileo's mathematical education and the manner in which he approached and solved the problems of Aristotle's physics render efforts to divorce the context of discovery and its cognitive justification extremely problematic. The typical empiricist 'logical reconstruction' saw Galileo 'appealing to the facts against Ptolemy and Aristotle,' but he actually gave a new account of *what an appeal to the facts had to be.*'[8] His work underscores the profound connection between technological change and intellectual progress in our culture. Indeed, the very possibility of perceiving a 'crisis' in Aristotle's physics reveals the process by which engineering and its methods 'gradually rose from the workshops of craftsmen and eventually penetrated the field of academic instruction.'[9]

In a famous letter to Marsili, Galileo states that he discovered the relativity of motion and the law of circular inertia through work on the problem of falling bodies raised in connection with his studies of ballistics and gunnery.[10] In his youth, when he studied medicine at the University of Pisa, mathematics was not yet taught. He came to study it privately with Ostilio Ricci, a former teacher at the Academia del Disegno in Florence, founded in 1592 by Vasari for young artists and artist-engineers. Upon his arrival at the University of Padua, where he spent nearly two decades (1592–1610), as a professor of Mathematics and Astronomy, Galileo established several work-rooms in his house with craftsmen-apprentices and began studies on pumps, the control of rivers, and the construction of fortresses. His first published work was a description of a measuring device for military purposes which he had invented; and the dialogue in his *Discorsi* (1638) takes place in the arsenal of Venice. The difficult problem which he solved 'had often been discussed by the gunners of the period,'[11] but they lacked the tools of mathematical analysis.

Edgar Zilsel points out that the different social origins of the two components of Galileo's method – the empiricism of technics and the rationalism of mathematics and logic – are obvious in *Discorsi*, 'since he gives the mathematical deductions in Latin and the experiments in Italian.'[12] After 1610, Galileo gave up writing Latin and addressed most of his work to non-scholars, in the vernacular. By appealing to an audience temperamentally opposed to the old ideas and standards of learning, Galileo combined a new account of 'what the facts had to be' with a clear conception of the appropriate methods and organization of scientific practice. Galileo's work-rooms exemplified the new understanding and division of intellectual activity. Thereafter, in one country after another, academies of science and learned societies were founded, where methodical training of the mind (above all, through mathematical analysis) could be systematically combined with the experimental, utilitarian, and causal approach of engineers and craftsmen. It would be hard to overestimate the practical implications of this new style of philosophizing. As Whitehead noted, 'Every university in the world organizes itself' in accordance with 'the scientific philosophy which closed the 17th century,' above all with its 'grand doctrine of nature as a self-sufficient meaningless complex of facts – the doctrine of the autonomy of physical science.'[13]

These academies and societies fashioned new standards of intellectual merit, achievement, and responsibility. Their primary function was to safeguard the 'advancement of learning' and the control of nature through 'a line and race of inventions that may in some degree subdue and overcome the necessities and miseries of humanity.'[14] Partisans of the 'new science' contended that the fate of Western civilization depended on the patient co-operation of successive generations of experts, tackling problems in 'the right way.' Progress in mind and society was nearly coterminous with the growth of scientific knowledge – enchantment as validation. As we shall see, these hopes and ideals resonate deeply in the philosophies of Kant and Popper.

An early expression of the new style of scientific philosophizing is

found in the writings of Francis Bacon. Against the 'niceties' of scholasticism and the antique idols of the humanistic literati, Bacon put forward a passionate argument for the superiority of the 'mechanical arts'
and their inductive method: there, knowledge was indeed power. Any
belief to the contrary was dismissed as literally childish. In *New Atlantis*
(1627), for instance, the 'Ancients' were portrayed as seldom, if ever,
rising above a state of 'choked and overgrown' intellectual stagnation,
whereas tireless groups of specialists made unending, cumulative progress toward establishing 'the power and dominion of the human race
itself over the universe.'[15] Similarly, in the *Wisdom of the Ancients*, Pan is
said to represent the 'Universe or the All of Things.' Pan wants for
nothing substantial outside of itself, for eros, Bacon warns us, is a desire
of something lacking. Consequently, Pan's only possible object of love
comes to be found in Echo, and their ensuing marriage is ingeniously
intended to signify the self-sufficiency and underlying unity of nature,
presuppositions bitterly opposed by schoolmen and literati alike. Bacon
reassures us, however, that 'it is well devised that of all words and voices
Echo alone should be chosen for the world's wife; for it is the true
philosophy which echoes most faithfully the world itself, and is written
as it were at the world's own dictation; being nothing else but the image
and reflection thereof, to which it adds nothing of its own, but only
iterates and gives it back.'[16]

Echoing Galileo's war-cry against Aristotelianism, that 'nature is written in mathematical language,'[17] René Descartes observed that earlier
attempts to lay a genuine foundation for knowledge had been like trying
'to find a knot in a bulrush.' Expanding upon this charge in *Rules for the
Direction of the Mind* (apparently written in 1628, though published posthumously), Descartes argued that Aristotelianism had been unable to
draw 'methodical' distinction (vita methodica) between 'clear and distinct
ideas' and the 'fluctuating testimony of the senses' – between that which
we can know scientifically (certainly) and the 'misleading judgement that
proceeds from the blundering construction of the imagination.'[18]

'Whenever men notice some similarity between two things, they are
wont to ascribe to each, even in those respects in which they differ, what
they have found to be true of the other. Thus they erroneously compare
the *sciences*, which entirely consist in the *cognitive exercise of the mind*, with
the arts, which depend upon an exercise and disposition of the body.'[19]
Philosophers and natural scientists must 'methodically' repress their 'bodily
dispositions,' the 'fluctuating testimony of the senses,' and their nature
as historical beings and agents. They must follow the 'sure speedy path

of Arithmetic and Geometry,' which 'alone was free from any taint of falsity or uncertainty.' The 'clarity and simplicity of the mind,' with its 'firm and lasting structure in the sciences,' could be progressively extended as a program of 'universal mathematics' until we finally possessed a unified, all-encompassing corpus of impersonal, totally indubitable, objective knowledge. One would be hard pressed to find a clearer justification for the historical divorce, and recently felt estrangement, of the sciences from the humanities.[20] Perhaps of even more consequence are its implications for disciplines, such as the various 'policy sciences,' wishing to embrace the callings of both of the 'two cultures.'

Nature itself came to be seen as a vast mechanism. 'Bits of matter qualified by mass spatial relations, and the change of relations' were how Descartes conceived of the cosmic machine.[21] Thinkers such as Hobbes, Spinoza, and Harvey paved the way for a similar understanding of mankind. But, despite the surface optimism propelling this endeavour, severe tensions emerged with regard to the logical incompatibility and 'disharmony between the object of science and the human ends science is made [or intended] to serve.'[22] While Newtonian cosmology presupposed (and strove after) universal order, lawfulness, and regularity in nature, man's status as a free, autonomous, goal-setting agent had been jeopardized. If nature and human nature were understood according to the Enlightenment's 'geometric spirit' and *libido sciendi*, as in Condillac's *Treatise on Sensations* and Hobbes's *Elements of Philosophy*, what was the epistemological status of human purposiveness, or enchantment itself?[23] This is perhaps the most urgent and controversial problem in modern philosophy. These two competing and incompatible ideas – nature as a vast, self-regulating mechanism and knowledge as purposeful power – are equally fundamental to Western society and deeply entrenched within its traditions and institutions. Indeed, they take us to the heart of modernity. 'Man, it appears, can only be maintained in the style to which he wishes to be accustomed at the price of abstract science, powerful technology and large-scale organization, ... [and] these in their turn destroy warmth, idiosyncracy, individualism, magic, and enchantment.'[24]

Many of Kant's predecessors were acutely aware of this tension. Four distinct philosophical strategies were advanced as possible solutions: Some, such as Descartes and many orthodox Christian thinkers, denied the problem by exempting man from the laws of nature through various ad hoc hypotheses. Others, like Malebranche, Descartes, at times, and many orthodox Christian philosphers, argued that the problem was insoluble and transferred it to a higher court of 'faith.' Thinkers such as Hobbes and Spinoza maintained that the problem itself was illusory, because purpose is not an ultimate vocation, even for mankind. And still others, like Leibniz and Berkeley, also thought that the problem was illusory, but because mechanism is not ultimate even in nature.[25]

Kant's greatness, as well as the deepest problematic in his thought, stems from his refusal to lessen the conflict by weakening one or both of the contending commitments. Both knower as purposeful agent and known were givens, not to be sacrificed or compromised. And Kant drove the tension between the two – 'the starry heavens above' and 'the moral light within' – to its logical extreme, integrating his predecessors' 'dogmatic' answers into a new system that strove to limit or demarcate their potentially antagonistic demands.[26]

A useful way of understanding Kant's epistemology is in terms of what he was reacting against. While having been trained in the 'Leibniz-Wolffian' rationalism that dominated the German Enlightenment, Kant none the less had been exposed to the ideas of British empiricism and Newton's mechanics through his many friends at the Berlin Academy and took the certainty of Newtonianism far too seriously to remain silent in the face of Hume's trenchant critique of causation. Kant's greatest challenge, accordingly, was to 'answer Hume' by proving the validity and legitimate foundation of scientific knowledge, while simultaneously destroying the excessive claims of the older speculative metaphysics. Thus, from his own early love for 'dogmatic metaphysics,' Kant painfully struggled to censure reason's 'leap out beyond the context of sensibility' (A 563-B 591), its 'soaring so far above all possible experience' (A 638-B 666), or any movement that indicates its leaving 'the ground of experience' (A 689-B 717), such as wandering into the realm of 'mere possibilities' (A 630-B 658), where it cannot legitimately operate.[27] Kant ultimately came to believe that rationalism and empiricism both needed revision before they could stand the acid test of his 'critical philosophy' and its 'transcendental method,' which was to subject reason itself to a critique of its own powers to know.[28] As we shall see, Popper has performed a similar operation on the epistemological maladies of our time.

The groundwork of Hume's empiricism is contained in part I of the first book of *A Treatise of Human Nature*. There, he states three simple principles of momentous and devastating import to the rationalist of his day and age. There was the genetic principle: 'All our simple ideas, in their first appearance, are derived from simple impressions which are correspondent to them and which they exactly resemble.' According to the atomic principle: 'There are not any two propositions which are perfectly separable.' The associative principle involved the assertion of a 'gentle force, which commonly prevails (sc. to unite ideas), and is the cause why, among other things, languages so nearly correspond to each other, nature, in a manner, pointing out to every one those simple ideas, which are most proper to be united into a complex one.'[29]

Reason, while clearly an instrument for advancing knowledge, was to be whittled down to a circumscribed sphere of activity through rational analysis and the 'experimental method': 'Reason is the discovery of truth or falsehood. Truth or falsehood consists in an agreement or disagreement either to real relations or ideas, or to real existence and matters of fact. Whatever, therefore, is not susceptible of this agreement or disagreement is incapable of being true or false, and can never be an object of reason.'[30] Thus, for Hume, facts ultimately are derived from commonsense observation rather than reason, and what people describe as cause-and-effect is not a deductive conclusion of reason but the product of experience. That is, the belief that every event must have a cause has no rational justification and, instead, simply represents our habit of expectation which results from the constant association of continuous experiences in the past (cf book I, part 3, of *A Treatise of Human Nature*). Moreover, in so far as facts are derived from common sense, reason can neither prove nor disprove their existence. Hume viewed human behaviour as being governed by unanalysed experience (the 'gentle force of association' and 'certain manners') and habit: 'Custom is the great guide of human life.'[31]

The logical conclusion of Hume's empiricism was to deny the validity of much of what we cannot avoid assuming. Humean empiricism forces us to view 'things' as nothing but the sum of their properties and implies that we no longer have the right to use the word 'property' at all. Further, many of the concepts we employ in our dealings with the external world seem to collapse if Hume's premises are granted. For example, if a 'thing' (such as a piece of wax) undergoes a change (in temperature), we could not maintain that it was the same thing if we argue that a thing is the sum of its properties. Also, the distinction we ordinarily make between an event caused by another event and an event merely following another is unjustified. Ultimately, Hume's empiricism denies us certainty that things will continue to happen in the way they always have happened. As Hartnack observes: 'The result of Humean empiricism, the result of thinking that knowledge builds upon and contains nothing other than that which is given in sense experience, is consequently a denial of knowledge and the collapse of those concepts we employ in order to speak about and to understand reality. If Humean empiricism is true, then there is no knowledge. And conversely, if there is knowledge, then Humean empiricism is false.'[32] In short, not to 'answer Hume' would have been to abandon a necessary precondition of modernity's optimism and self-confidence, a concession hardly palatable to Kant. Popper came to the same conclusion in the 1930s when confronted with the profound intellectual crisis precipitated by the discoveries of Einstein, Planck, and their associates.

If Hume's world had no non-sense, it also had no sense either, for there was nobody in it.[33] For Hume, the self is simply a bundle of 'impressions,' and, on his own principles, there is nothing else that the self possibly could be. As he conceded in the Appendix to the *Treatise*, 'associative mechanisms' cannot ever make a 'person.' If, as he held, there is no logical or rational necessity to what we know, then there is no responsible agent to assent to our knowing it. Since the mind passively received sense impressions or perceptions, and all perceptions are necessarily separable, how do we then account for the togetherness, cohesiveness, or unity of that 'bundle' we commonly designate as 'mind' or 'self'? Hume's response was: 'For my part, I must plead the privilege of a sceptic, and confess that this difficulty is too hard for my understanding.' Here, more than in his critique of causation, lies Hume's ultimate scepticism.

Though much impressed by Hume's courage and philosophic rigour, Kant could not accept his scepticism, since it entailed that Newton's laws did not describe objective relations in nature but merely reflected the habitual and subjective judgments of individuals or societies. Yet as early as 1770, in his *Inaugural Dissertation: Form and Principles of the Sensible and Intelligible World*, Kant admitted that empiricists were right to emphasize that sense experience is essential to human knowledge. Therefore, by 1781, when the *Critique of Pure Reason* appeared, Kant had come to believe that his celebrated 'Copernican revolution' in philosophic method had to, and could, overcome the anomalies in both empiricism and the 'dogmatic rationalism' of his time. In Kant's view, while the former could not explain the validity of objective knowledge in the natural sciences, the latter ultimately produced a series of 'antinomies' that arise from the inability of reason to meet its own demands on thought. The crux of Kant's critical epistemology is captured in his 'answer to Hume' and the so-called 'Copernican revolution' in thinking it represented. A brief review of these two aspects of his thought will complete the background for a more extended discussion in the next chapter of Popper's philosophy of mind, his views on language, and his conception of objective knowledge.

Ever since Aristotle, it has been customary to consider a judgment about reality as consisting of a subject and a predicate. The subject is that about which the judgment affirms something; the predicate is that which is predicated of the subject.[34] For centuries to come, there was little revision in this logical schema of Aristotle's; philosophers before Kant accordingly maintained that judgments were either analytic or synthetic. In an analytic judgment, such as 'a triangle has three angles,' the predicate is found by analysis of the concept of the subject; such judgments are very important in organizing and articulating our knowledge. But analytic judgments do not extend our knowledge beyond what we already know. Thus, they are true a priori and necessarily true regardless of empirical referent and sense data. In a synthetic judgment, the predicate is not logically included in the concept of the subject, as in 'the woods are green.' The truth or falsity of such judgments can be determined only through recourse to experience; that is, they are a posteriori. But, even if true, such a judgment is not necessarily true; our senses can betray us, and so on.

Hume recognized this type of classification, and he and Kant agreed that analytic judgments do not give us any scientific knowledge of reality. They also concurred on the existence of synthetic a posteriori judgments. For Hume, however, these judgments deal with that with which our senses provide us. But, as we have seen, if knowledge consists only of successive sense impressions, there can be no logical or rational grounds to our knowledge, including that of natural science. Suffice to say, these sceptical implications posed the gravest of problems for the validation of a newly emergent scientific and industrial civilization.

Kant believed that in the natural sciences and mathematics there exists a third type of judgment, which is both synthetic (going 'beyond' the subject) and a priori (requiring no experience in order to amplify the subject). Kant was the first in the history of philosophy to posit such synthetic a prioris; before his first *Critique*, they would have been dismissed as a contradictio in adjecto. But, for Kant, they were absolutely essential even for synthetic a posteriori judgments, since any judgment based upon experience presupposes an a priori synthetic judgment for connecting or linking one event to another as cause-and-effect. Thus Kant's general 'answer to Hume' was to show that Hume's own thesis gains its very plausibility only by presupposing the principle the necessity of which he is denying.[35] Accordingly, the main epistemological task of *Critique of Pure Reason* is to answer the question 'How are synthetic a priori judgments possible?'

Kant's reply is most vividly described in what has become known as his 'Copernican revolution' in philosophy.[36] In the famous Preface to the second edition of the *Critique* (1787), Kant observed that the 'students of metaphysics' could manage so little agreement that 'metaphysics [should] rather ... be regarded as a battleground,' though one where very little territory had been gained or lost (B xv). While metaphysicians were 'groping and fumbling,' caught in the throes of totally inconclusive 'opinion-mongering,' Kant was convinced that mathematics and the physical sciences had obtained 'the sure path of science':[37] 'The mathematician does not inspect what he discerns either in the figure or the mere concept of it, and from this, as it were, read off its properties, but brings out what was necessarily implied in the concepts he has himself formed a priori and has put into the figures in the construction by which he presents it to himself' (B xii).

According to Kant, the 'sure path' in mathematics had been discovered by the Greeks: 'The transformation must have been due to a revolution brought about by the happy thought of a single man in an experiment – an experiment after which the road that must be taken could never again be missed, and the sure path of a science was entered upon and sign-posted for all time to come and into the infinite distance' (B x–xi). The 'revolutionary experiment' that Kant had in mind was clearly the first ancient geometrical construction: 'A light flashed upon the mind of the first man ... who demonstrated the properties of the isosceles triangle' (B xi–xii).

Thus the great achievement of the ancient geometers was their discovery of a 'true method,' a Cartesian-style vita methodica, which transformed their fumbling guesswork into the cumulative, incremental development of objective, scientific knowledge. Specifically, their discovery was that 'if he is to know anything with a priori certainly he must not ascribe to the figure anything but what necessarily follows from what he has himself put into it in accordance with his concept' (B xii). The development of the natural sciences has been similar to that of mathematics, although somewhat slower: 'Natural sciences was much longer in entering upon the highway of science. It is, indeed, only about a century and a half since Bacon, by his ingenious proposal, partly initiated this discovery, partly inspired fresh vigour in those who were already on the way to it. In this case also the discovery can be explained as being the sudden outcome of an intellectual revolution' (ibid).

After discussing the contributions of Galileo, Torricelli, and Stahl to this irreversible 'intellectual revolution,' Kant notes, 'A fresh light broke upon all students of nature. They learned that reason has insight only into that which it produces after a plan of its own, and that it must not allow itself to be kept, as it were, on nature's leading-strings, but must itself show the way with principles of judgement based on fixed laws, constraining nature to give answers to questions of reason's own determining' (B xi–xii). Nature will answer only such questions as we ask of it. We can have certain, universal knowledge, an accumulated body of synthetic a priori judgments, only in so far as our mind actively contributes to nature itself the concepts through which we come to understand it: 'Reason, holding in one hand its principles, according to which alone concordant appearances can be admitted as equivalent to laws, and in the other hand the experiment which it has devised in conformity with these principles, must approach nature in order to be taught by it. It must not, however, do so in the character of a pupil who listens to everything that the teacher chooses to say, but of an appointed judge who compels the witnesses to answer questions which he himself formulated' (B xiii).

In metaphysics, however, such a 'sure path' and 'true method' had not yet been found. 'It has hitherto been assumed that all our knowledge must conform to objects. But all attempts to extend our knowledge of objects by establishing something in regard to them a priori by means of concepts have, on this assumption, ended in failure. We must therefore make trial whether we may not have more success in the tasks of metaphysics if we suppose that objects must conform to our knowledge ... We should then be precisely along the lines of Copernicus' principal thought' (B xvi).

Kant's allusion to Copernicus emphasizes that in the great discoveries of Bacon, Galileo, Torricelli, Stahl, and, above all, Copernicus the mind was somehow attending to what it itself had 'put into' its objects. Analogously, philosophers before Kant (including Hume) had found it impossible to explain how there could be a priori knowledge of things on the assumption that knowledge of things consists of passive conformity to an object. Therefore, as Copernicus had hypothesized that the complex observed planetary motions were not real motions, but rather apparent motions dependent upon the real motion (i.e. the perspective) of the observer, so Kant maintained that if the phenomenal characteristics

of objects are explained in terms of the constructions of the active knowing mind, knowledge of them can be, indeed must be, a priori. Rather
than 'turning the knower around the world, we change our direction
and move the world around the knower.'[38] All objects of knowledge must
conform to the structure and activity of the knowing mind, which, in
turn, constitutes the ground or possibility of such knowledge. Ultimately,
we can be certain only of our own constructions.

Kant's 'Copernican revolution' in philosophy thus yielded a powerful
method of transcendental analysis with which he tried to answer three
principal questions of the *Critique*: What are the grounds of the possibility
of mathematics? This was answered in the transcendental aesthetic. What
are the grounds of the possibility of pure natural science? This was
answered in the transcendental analytic. Given both of the above answers, is a science of metaphyics possible? This was answered in the
transcendental dialectic.[39]

In light of their significance for those, like Popper, who develop a
similar metaphysical position in the wake of Einstein's theories of relativity, two other aspects of Kant's philosophy deserve mention: his conception of the mind and the atinomies of reason itself. First, the emphasis
placed on the active, constructive, and synthetic capacity of the mind
necessitates and presupposes a clear distinction between phenomenal
and real characteristics of objects. Kant was the first philosopher to
formulate consistently a 'three-faculty' conception of the mind – though
Johann Tetans (the 'German Locke,' according to Herder) clearly an-
ticipated him in this – and it was upon this foundation that Kant distinguished the real from the phenomenal realms of existence.

According to Kant, the mind is composed of three cognitive faculties:
sensibility, understanding, and reason. Sensibility, or our receptivity to
sense data, is the faculty by which we gain sensations for our conceptions
and through which our conceptions are, in turn, related to actual objects.
The a priori 'forms of sense intuition,' to which all objects we can ever
know must conform, are space and time. In other words, all objective
knowledge, viz. possessing a priori universality and necessity, must be
spatio-temporal in nature. In some of the most frequently cited passages
from the *Critique*, Kant makes it clear that we cannot bring a priori
concepts, principles, and forms to bear upon objects without sense intuition, and this bears a striking similarity to Hume's 'certain manners':
'In whatever manner and by whatever means cognition may relate to
objects, intuition is that through which it is in immediate relation to
them, and to which all thought as a means is directed ... All thought

must directly or indirectly be related to intuitions' (A 19-B 75). 'Thoughts without contents are empty, intuitions without concepts are blind' (A 51-B 75).

Understanding (Verstand) is the second faculty of the mind, and its function is to connect our perceptual conceptions of things into synthetic judgments of knowledge about phenomenal objects. Kant explicates these (four) a priori rules for the syntheses of concepts into judgments about objects in the transcendental analytic and calls them 'principles of pure understanding.' Basically, he derives these 'categories' from traditional (Aristotelian) logic, and they can be summarized as follows.

In 'axioms of intuition' the mind employs the three categories of quantity (unity, plurality, and totality). 'Anticipations of perception' refer to the categories of quality (reality, negation, and limitation). These two sets of categories together simply state the grounds by which mathematical operations can be applied to objects (e.g. all phenomena must be spatio-temporal, extensive, and intensive if we are to measure 'forces,' etc).

In 'analogies of experience' the mind employs the three categories of relation (substantiality/inherence, causality/dependence, and community/interaction). These are the most important categories inasmuch as they constitute the foundation of Newtonian physics: the first, stating the 'conservation of matter,' the second, 'the law of uniformity' or universal determinism, and the third, Newton's third law of motion. They are the crux of Kant's more specific 'answers to Hume' and of his re-validation of modern science against scepticism.

'Postulates of empirical thought' refer to the categories of modality (possibility, existence, and necessity). Kant argued that these were necessary in order to justify the application of scientific hypotheses to phenomena and to confirm inductive inferences.[40]

Kant's main point is that without these 'categories' we would be left simply with a 'blind, buzzing confusion' of chaotic sensations. Thus he drew a rigid demarcation between the form of knowledge, which is supplied by our understanding, and its content or substance, which we 'intuit' from the phenomenal world. A battle, at times fierce, has waged ever since over the rigidity and transcendental nature of this dualism of nature and mind.

The combined constructions of sensibility and understanding are 'subjective' in that they are the form or structure of our experience and do not correspond to metaphysical realities or 'things-in-themselves.' Moreover, as 'pure' systems of measurement and frames of reference, they extend beyond the limits of our fragmentary observations and therefore are transcendentally ideal. Yet they are also 'objective' (or empirically real) in that they are not personal, subjectivistic, or psychological peculiarities of a given person; they are the boundaries of our ordered, conceptual, public knowledge of phenomena. Thus Wittgenstein's famous claim in the *Tractatus* that language limits the world is decidedly Kantian in inspiration and design.[41] Reminiscent of Leibniz's *New Essays* in this respect, Kant observes, 'There can be no doubt that all our knowledge begins with experience ... But though all our knowledge begins with experience, it does not follow that it all arises out of experience. For it may well be that even our empirical knowledge is made up of what we receive through impressions and of what our own faculty of knowledge supplies from itself' (B i).[42]

As we will see in the next chapter, Popper specifically refers to this insight as holding the key to 'the riddle of natural science' – that is, though science is based upon experience, our theories are not derived from observations (cf *CR* chapter 8).

While in sensibility and understanding, and the world of experience they underlie, there is no way to prevent an infinite regress of phenomenal conditions (i.e. every phenomenon has other phenomena as its condition), reason, Kant's third faculty of the mind, demands a totality of these conditions. Otherwise, everything remains contingent. For Kant, reason is the faculty of systematic thought, of providing 'a wherefore for every therefore,' as Beck observes,[43] and its demands cannot be met by a faculty such as our understanding, which merely seeks out fragmentary, proximate (or 'efficient') causes. Therefore, if reason is to achieve its own demands for a causa sui, it must speculate beyond any possible experience to find the unconditioned, the supersensible realm of 'things-in-themselves' (dinge-an-sich).

Kant accordingly maintains that in speculating beyond and negating the restrictions of the 'categories' – that is, beyond nature itself in so far as it is simply phenomena under the laws of understanding – reason necessarily transcends the spatio-temporal order. As Randall notes, 'The pattern of 'pure reason' [is] timeless and eternal.'[44] Thus, while a category and its schema are constitutive of nature, the object of speculative reason can function only as a 'regulative idea.' In other words, the 'regulative principles of Reason' do not extend our objective knowledge in the sense that the categories do, but guide reason in its quest for greater unity (or totality) beyond sensibilia (cf. A 680-B 708). But to recall an earlier point, since categories can be applied, or 'schematized,' to objects only via a sensuous representation (or 'intuition'), they will not permit us to know the supersensible realm, but only to think of it. Again, as we will see in the following chapter, Popper also tries to take advantage of these assumptions in formulating the logical demarcation between genuine 'scientific' knowledge and metaphysics. By so doing, he hopes to preserve the empirical foundation of cognitive progress without denying the positive role of speculative reasoning in the process.

Kant's epistemology thus necessarily reflects reason divided against itself. While theoretical reason does its best to organize and reduce our knowledge into logically formal and mathematical systems which give us parsimonious explanations of phenomena, speculative reason pushes onward and upward for 'final answers,' outside and beyond our causally ordered knowledge of 'objective reality,' toward the noumenal realm of the 'ding-an-sich.' Although speculative reason must cut itself off from the world of conditioned or 'determined' phenomena, it must rely on the 'categories' of thought in order to do so. In short, Kant met modernity's underlying tension between the validation of scientific knowledge and the enchantment or meaning of its effects on modern life by finding virtue in both their demands.

This leads us to one final dimension of Kant's epistemology, namely, the 'antinomies of the Pure Reason' found in the transcendental dialectic (A 444–558-B 472–586). In *Critique of Practical Reason* (1788), Kant wrote: 'The antinomy of pure reason, which becomes obvious in its dialectic, is, in fact, the most fortunate perplexity in which human reason could ever have become involved, since it finally compels us to seek to escape from this labyrinth.'[45] Indeed, some ten years later, Kant wrote to his good friend and follower Christian Garve that the discovery of the antinomy of speculative reason was the beginning of his 'critical philosophy.'[46] In *Critique of Pure Reason*, Kant tries to explicate the problem by exploring four 'antinomies' within speculative reason. He demonstrates that for every synthetic a priori judgment, there is an equally valid and 'necessary' argument that could prove its contradiction and which also expresses an inescapable interest of reason. The 'third antinomy' exposes the conflict within the idea of causality itself. The thesis posits the existence of causes not subsumed under the laws of nature, or causation other than mechanical causation; the antithesis asserts the sufficiency of natural causation, or causation under the laws of nature (both those already known and those yet to be discovered).

Kant believed that uncovering such antinomies was 'the most fortunate perplexity' into which reason could ever fall, because 'critically' understood they need not be taken seriously at all. Instead, 'they can be laughed at, as mere child's play' (A 743-B 771). 'Both parties beat the air, and wrestle with their own shadows, since they go beyond the limits of nature, where there is nothing they can seize and hold with their dogmatic grasp. Fight as they may, the shadows which they cleave asunder grow together again forthwith, like the heroes of Valhalla, to disport themselves anew in bloodless contests' (A 756-B 786; Kemp-Smith translation). Therefore, the only adequate resolution of the third antinomy, Kant maintained, lies in the recognition that both the thesis and antithesis may be true if their respective spheres of application are distinguished. Each is defined by the nature of the experience supporting it, and neither can possibly be valid if employed beyond the realm to which its proofs extend.

The thesis presents the claims of reason, which requires a sufficient cause for every phenomena. However, as we have seen, such a sufficient cause cannot be found within the realm of phenomena due to an infinite regress of phenomenal conditions. The antithesis represents the interest of understanding in its efforts to apply the law of causality to a spatio-temporal series of events.

As Beck rightly notes, the whole argument shows 'that the assumption of a free cause among phenomena would interrupt the continuity required by natural law.'[47] The contradiction disappears, however, when the thesis is applied to relations between noumena ('things-in-themselves') and the antithesis to relations among phenomena. As Kant observes in *Critique of Practical Reason*,

There is no true conflict if the events and even the world in which they occur are regarded as only appearances (as they should be) ... One and the same being acting as appearance (even to his own inner sense) has a causality in the sensuous world always in accordance with the mechanism of nature; while with respect of the same event, so far as the acting person regards himself as noumenon (as pure intelligence, existing without temporal determination), he can contain a determining ground of that causality according to natural laws, and this determining ground of natural causality is free from every natural law. (118–19)

Without this dualism between noumenon and phenomenon, obviously of Platonic provenance, Kant's entire 'critical' project collapses into either one of its dominant moments or polarities: logical empiricism or positivism, on the one hand, or some variety of absolute idealism or romanticism, on the other.[48]

For his part, Kant argued for the necessity of the dualism to the very last. Against the disenchantment and 'unhappy consciousness' of the early German Romantics (or Sturm und Drangers), especially Herder and Jacobi, Kant repeatedly criticized their claims of being able to 'know' the supersensible realm of noumena and for having ignored the necessity of both poles of his 'critical' revision of metaphysics. For instance, Fichte's absolute idealism, with its claim of being a more faithful descendant of 'critical philosophizing' than even Kant's own later work, had brought stern rebuke from the old master himself. Kant argued to the end that it was only by embracing such a transcendental dualism that we can consistently defend ourselves against Hume's scepticism and be able to affirm our practical freedom. Thus, as he observed in the Preface to the second edition of the first *Critique*, 'I have found it necessary to deny knowledge in order to make room for faith' (B xxx). Theoretical knowledge of the noumenal realm, he argued, would destroy the very possibility of 'free,' undetermined actions. And only such an assumption can justify our belief that the moral demands we place upon ourselves can be met; in other words, only through theoretical ignorance of the future can there be a secure basis for our practical faith in the improvement of mankind. Popper extends this view in several interesting directions in his denial that there can ever be such a thing as 'laws' in history, but that none the less, though 'history as such' has no 'meaning' or enchantment, there is still hope in proceeding as if we can 'give it meaning' through our endeavours. I will return to these themes, especially in chapter 7, and some of the problems that arise in connection with Kant's and Popper's dualistic transcendentalism will be the subject of chapter 8.

In the first *Critique*, Kant's defence of the rationality of our faith in freedom – and, by implication, of the possibility of progress upon which it rests – as a supersensible, noumenal mode of causality was limited to his fixing a boundary beyond which scientific knowledge cannot validly aspire and to his proof that mechanism is not the only possible form of causality. But, for Kant, the reality of freedom has to be grounded in the same transcendental manner as pure theoretical reason had been defended against Hume's empiricism and scepticism. Therefore, in *Groundwork for the Metaphysics of Morals* (1785) and *Critique of Practical Reason*, Kant justifies freedom more positively by indicating its existence as a necessary a priori condition of a certain type of experience, namely, of morality, with its universal and necessary injunctions. Kant's point is that, in order to justify rationally the possibility and phenomenon of moral necessitation, we must presuppose a 'free cause.' Only if free causes are held to exist can the unconditional necessity of moral law be explained: 'Freedom ... among all the ideas of speculative reason is the only one whose possibility we know *a priori*. We do not understand it, but we know it as the condition of the moral law which we do know ... There really is freedom, for this Idea is revealed by moral law.'[49]

There is thus a perfect parallelism between Kant's 'theoretical' and 'practical' philosophies in so far as the function of reason is concerned. In both phases, reason functions as the active law-giver and is bound by the laws or rules that it gives. While the a priority of knowledge can be guaranteed and secured only by rooting it in our transcendental understanding, so too the a priority of moral duty and obligation can be preserved only by basing it on an equally 'pure,' albeit acting, practical reason. Kant compares the two functions as follows: 'The Legislation of human reason (philosophy) has two objects, nature and freedom, and therefore contains not only the laws of nature, but also the moral law, presenting them at first in two distinct systems, but ultimately in one single philosophical system. The philosophy of nature deals with all that is, the philosophy of morals with all that which ought to be' (A 840-B 868).

Accordingly, there is much wisdom in Tarbet's observation that 'there is justice in calling the legal metaphor the main structural metaphor of the (first) *Critique*'[50] and in affirming Kant's belief that 'the critique of pure reason can be regarded as the true tribunal of all disputes of pure reason, ... in which our disputes have to be conducted by the recognized methods of legal action' (A 751-B 779). On Kant's view, the only rational response to the crisis of Enlightenment ideals – especially the potentially destructive rift between the validation of the Baconian maxim that knowledge is power and the threat this poses to the enchantment and meaningfulness of modern life – was to settle the matter 'in court,' as it were, before the tribunal of a once-again sovereign, because methodically fortified, reason.

Nietzsche observed: 'The most valuable insights are arrived at last; but the most valuable insights are methods.'[51] It would be difficult to overestimate the impact of Kant's 'critical' philosophy of nineteenth- and twentieth-century philosophy and social science. Hence the widespread view referred to in the previous chapter that one may philosophize for or against but not without a serious consideration of his thought.[52] With regard to the general function of philosophy, Kant's greatest concern was to retrieve our rational faith in 'progress,' understood as the possibility of ultimately knowing reality and of increasing human autonomy. As we have seen, while scepticism and irrationalism had come to pose the severest of challenges to the first of these philosophical pillars of modernity, the validity of Newtonian mechanism seemed to jeopardize our status as 'free,' self-determining historical agents. To the extent that this crisis in optimism and intellectual self-confidence went unanswered, Kant knew all too well that we would be left in a state of unenlightened 'self-incurred immaturity,' inconclusive 'opinion-mongering,' and blind 'fumbling and guess-work' as to the future course of events. In the absence of an adequate response, no longer – indeed, perhaps never again – would we be able to believe (as had been the custom since the Renaissance and Enlightenment) that 'what mind might encompass of knowledge of the physical universe has a direct bearing upon the quality of human existence, and ... that mind can ... be decisive in political life.'[53]

Kant's solution to this dilemma was a set of radically new 'methodical' criteria and philosophical premises for the re-enchantment of reason, thus renewing our faith in the prospects and possibility of orderly, purposeful growth in mind and society alike. Above all, this entailed subjecting reason itself to a transcendental critique of its own powers of knowing. And ultimately, this meant setting limits to the potentially destructive, contradictory aspirations that thought itself can be seen to embody – recklessly 'leaving the ground of experience' in quest of a sense of greater 'totality' and the discovery of an ultimate causa sui. As Kant observed in *Critique of Pure Reason*, he considered himself, along with David Hume, 'one of those geographers of human reason' (A 760-B 788), forever mapping or demarcating the respective spheres and interests of our understanding nature, as an order of contingent, 'efficiently' caused (but 'meaningless') phenomena, and of reason, which continually presses 'onwards and upwards' beyond the categories of our phenomenal sensibility and de facto determination toward the mundus intelligibus of 'ends.' Unfortunately, Kant left all the relationships and precise mediations between the two values – the realms of necessity and freedom – quite obscure in light of his purely formal characterization of the 'transcendental' and a priori nature of the self. I will return to this problem, in connection with Popper's thought, in chapter 8.

This emphasis, in Kant, on the preventative or prophylactic function of philosophy as a necessary precondition for progress toward 'enlightenment' ideals is far from accidental. On the contrary, it takes us to the centre of his metaphysics and universe of discourse. Whether it be in the Preface to the first *Critique*, where he recalls 'having found it necessary to deny knowledge in order to make room for faith' (B xxx), or the concluding paragraph of *Critique of Practical Reason*, where he characteristically notes 'that the inscrutable wisdom through which we exist is not less worthy of veneration in respect to what it denies us than in what it has granted,'[54] Kant's underlying presupposition was the same: nature itself fixes limits to how we should conduct our investigations, limits which we ignore only at great peril to the future development of the species.

In this context, it is also interesting to note the centrality of Seneca's Stoicism in Kant's political thought and philosophy of history, best evidenced by his frequent reference to one of the Epistles, 'Duncunt volentum fata, nolentum trahunt / The fates lead him who is willing, but drag him who is unwilling.'[55] Kant's project is thus best understood as an attempt to formulate the necessary, logical limits to what we can know and, accordingly, what we ought to do and may hope for. Above all else, his is a metaphysics of orderly, lawful growth, of possibilities and progress within predetermined limits.

Seldom have these central assumptions and ideals of liberalism and the Enlightenment suffered from as many assaults and from as many directions of both an intellectual and social kind as during the first half of Popper's life. If, as George Lichtheim observed, 'the decade 1914–24 witnessed the greatest upheaval Europe had undergone since Napoleon,'[56] the next decade and a half was even more unsettling for intellectuals such as Popper, who not only endured the aftermath of the war but tried to make sense of its causes and provide the means with which to combat their possible recurrence. And it is precisely in that context that the metaphysical structure of Kant's thought emerges as of such importance in situating Popper's work vis-à-vis the series of crises his theories were intended to address.

More specifically, for Popper the underlying motivation and structure of Kant's 'reply to Hume' came to serve as the corner-stone of a systematic defence of rationality and progress during a period in which they were under far more serious attack than anything Kant ever envisioned. If Enlightenment ideals about the efficacy of reason in clarifying and helping us to solve social and political problems are once again 'becoming increasingly thin and unconvincing' to many sensitive thinkers among us,[57] so much less secure must their stature and place have been in what Popper recalls a 'starving postwar Vienna' – the aftermath of a war that 'had destroyed the world in which [he] had grown up.' There is strong evidence that Popper's experience during the 1920s and 1930s in Vienna of the widespread assault upon Enlightenment ideals, not only in social and political affairs but within the natural sciences and epistemology as well, is of decisive importance to an understanding of his thought and the widespread reception it subsequently received.

As we shall see in the chapters to follow, the doctrines and 'enemies' Popper initially chose and continues to attack, the weapons he uses to counteract their credibility and potential influence, and the positive thrust of his own philosophy are profoundly Kantian and deeply committed to defending the prospects – or what Weber and, more recently, Dahrendorf call the 'life chances'[58] – of a rational, liberal way of life against forms of irrationalism and authoritarianism endemic in post-war Austria.

Popper himself, like Kant, tells us that philosophy, understood as the 'legislation of human reason,' has 'two objects, nature and freedom.' And, like Kant, Popper contends that these 'two objects' must ultimately be presented in one unified philosophy, for, in both contexts, it is man's reason, the knowing mind that determines their respective natures and the conditions of their possibility. Thus, in the opening section of *The Self and Its Brain*, fittingly entitled 'Kant's Argument,' Popper observes that 'Kant is essentially right' in seeing the seriousness of the potential contradiction between the validation of scientific knowledge and the prospects of leading an enchanted, meaningful existence. But, for both Kant and Popper, disenchantment with the possibility of progress and 'enlightenment' need not follow. Theirs are philosophies of hope in orderly growth. In Popper's own words, though scientific knowledge 'annihilates the importance of a man, considered as a part of the physical universe,' a proper understanding of 'the invisible self' and the human personality 'raises immeasurably his value as an intelligent and responsible being' (*SB* 3).

Echoing Josef Popper-Lynkeus (1838–1921), a well-known-engineer-inventor, social reformer, and leading literary figure in Vienna during the first two decades of the century, Popper notes: 'Every time a man dies, a whole universe is destroyed. (One realizes this when one identifies onself with that man.)' Human beings, he continues, 'are irreplaceable; and in being irreplaceable they are clearly very different from machines. They are capable of suffering, and of facing death consciously. They are selves; they are ends in themselves, as Kant said' (*SB*, 3). Underlying everything that Popper has written is this conviction that individual human beings are 'irreplaceable'; their preservation and development should govern all our attitudes and actions. As he characteristically observed in a recent essay, 'How I See Philosophy':

We do not know how it is that we are alive on this wonderful little planet – or why there should be something like life, to make our planet so beautiful. But here we are, and we have every reason to wonder at it, and to feel grateful for it. It comes close to being a miracle ... There may be many other planets with life on them. Yet if we pick out at random a place in the universe, then the probability ... of finding a life-carrying body at that place will be zero, or almost zero. So life has at any rate the value of something rare; it is precious. We are inclined to forget this, and treat life cheaply, perhaps out of thoughtlessness; or perhaps because this beautiful earth of ours is, no doubt, a bit overcrowded ... There are those who think that life is valueless because it has an end. They do not think that the opposite argument might also be proposed: that if there were no end to life, it would have no value; that it is, in part, the ever-present danger of losing it which helps to bring home to us the value of life. (HSP 55)

Treating human beings as 'ends in themselves' rather than as mere 'means' is thus incompatible not only 'with the materialist doctrine that men are machines' but equally, if not more importantly, with any and all denials that mind or 'critical' rationality can be 'decisive' in intellectual and political affairs. This Kantian-inspired critique of all 'determinisms' because of their intellectual and moral consequences – above all, their anti-humanitarian implications – represents the underlying and sustaining motivation to Popper's better-known views concerning epistemological fallibilism, methodological falsificationism, and the philosophies of history and of politics (the subjects of the next four chapters of this study).

In the following chapter, I will characterize this moral and intellectual consequentialism of Popper's thought as a kind of logical pragmatism, the view of 'truth as consequences.' There, we shall see that what distinguishes Popper's thought from other varieties of neo-Kantianism is its pragmatic, problem-solving, evolutionary core, while what distances his thought from most other types of pragmatism (that of C.S. Peirce being the one notable exception) is his logicism, the presupposition which he shares with the members of the Vienna Circle that formal logic occupies a privileged, essentially normative, juridical role in the philosophy of science which, in turn, represents our best standard of rationality, the growth of knowledge, and a free and 'open' society as a whole. And, uniting the two poles of Popper's thought – the dynamic and the static, the anthropological and the transcendental, the pragmatic and the logical, the demands of order and of growth – is Kant's conception of human autonomy, the view of man as potentially 'citizen and builder of his own world.'[59] This, Popper never tires of reminding us, is a hope worth fighting for in the realm of ideas.

I believe that this aspect of Popper's thought is one of the primary reasons for the tremendous – some have claimed, unprecedented – following his thought now enjoys, evidenced by both the quantity of secondary literature and commentary his writings have commanded and the presence of organized bodies and institutions now conducting themselves with the inspiration and doctrinal guidance of Popper foremost in mind.[60] In a century known primarily for its wars and brutalities, its sense of quiet desperation and meaninglessness, and a profound resignation to a future of negligible, if any, improvements in the condition of the species as a whole, Popper's is a message of hopeful but limited possibilities – of survival and purposeful growth for those still willing to learn.

As we shall see at greater length in the next chapter, Popper's intellectual odyssey began in educational psychology and learning theory. And, in spite of his subsequent 'changeover' from the psychology to the methodology of knowledge, Popper's thought is reminiscent of John Dewey's in its life-long attempt to link the survival and proper understanding of the values of purposes we cherish most with the reform of our habitual ways of thinking, educational practice, and pedagogical methodology. The rationality of free, open, and progressive society, he tells us, is above all else successful problem-solving understood as the methodical elimination of error. More than anything else, we must learn to teach our society how to live within the logic and limits of our experience.

Though many have rightly taken offence at Popper's frequently combative style and the strident tone of his prose (in many but the more technical of his writings), one would do well to bear in mind the moral consequentialism and the radical humanitarianism and individualism that motivate and sustain such rhetoric and his use of the language. Time and time again, Popper argues,

The choice before us is not simply an intellectual affair, or a matter of taste. It is a moral decision. ... For the question whether we adopt some more or less radical form of irrationalism, or whether we adopt ... 'critical rationalism', will deeply affect our whole attitude towards other men, and towards the problems of social life ... [And] whenever we are faced with a moral decision of a more abstract kind, it is most helpful to analyse carefully the consequences which are likely to result from the alternatives between which we have to choose. For only if we can visualize these consequences in a concrete and practical way, do we really know what our decision is about; otherwise we decide blindly. (*OS* II 232)

Ideas, he notes in one of his later collections of essays, 'are dangerous and powerful things' (*CR* 5). Though the theory of knowledge or epistemology is 'reputed to be the most abstract and remote and altogether irrelevant region of pure philosophy,' Popper reminds us of Kant's attitude toward the subject. Popper believes that Kant and Russell were right in attributing 'to epistemology practical consequences for science, ethics, and even politics' (*CR* 4). Citing Russell's *Let the People Think* (1941), Popper concurs with the view that 'epistemological relativism, or the idea that there is no such thing as objective truth, and epistemological pragmatism, or the idea that truth is the same as usefulness, are closely linked with authoritarian and totalitarian ideas' (*CR* 4–5).

The situation is really very simple. The belief of a liberal – the belief in the possibility of a rule of law, of equal justice, of fundamental rights, and a free society – can easily survive the recognition that judges are not omniscient and may make mistakes about facts and that, in practice, absolute justice is hardly ever realized in any particular legal case. But this belief in the possibility of a rule of law, of justice, and of freedom, cannot well survive the acceptance of an epistemology which teaches that there are no objective facts; not merely in this particular case, but in any other case; and that the judge cannot have made a factual mistake because he can no more be wrong about the facts than he can be right. (*CR* 5)

Indeed, Popper has argued that it is the acceptance of a conception of standards of rational criticism and objective truth

which creates the dignity of the individual man; which makes his responsible, morally as well as intellectually; which enables him not only to act rationally, but also to contemplates and adjudicate, and to discriminate between competing theories. These standards of objective truth and criticism may teach him to try again, and to think again; ... They may teach him to apply the method of trial and error in every field, and especially in science; and thus they may teach him how to learn from his mistakes, and how to search for them. These standards may help him to discover how little he knows, and how much there is that he does not know. ... They may help him to become aware of the fact that he owes his growth to other people's criticisms, and that reasonableness is readiness to listen to criticism. And in this way they may even help him to transcend his animal past, and with it that subjectivism and voluntarism in which romatic and irrationalist philosophies may try to hold him captive. (*CR* 384)

One would be hard pressed to find a more principled and outspoken heir to Kant's defence of the possibility and ideals of 'enlightenment' than Popper. It is too frequently forgotten that Kant ultimately answered the question, 'What is Enlightenment?' in terms of the philosophy of history, not metaphysics or epistemology.[61] In 1784, he defined enlightenment as mankind's departure from its own self-incurred immaturity and servitude – in short, as autonomy. And, significantly, Kant defined the historical place and significance of his own philosophy by viewing the epoch in which he lived as one of enlightenment. To the extent that enlightenment could be achieved, Kant contended, it was not as a private accomplishment but as a general cultural and historical, universal process. As a keen student of the concept observes, 'In religion, it means the struggle for tolerance against superstition and a revolt of reason against the orthodox priesthood; in politics, the struggle for freedom before the law against the arbitrary despotism of estates; in natural science, empiricism; in philosophy, the liberation from the tutelage of theology and the fight against dogmatism and metaphysics.'[62]

Confronted with the imminent threat of a new dark age, Popper was understandably wary of all 'progressivist' philosophies of history which Kant's thought inspired, but, none the less, he realized the depths of our longing for meaning and purpose in life, for having some rational grounds for hope and progress. And, like Kant, these he would eventually locate in our understanding of the orderly and methodical growth of knowledge: 'Our mind grows and transcends itself. If humanism is concerned with the growth of the human mind, what then is the tradition of humanism if not a tradition of criticism and reasonableness?' (*CR* 384). Thus 'although history has no meaning, we can give it a meaning,' provided we learn to live within the limits of how little we really know (*OS* II 269, 278). Like the jurist in Musil's *Man without Qualities*, Popper 'does not go to Nature for his concepts; what he does is to penetrate into Nature with the flame of intellect and the sword of the moral law.'[63]

The remainder of this study traces the impact of this metaphysical structure and moral impulse of Kantianism on Popper's epistemology and methodology of the natural sciences (chapter 4), his corresponding recommendations for the conduct of social inquiry (chapter 5), and his defence of liberal democracy against a host of challenges, both intellectual and practical (chapter 7). Then, in chapter 8, I take up the so-called 'Darwinian turn' of Popper's later thought and express some critical reservations about the consistency, implications, and limits of his attempt to conserve the liberal way of life in the manner he suggests.

4

Truth as consequences:
the unity of Popper's thought

Find a scientific man who proposes to get along
without any metaphysics ... and you have found one
whose doctrines are thoroughly vitiated by the crude
and uncriticized metaphysics with which they are
packed.[1]

C.S. Peirce

The history of science, like the history of all
human ideas, is a history of irresponsible dreams,
of obstinacy, and of error.

Popper, *Conjectures and Refutations* 216

In Popper's hands, the metaphysical impulse and structure of Kant's
philosophy become a powerful exemplar of contemporary liberalism, a
fortified variety of scientific moralism – at once an ethic and a methodology of orderly growth in mind and society. I believe that Popper's
epistemology is best described as a distinctively twentieth-century variety
of Neo-Kantianism, which ultimately I will characterize as a type of
logical pragmatism. The intellectual foundations of this outlook are best
expressed in the view of 'truth as consequences,' the components of
which were all laid by the time Popper fled his native Vienna for New
Zealand. As opposed to the intellectual development of Russell or Carnap, both of whom regularly revised their views, Popper has not significantly altered the major tenets of his early philosophy. Instead, as
Lieberson points out, Popper has elaborated his early views 'again and
again, extended, refined, and generalized them in an effort to explain
and understand even broader and more areas of human inquiry.'[2]

Differentiating an 'early' from a 'later' Popper, let alone seeing three of him – 'P_0, P_1, P_2' – can be justified only on the explicitly 'whiggish' desire to regard his thought as a continuous but unfinished stage in the development of someone else's philosophy (in this case, that of the late Imre Lakatos).[3] I believe, to the contrary, that a close reading of Popper's work against the philosophical background of its formation in Vienna yields but one Popper, the unity of whose thought is a decidedly Kantian interpretation and justification of intellectual – above all, scientific – progress and of the moral autonomy that modernity once promised and, at least to some, still potentially embodies. I accordingly intend to underscore the already well-documented affinities between Popper's scientific philosophizing and the 'pragmaticism' of Charles Saunders Peirce.[4] But I will emphasize that the corner-stone of both their philosophies of fallibilism is the specifically Kantian understanding of the dependence of logic on ethical and moral considerations, the truly revolutionary insight that all conceptual thought is, in the words of Richard Bernstein, 'essentially normative.'[5] And let us not forget yet another momentous debt we owe to Kant: that all thought is necessarily conceptual!

Kant believed that the objects of science are actively constructed by the mind (and, therefore, are 'hypothetical' or conjectural in nature), that science itself represents our best system of conceptual knowledge, and that philosophy as a whole should aspire to the ideals of scientific clarity, rigour, objectivity, and explanation. These three principles have been central assumptions in the movement of ideas within which Popper's thought should be viewed: that of 'scientific philosophizing.'[6] According to another participant, Herbert Feigl, Russell, Frege, Tarski, and, above all, the physicists and mathematicians-turned-philosophers of the Vienna Circle constructed 'philosophies for our age of science' – tough-minded (William James's term), opposed to obscurantist metaphysics and mysticism, and in favour of the spirit of Enlightenment and clarification.[7] Above all, the movement opposed what Feigl calls 'verbal sedatives,' that is, 'high-sounding phrases that may tranquilize scientific curiosity and thus impede the progress of research.'[8]

In a lecture to the Aristotelian Society, delivered in 1948, Popper gave a clear indication of his intellectual orientation: he had 'always felt much sympathy with Kant, the positivists and all others who, repelled by the extravagant claims of some philosophical system builders, began to doubt whether there was anything at all in philosophy. I have only admiration for those who reacted against apriorism – the attitude of possessing if not all fundamental knowledge, at least the key to it – and against all empty verbalism.'⁹

Elsewhere, he recalls: 'What attracted me most to the Vienna Circle was the "scientific attitude" or, as I now prefer to call it, the rational attitude' (IA 70). Citing approvingly Carnap's *Der Logisch Aufbau der Welt* (1928), Popper notes that his own widely publicized criticism of Carnap's inductionism and reductionism is insignificant given their shared assumption about the nature of philosophizing. He lauds Carnap's plea 'for rationality, for greater intellectual responsibility, ... [and for us] to learn from the way in which mathematicians and scientists proceed, and ... contrasts with this the depressing ways of philosophers.' It is, Popper concludes, 'in this general attitude, this attitude of enlightenment, and in this critical view of philosophy – of what philosophy unfortunately is, and of what it ought to be – that I still feel very much at one with the Vienna Circle and with its spiritual father, Bertrand Russell. This explains why I was sometimes thought by members of the Circle, such as Carnap, to be one of them, and to overstress my difference with them' (IA 70). Thus, although his disagreements with logical positivists were fundamental at some levels of analysis, these 'arose only because of a shared conviction about what questions and ideals are important.'¹⁰

In the 1948 lecture Popper underscored the depths of his Kantianism and its role in differentiating his thought from the Humean empiricism and physicalism of the Circle. Although the logical positivists were anti-apriorists, who believed that 'there is no room for a third realm of studies besides the empirical sciences on the one hand and knowledge of logic and mathematics on the other,' they found themselves entangled in a series of intellectual culs-de-sac when asked to produce a criterion of empirical knowledge (LP 142). So, too, did the scientific empiricism of Hans Reichenbach and other members of the Berlin Society for Scientific Philosophizing, with whom members of the Circle were in regular contact and whose epistemology was similar to their own. 'When confronted with the task to explain the criterion of meaningful language, as opposed to meaningless verbiage, [the logical positivists] got themselves into many difficulties, proposing, for example, criteria in terms which turned out to be themselves meaningless' (LP 143).

The criterion Popper is referring to here is the Circle's principle of verifiability, formulated by Friedrich Waismann and subsequently and more widely associated with Carnap (converted to physicalism by Otto Neurath).

According to Popper, these positivists, 'who had started by denouncing philosophy as merely verbal, and who had demanded that ... we should turn away from the verbal problems to those which are real and empirical, found themselves bogged up in the thankless task of analysing and unmasking verbal pseudo-problems' (ibid). Popper saw the underlying problem with both the Machian phenomenalists and the Wittgensteinians of Schlick's seminar as being their a priori and ultimately self-defeating hostility toward metaphysics. 'The Circle had become not only antimetaphysical, but antiphilosophical' (HSP 45).

Tracing the inspiration of Wittgenstein's *Tractatus* to Russell's solution of the logical paradoxes as pseudo-propositions that are neither true nor false but meaningless, Popper charges that the work dismisses most of the traditional issues of philosophy as 'pseudo-problems which arise from speaking without having given meaning to all one's words.' Much to Popper's consternation, this led to the technique' of branding all sorts of inconvenient propositions and problems as "meaningless" ' (HSP 45–6).

Since, in Popper's view, metaphysical ideas are often forerunners to scientific ones, he believes that restricting questions of science to factually verifiable or 'meaningful' knowledge may limit our ability to solve our most pressing problems: 'The existence of urgent and serious philosophical problems and the need to discuss them critically is the only apology for what may be called professional or academic philosophy' (HSP 45). Popper emphatically rejects the view of thinkers such as G.E. Moore 'that the need to correct what professional philosophers say would be a sufficient excuse for philosophy to exist,' which leads to something 'like philosophic inbreeding.' This 'would make a specialism of philosophy, after the model of modern science. Now I think that a strong case can be made against this all too fashionable specialization in the sciences; and the case against specialization in philosophy is stronger.'[11]

Echoing the modernism and pedagogical progressivism of Glöckel's school reform movement, Popper argued before the Aristotelian Society that 'most of us think too much in terms of subject-matters or disciplines' (LP 144). Such disciplines or bodies of knowledge are 'largely didactic devices designed to help in the organization of teaching. The scientist – the man who does not only teach but adds to our knowledge – is fundamentally a student of problems, not subject-matters' (ibid). Again we see the fundamentally Kantian structure of Popper's philosophy of mind.

The verification theory of meaning – the central doctrine of logical positivism – seemed to Popper a fatally misconceived criterion for demarcating science from pseudo-science, 'merely a translation of Aristotelian subject-predicate logic into psychological terms' (IA 60). It was akin to the 'passive storehouse conception of the mind.' According to Popper, this school committed the cardinal sin of Kant's dogmatists – subreption, extending a category's logic beyond the sphere of its competence, thereby depriving scientific growth and progress of the necessary foundation or a priori condition of its validation as objective knowledge.

Popper's illustration of the limitations of Aristotelian logic focuses on the statement 'Men are mortal.' A 'copula' links the two 'terms' (subject and predicate). If we translate the statement into psychological terms, 'You will say that thinking consists in having the "idea" of man and mortality "associated"' (ibid). Such a 'subject-predicate logic is a very primitive thing. (It may be regarded as an interpretation of a small fragment of Boolean algebra, untidily mixed up with a small fragment of naive set theory). It is incredible that anybody should still mistake it for empirical psychology' (ibid). Elevating such a pseudo-empirical psychological criterion to the standard to distinguish scientific from pseudo-scientific knowledge jeopardizes science by transferring atomism from physics to psychology.

Kant's criticism of Hume's atomism led Kant to believe that our understanding supplies the categories and principles by which we order our experience. So Popper came to believe that the sort of sense data – 'simple ideas' or impressions – assumed in Mach's phenomenalism or the early Wittgenstein's notion of 'facts' simply did not exist; 'they were fictitious' (IA 60). Drawing on Oswald Külpe and his Würzburger School, Otto Selz, and, especially, Bühler (with this theory of 'imageless thought'), Popper concluded early that 'we do not think in images but in terms of problems and their tentative solutions' (IA 60).

A further step showed Popper that the mechanism of translating a dubious logical doctrine into one of an allegedly empirical psychology was still at work, and had its dangers, even for such an outstanding thinker as Bühler' (IA 60). Following Külpe's Logic,[13] Bühler conceived of arguments as complex judgments – 'a mistake from the point of view of modern logic.' Because of this error, 'there could be no real distinction between judging and arguing.' Moreover, such a view tends to blur the original distinction between the descriptive function of language (which corresponds to 'judgments') and the argumentative. In short, Bühler had not succeeded in 'seeing that they [judging and arguing] could be [as] clearly separated as the three functions of language which he had already distinguished' and which Popper certainly accepted as opposed to the atomism of Hume, Mach, and Russell (ibid).

Popper's elaboration of this dimension of Bühler's thought represents the most visible and significant shift of perspectives of his entire career – his 'turnaway' from psychology and 'changeover to methodology' (IA 61). Bühler's expressive function could be logically separated from the communicative (signal, or release) function 'because an animal or man could express himself even if there were no "receiver" to be stimulated.' Both functions could in turn be distinguished from the descriptive because 'an animal or a man could communicate fear (for example) without describing the object feared' (IA 60–1).

Popper recalls that the descriptive function, '(a higher function, ... and exclusive to man) was, I then found, clearly distinguishable from the *argumentative* function, since there exist languages, such as maps, which are descriptive but not argumentative' (IA 61).[15] Because of these differences in functions and, above all, of his view of the pivotal role of arguments in the growth of knowledge, Popper characterizes Wittgenstein's familiar analogy between scientific theories and maps as a 'particularly unfortunate one.' Maps, Popper contends, are non-argumentative, whereas theories 'are eseentially argumentative systems of statements: their main point is that they explain deductively' (IA 61).

Popper credits this critical interrogation of Bühler's thought, as well as extensive conversations with Heinrich Gomperz, with showing him '*the priority of the study of logic over the study of subjective thought processes*' (ibid). Ever since that period (1926–7), he has been 'highly suspicious' of many widely accepted psychological theories. 'I came to realize that *the theory of conditioned reflex was mistaken. There is no such thing as conditioned reflex*' (ibid). Popper contends that Pavlov's dogs should not be seen as 'conditioned' – their learning process a mere reflex. Instead, they search for 'invariants in the field of food acquisition (which is necessarily "plastic", in other words open to modification by trial and error) and as fabricating expectations, or anticipations, of impending events' (IA 61).

Popper's scientific naturalism thus extends Kant's insight into the conceptual foundations of human cognition so far as to include other animals in the evolutionary chain of 'problem-solvers' – an evolutionism completely in keeping with the thrust of Kant's *Critique of Judgement* (1790).[16] As Popper remarks in another context,

Animals and men are born with a great storehouse of instinctive knowledge – of ways of reacting to situations, of expectations. The new-born child expects to be fed and cared for. Its expectations, its inborn conjectural knowledge, may be disappointed. In this case it may die ... The fact that our inborn knowledge may be disappointed shows that even this inborn knowledge is merely conjectural ... We do not learn by observation, or by association, but by trying to solve problems. A problem arises whenever our conjectures or expectations fail. We try to solve our problems by modifying our conjectures ... The solution, the new behaviour, the new conjecture, the new theory, may work; or it may fail. Thus we learn by trial and error; or more precisely, by tentative solution and by their elimination if they prove erroneous. As H.S. Jennings showed in 1910, this method is used even by the amoeba (CKP 96)

The intimate connection between human fallibility and the evolutionary importance of problem-solving takes us to the heart of Popper's intellectual universe. 'From a Darwinian point of view, we are led to speculate about the survival value of mental processes' (RPE 183). Popper's life-long belief in the inherently irrationalist consequences of all varieties of 'subjectivistic' epistemology and so-called belief philosophies has led him to 'a somewhat daring conjecture in the psychology of cognition,' the principle of transference: 'What is true in logic is true in psychology,' and, by extension, 'what is true in logic is true in scientific method and in the history of science' (OK 6; cf 24, 26, 67–8, 80).

Echoing Hegel and Nietzsche, George Santayana once observed that those who are ignorant of the history of thought are destined to re-enact it. A well-known study of Austrian intellectual history added the important corollary, 'that those ignorant of the context of ideas are, similarly, destined to misunderstand them.'[17] Those who would have us believe that Popper's primary background and training were those of a natural scientist (typically, a physicist) and/or a formal logician commit such an error by ignoring, or drastically underestimating the significance of, Popper's intellectual engagement with Bühler's Gestaltist psychology, including his doctoral examinations and thesis.

These types of assumptions, and neglect of the early formative period of Popper's thought, have licensed a deep misunderstanding about the place and relative importance of methodology in his philosophy. Some writers insist on dividing Popper's thought into a youthful, 'methodological' phase (represented by his *Logik der Forschung*) and a later, 'metaphysical' one (*Conjectures and Refutations*, *Objective Knowledge*, and *The Self and Its Brain*).[18] This increasingly influential interpretation sees the main target of Popper's earlier period as the logical positivism of the Vienna Circle, and his later chief concern as the 'relativism' of philosophers such as Michael Polanyi, Thomas S. Kuhn, and proponents of the later Wittgenstein's philosophy, particularly Peter Winch.

Some commentators portray Popper as a logical positivist or as having 'been trained in physics' or the 'natural sciences'; some neglect the fact that most of his ideas and arguments published in the 1960s and 1970s were formulated much earlier and under the influence of non-Anglo-Saxon traditions of thought. These exegetical habits skew the priority inherent in the Kantian structure of Popper's thought between its sustaining moral and 'metaphysical' concerns and those of a narrower 'methodological' kind.

As we shall see, the heat of Popper's vision[19] flows from an explicitly metaphysical and moral commitment to consequentialism in scientific methodology and the analysis of politics and society. Throughout his career, the potential 'survival value' of alternative mental processes – and perceived threats thereto – have unified Popper's work. The role of logic and formal analytical tools are ancillary to this overriding concern for 'the rational and imaginative analysis' of the consequences of proposed solutions to our most pressing scientific and political problems (cf *OS* II 232–3).

Popper's immanent critique of Bühler's theory of language has profoundly affected the metaphysical structure of his thought, particularly his objectivist conception of mind and the 'transcendental' justification of freedom. Popper believes that 'dogmatic ways of thinking' arise from an inborn need for regularities and our 'inborn mechanisms of discovery, mechanisms that make us search for regularities' (IA 37). In spite of 'an important environmental component' in language acquisition and other successful problem-solving contexts, 'genetic factors are much more important' to the long-term adaptability of a given species (IA 38). Popper drew on this Gestaltist-inspired notion that successful learning presupposes certain 'inborn dispositions' – above all, to theorize – and developed it systematically in rejecting Hume's psychological theory of learning by induction, as well as in arriving at the Kantian conclusion that 'there is no such thing as passive experience; no passively impressed association of impressed ideas' (IA 40).

Echoing Kant and Dewey,[20] Popper adds: 'Experience is the result of active exploration by the organism, the search for regularities or invariants. There is no such thing as perception except in the context of interests and expectations, and hence of regularities or "laws"' (ibid). Thus, with reference to Kant's central idea, 'without theories we cannot even begin, for we have nothing else to go by' in trying to cope with our environment and the problems it presents us with (IA 46). But if there is 'no such thing' as passive experience, experience plays a crucial negative role in the survival and successful evolution and learning of the species.

On a 'pre-scientific' or 'dogmatic' level, Popper notes, 'we hate the very idea that we may be mistaken' and do our best to cling to our previous conjectures just 'as long as possible.' It is the hallmark of science to 'systematically search for our mistakes, for our errors' (CKP 96). Popper points out that 'dogmatic theory formation comes very close to [Lorenz's] imprinting' (IA 34–5). However, whereas imprinting is 'an absolutely irreversible process of learning, ... not subject to correction or revision,' critical thought, best exemplified by science, consists of giving up a dogma 'under the pressure of disappointed expectations, and in trying out other dogmas' (IA 35). In science 'we are consciously critical in order to detect our errors,' and criticism thus understood 'may be said to continue the work of natural selection' (CKP 96 and IA 112, respectively). As long as we remain pre-scientific, 'we are often destroyed, eliminated, with our false theories.' But once we cultivate the fruits of fallibilism and attempt systematically to eliminate false theories, we can happily 'try to let our false theories die in our stead' (CKP 96–7).

This, Popper concludes, 'is the *critical method of error elimination*' and constitutes nothing less than '*the method of science*' (ibid). In fact, 'there is no better idea of rationality than that of readiness to accept criticism' (IA 81). By 1937, Popper notes, he had sharpened and condensed this conception of rationality and the best methodology of science into the following schema: $P_1 \rightarrow TT \rightarrow EE \rightarrow P_2 \rightarrow$, where P_1 is an initial problem with which scientific discussion begins, TT is a tentative theory, which after criticism undergoes EE, or error elimination, which in turn produces P_2, a new problem, ad infinitum (IA 205; cf *OK* 121, 126, 174–7).

Popper shares this century's overriding concern with the unique place of language in our evolutionary development.[21] Unlike imprinting in lower organisms, in humans error elimination presupposes 'that we can look at our theories critically – as something outside ourselves. They are not any longer our subjective beliefs – they are our objective conjectures' (CKP 97). Therefore language is the foundation both of criticism and of our humanity, since 'human consciousness – the consciousness of self – is the result of language' (CKP 102).

The development of the descriptive use of sentences and our innate capacity and need to criticize them makes possible the cumulative growth of knowledge. Thus it is only with the development of the descriptive function that 'the regulative idea of truth emerges, that is, of a description which fits the facts' (*OK* 120). The argumentative function 'presupposes the descriptive function: arguments are fundamentally about descriptions: they criticize descriptions from the point of view of the regulative ideas of truth; content; and verisimilitude' (ibid). To the combined development of these two functions 'we owe our humanity, our reason. For our powers of reasoning are nothing but powers of critical argument' (*OK* 121).

Of late, Popper has developed his theory of language within the explicitly 'metaphysical research program' of Darwinian evolutionism, a turn in his thought I will address in chapter 8. But the connection between this more recent evolutionism and his earlier critique of Bühler's ideas indicates the unity and continuity in Popper's thought. Popper distinguishes two senses of thought and knowledge – subjective, 'consisting of a state of mind or consciousness or a disposition to behave or react,' and objective, 'consisting of problems, theories, and arguments as such' (*OK* 108–9). In the former, '*my* knowledge consists of *my* disposition, [and] *your* knowledge consists of *your* disposition'; in the latter, knowledge 'consists of spoken or written or printed statements' (CKP 98). Like Kant, and more recently Bolzano, Frege, and Tarski, Popper has always maintained the crucial importance of drawing this distinction with all the intellectual resources at our disposal; without it we lose all hope of understanding and preserving that which is distinctively human: our ineradicable fallibility and our capacity to survive our errors by gradually eliminating our mistaken theories or conjectures.

Although both kinds of knowledge are inherently 'uncertain or conjectural or hypothetical,' Popper maintains that it makes an important evolutionary difference for the human race that we put our ideas into words, 'or better, writing them down ... For in this they become criticizable. [Whereas] before this, they are part of ourselves' (CKP 98). One of the clearest statements of this anthropological and evolutionary core of Popper's thought comes at the end of *Conjectures and Refutations*:

In this way [by explicitly formulating our conjectures into theories], rational *criticism* may develop and standards of rationality – some of the first intersubjective standards – and the idea of an objective truth ... It is by this mutual criticism that man, if only by degrees, can break through the subjectivity of a world of biological release signals, and, beyond this, through the subjectivity of his own imaginative inventions, and the subjectivity of the historical accidents upon which these inventions may in part depend. For these standards of rational criticism and of objective truth make his knowledge structurally different from its evolutionary antecedents ... It is the acceptance of these standards which create[s] the dignity of the individual man; which makes him responsible, morally as well as intellectually ... These standards may help him to discover how little he knows, and how much there is that he does not know ... And in this way they may even help him to transcend his animal past, and with it that subjectivism and voluntarism in which romantic and irrationalist philosophies may try to hold him captive. (*CR* 384)

'Breaking through the subjectivity' of the biological and historical dimensions of existence takes us to the centre of one of the most controversial aspects of Popper's metaphysics: his determination to eliminate all traces of psychologism from epistemological and methodological inquiry. According to Popper, traditional epistemology (perhaps best evidenced in Descartes) has been bedevilled by one variety or another of subjectivism – the assumption that objectivity, rationality, and scientific knowledge are 'identical with the psychological process by which we come to make use of them.'[22] On such a view, given its classical modern formulation in J.S. Mill's *Examination of Sir William Hamilton's Philosophy* (1865), rationality is a function of one's beliefs or a state of mind in which one is open to arguments, and objectivity a willingness to make an effort to avoid bias. Thus Mill observed of logic that 'as far as it is a science at all, its theoretic grounds are wholly borrowed from psychology.'[23]

In the latter half of the nineteenth century, a number of thinkers became increasingly critical of such psychologism, arguing that it ultimately succumbs to epistemological relativism and/or scepticism concerning our ability to know, being dependent on a state of mind, an attitude, or the psychology of the knowing (and fallible) subject.[24] In his *Critique of Pure Reason*, Kant had already advanced the major premisses for such a critique of psychologism. He criticized Locke for having failed to distinguish between the quaestio facti, or the 'physiological derivation,' of a priori concepts (i.e. their factual occurrence in the mind or consciousness of man) and the quaestio juris, or their validity, which depends entirely upon certain 'transcendental' universals, or a priori categories, for their determination. Passmore notes: 'Psychological laws are no more than inductive generalizations, subject therefore to correction in the light of further experience, whereas logical and mathematical principles are "necessary" – they *must* be true – and therefore cannot be "grounded" upon inductively derived premises.'[25]

Kantian premisses figured prominently in the work of those imme-diately preceding Popper in rejecting psychologism. For example, in his *Logik* (1874), Rudolf Lötze maintained that the psychological act of think-ing is categorically distinct from the content of thought; whereas the former is inherently a determinate, temporal phenomenon, the latter partakes of another 'mode of being,' validity.[26] In mathematics, Frege observed in *Die Grundlagen der Arithmatik* (1884) that we should 'never take a description of the origin of an idea for a definition, or for an account of the mental and physical conditions through which we become conscious of a proposition for a proof of it. A proposition may be thought, and again it may be true; never confuse these two things. We must remind ourselves, it seems, that a proposition no more ceases to be true when I cease to think of it than the sun ceases to exist when I shut my eyes.'[27] Frege maintained that there is a deep, underlying philosophical flaw in psychologism, that of being forced to choose between the false antithesis of treating numbers either as spatial (whether as groups of objects or as marks on a page) or as merely subjective. For Frege (as for Peano, Russell, and Whitehead and other proponents of the new math-ematical logic), 'numbers are neither spatial nor physical nor yet sub-jective like ideas, but non-sensible and objective.'[28] In other words, numbers are applied not to 'things' but to 'concepts,' and concepts (in true Kantian fashion) are to be understood not as an image in an individual mind but as an 'object of Reason.'

Perhaps the most systematic pre-1914 critique of psychologism was contained in Edmund Husserl's early efforts to develop a 'pure' or pre-suppositionless logic and phenomenology. Husserl argued that if psy-chologism were true and logic were indeed a branch of psychology, the laws of logic would be like those of psychology: vague and approximate; like all empirical laws, based on induction, which yields only probable knowledge; and presupposing mental phenomena, such as representa-tion and judgment. On each count, Husserl found serious fault in this reasoning: it is absurd to consider logical laws merely probable, since they possess apodictic certainty and reflect necessary relations existing independently of empirical facts.

Although Popper sees Husserl's 'phenomenology' as 'a systematic re-vival of the *methodological essentialism* of Plato and Aristotle' (*OS* I 216), phenomenology, like the critical realism inspired by Kant's thought, considered 'psychologism' and the relativism it can engender a major problem of modern epistemology.

Popper readily concedes 'that every discovery contains "an irrational element" or a "creative intuition", in Bergson's sense' (*LSD* 32). He approvingly notes Einstein's conception in *Mein Weltbild* (1934) of 'the search for those highly universal laws ... from which a picture of the world can be obtained by pure deduction. There is no logical path leading to these ... laws. They can only be reached by intuition, like an intellectual love *"Einfuhlung"* of the objects of experience' (*LSD* 32). But, for Popper, the role of 'intuition' in discovery should not be confused with logical evaluation of questions such as 'Can a statement be justified? And if so, how? Is it testable? Is it logically dependent on certain other statements? Or does it perhaps contradict them?' (*LSD* 31).

Referring to Kant's dichotomy between quid facti and quid juris modes of discourse, Popper insists on separating 'the process of conceiving a new idea and the methods and results of examining it logically' (ibid). The corner-stone of Popper's methodology – the falsificationist criterion of demarcating scientific from pseudo-scientific knowledge – is predicated upon this hostility toward psychologism and his life-long determination not to confuse the realm of objectivity and scientific knowledge with the realm of subjective feeling and conviction or belief.

And once again, Kant's 'critical' philosophy provides the inspiration and leading line of Popper's own variety of rationalism: 'My use of the terms "objective" and subjective is not unlike Kant's. He uses the word "objective" to indicate that scientific knowledge should be *justifiable*, independently of anybody's whim: a justification is "objective" if in principle it can be tested and understood by anybody. "If something is valid", he writes, "for anybody in possession of his reason, then its grounds are objective and sufficient" ' (*LSD* 44; cf *CR* 47–8). In Popper's estimation, 'Kant was perhaps the first to realize that the objectivity of scientific statements is closely connected with the construction of theories – with the use of hypotheses and universal statements' (*LSD* 45).

Against all attempts to 'ground' objectivity in either the 'authority' of sense-based 'observations' or in reason itself or our 'power of intellectual intuition,' Popper maintains that the objectivity of the statements of science resides in their being intersubjectively testable (*LSD* 47; cf *CR* 4, 20–6). We test such statements 'by their deductive consequences' (*LSD* 98). For Popper, consequentialism is as central in scientific matters as in consideration of moral issues: 'The empirical basis of objective science has ... nothing "absolute" about it. Science does not rest upon solid bedrock. The bold structure of its theories rises, as it were, above a swamp. It is like a building erected on piles. The piles are driven down from above into the swamp, but not down to any natural or "given" base; and if we stop driving the piles deeper, it is not because we have reached firm ground. We simply stop when we are satisfied that the piles are firm enough to carry the structure, at least for the time being' (*LSD* 111).

Though some commentators have interpreted such passages as signs of scepticism, such a reading ignores the fact that Popper continually emphasizes the non-arbitrary and rational – because critical, as opposed to dogmatic – nature of his proposals for testing and accepting such statements in science.[29] Popper admits that 'any basic statement can again in its turn be subjected to scientific tests' (*LSD* 104). Moreover, with reference to Pierre Duhem, Popper observes: 'No conclusive disproof of a theory can ever be produced; for it is always possible to say that experimental results are not reliable, or that discrepancies ... between the experimental result and the theory are only apparent and ... will disappear with the advance of our understanding' (*LSD* 50; cf 42, 82–3, 108).

In the *Logic of Scientific Discovery* Popper proposes over twenty methodologically prescriptive rules designed to increase the vulnerability of our most cherished theories or conjectures to potential falsification and refuting experiences. Because 'there are all kinds of sources of our knowledge' and 'no conclusive disproof of a theory can ever be produced,' Popper insists on methodological rules that forbid the use of '*ad hoc* auxiliary assumptions' or (more recently) 'conventionalist' and 'immunizing stratagems' (*CR* 24; cf 42 and 44, *OK* 15–16 and 30).

Among the many such prescriptions in the *Logic*, a few are particularly worth noting. (1) 'Adopt such rules as will ensure the testability of scientific statements; which is to say, their falsifiability' (49). (2) 'Only such statements may be introduced in science as are inter-subjectively testable' (56). (3) 'Only those [auxiliary hypotheses] are acceptable whose introduction does not diminish the degree of falsifiability or testability of the system in question, but on the contrary, increases it' (83). (4) 'We shall take it [a theory] as falsified only if we discover a *reproducible effect* which refutes the theory. In other words, we only accept the falsification if a lower-level empirical hypothesis which describes such an effect is proposed and corroborated' (86). (5) 'Those theories should be given preference which can be most severely tested' (121). (6) 'auxiliary hypotheses should be used as sparingly as possible' (273). (7) 'Any new system of hypotheses should yield, or explain, the old corroborated regularities' (253).[30] These are hardly the recommendations of a thinker who doubts that real progress can be made in our understanding of the laws of nature. In his own words, 'it seems clear that the growth of scientific knowledge is the most important and interesting case of the growth of knowledge [in general]' (*LSD* 19).

More recently, Popper has replied to allegations of scepticism or ir-rationalism: 'The position here defended [critical realism] is radically different from what has in modern times been called "sceptisicm", at least since the Reformation. For in modern times scepticism is described as the theory which is pessimistic with respect to the possibility of knowl-edge. But the view proposed here hopefully adheres to the possibility of the growth of knowledge. It merely removes the quality of certainty which common sense assumed as essential to knowledge' (*OK* 99). Thus, although Popper's epistemology and methodology deny that science can yield certainty, they suppose that our knoweldge none the less pro-gresses, or grows in a rational and directed fashion.

In his most recent works, particularly several essays in *Objective Knowledge* (1972) and *The Self and Its Brain* (1977), Popper has continued to forge the already tight link between the exclusively logical nature and evalu-ation of objective knowledge and the evolutionary, problem-solving con-cerns outlined above. His determination to reaffirm Kant's distinction between *quaestio juris* (context of justification) and *quaestio facti* (context of discovery) has led him to propose a pluralistic metaphysics which he calls 'the third world theory.'

In a 1967 address, 'Epistemology without a Knowing Subject,' Popper outlined his metaphysical pluralism: 'Without taking the words "world" or "universe" too seriously, we may distinguish the following three worlds or universes: first, the world of physical objects or physcial states; sec-ondly, the world of states of consciousness, or of mental states, or perhaps of behavioural dispositions to act; and thirdly, the world of *objective contents of thought*' (*OK* 106). 'Among the inmates of my "third world" are, more especially, *theoretical systems*; but inmates just as important are problems and *problem situations*. And ... the most important inmates of this world are *critical arguments*, and what may be called – in analogy to a physical state or to a state of consciousness – *the state of a discussion* or *the state of a critical argument*; and, of course, the contents of journals, books, and libraries' (*OK* 107).

Traditional epistemologists – Descartes, Locke, Berkeley, Hume, and even Kant and, to some extent, Russell – conceived of knowledge as a special kind of subjective belief and were particularly concerned with its 'basis or origin.' Popper insists on a clear distinction between two dif-ferent senses of knowledge or thought:

[1] *knowledge or thought in the subjective sense*, consisting of a state of mind or consciousness or a disposition to behave or to react, and
[2] *knowledge or thought in an objective sense*, consisting of problems, theories, and arguments as such. Knowledge in this objective sense is totally independent of anybody's claim to know; it is also independent of anybody's belief, or disposition to assent, or to assert, or to act. Knowledge in the objective sense is *knowledge without a knower*: it is *knowledge without a knowing subject*. (*OIC* 108–9)

Santayana provides us an instructive vantage point when he says, in *Realms of Being*, that two divisions are simply 'not enough when we turn to an attempt to formulate a world-view.' Popper readily concedes the affinity between his pluralism and Plato's theory of the forms – and, therefore, with a good deal of Hegel's conception of objective spirit, Bolzano's theory of a universe of propositions and truths in themselves, and Frege's universe of the objective contents of thought. For each of these thinkers, intelligibility and purposiveness require what Kelly characterizes as 'relational continuity of categories and terms – something only triadic and not dyadic systems can provide' (cf IA 180 n 302).[31] And throughout his career, Popper has rejected both monism and naïve dualism, for precisely this reason: the emergence of human consciousness, the growth of scientific knowledge, and the prospects for an 'open society' all presuppose three equally and irreducibly 'real' worlds – each developmentally 'emergent' though relatively autonomous (cf *OK* 153, *SB* chapters P2 and P4).

In 'On the Theory of the Objective Mind' (late 1960s), Popper explains that his 'central thesis is that any intellectually significant analysis of the activity of understanding has mainly, if not entirely, to proceed by analysing our handling of third world structural units and tools' (*OK* 166): 'The third world (part of which is human language) is the product of men, just as honey is the product of bees, or spiders' webs of spiders. *Like language* (and like honey), human language, and thus larger parts of the third world are the *unplanned product of human actions*, though they may be solutions to biological or other problems' (*OK* 159–60).

To illustrate the objectivity and autonomy of such products, Popper advances several arguments. Against those who hold that a book is nothing without a reader, Popper maintains that 'a book remains a book – a certain type of product – even if it is never read (as may easily happen nowadays).' Moreover, 'a book, or even a library, need not even have been written by anybody: a series of books or logarithms, for example, may be produced and printed by a computer' (*OK* 115). The figures in such a hypothetical book contain objective knowledge – 'true or false, useful or useless; and whether anybody ever reads it and really grasps its contents is almost accidental' (*OK* 115).

Similarly, even though the natural numbers are human creations,

there is an infinity of such numbers, more than will ever be pronounced by men, or used by computers. And there is an infinite number of true equations between such numbers, and of false equations; more than we ever pronounce as true, or false.

But what is even more interesting, unexpected new problems arise as unintended by-products of the sequence of natural numbers; for instance the unsolved problems of the theory of prime numbers (Goldbach's conjecture, say). These problems are clearly *autonomous*. They are in no sense made by us; rather, they are *discovered* by us; and in this sense they exist, undiscovered, before their discovery. Moreover, at least some of these ... may be insoluble. (*OK* 160–1)

Or, as he observed in *The Self and Its Brain*, 'One may say that World 3 is man-made only in its origins, and that once theories exist, they begin to have a life of their own: they produce previously invisible consequences; they produce new problems' (*SB* 40). One of Popper's former students characterizes the relations between the three worlds in the following manner:

These worlds are in a high degree autonomous, but they are also interconnected in that they have a feedback effect on each other. World 1 and World 2 can (and do) interact directly, as can (and do) Worlds 2 and 3; but Worlds 1 and 3 can interact only through the mediation of World 2. A book is a physical object (World 1), but it also contains ideas (World 3), and it is only through mental states (World 2) that those ideas (which may be ideas about objects in Worlds 1, 2, or 3) can be grasped by us. These ideas may be correctly grasped by you but incorrectly grasped by me, and this is possible because *they exist independently of my particular mind and yours*.[32]

Popper's *Logik der Forschung* already 'contained a theory of the growth of knowledge by trial and error elimination, that is by Darwinian selection' (IA 133). In his 1961 Herbert Spencer Lecture, Popper similarly observed:

The growth of our knowledge is the result of a process closely resembling what Darwin called 'natural selection'; that is, the *natural selection of hypotheses*: our knowledge consists, at every moment, of those hypotheses which have shown their (comparative) fitness by surviving so far in their struggle for existence; a competitive struggle which eliminates those hypotheses which are unfit ... What is peculiar to scientific knowledge is this: that the struggle for existence is made harder by the conscious and systematic criticism of our theories ... eliminating our mistaken beliefs before such beliefs lead to our own elimination (*OK* 261).

While all organisms 'are programmed to explore their environment' and possess an instinct for self-preservation, Popper notes in *The Self and Its Brain*, 'They do not take these risks consciously.' Consequently, 'they are not aware of death. It is only man who may consciously face death in his search for knowledge.' 'Only a human being capable of speech can reflect upon himself' and, in so doing, become conscious of (and able to modify) various courses of action (*SB* 144).

Popper intends his conception of consciousness and self 'in the sense of Kant's two statements: "A person is a subject that is responsible for his actions", and "A person is something that is conscious, at different times, of the numerical identity of its self" ' (*SB* 115; cf 145). Thus, only a man 'can make an effort to become a better man, to master his fears, his laziness, his selfishness; to get over his lack of self-control' (*SB* 144). In Popper's hands, the traditional ideals of 'enlightenment' are still secure and worthy of veneration.

Popper contends: 'In all these matters it is the anchorage of the self in World 3 that makes the difference.' Its basis 'is human language which makes it possible for us to be not only subjects, centres of action, but also objects of our own critical thought, or our own critical judgment. This is made possible by the social character of language; by the fact that we can speak about other people, and that we can understand them when they speak' (ibid). We thus owe to the development of language and the biological 'emergence' of the other products of world 3 not only our status as selves but our humanity and rationality as well (cf *OK* 120, 130–1, 147).

One of Popper's clearest expositions of rationality and freedom in the context of his evolutionism is in 'Of Clouds and Clocks,' his Arthur Holly Compton Memorial Lecture, delivered at Washington University in 1965:

The art of critical argument has developed by the method of trial and error-elimination, and it has had the most decisive influence on the human ability to think rationally. (Formal logic itself may be described as an 'organon of critical argument'.) Like the descriptive use of language, the argumentative use has led to the evolution of ideal standards of control, or of '*regulative ideas*' (using a Kantian term): the main regulative idea of the descriptive use of language is *truth* (as distinct from *falsity*); and that of the argumentative use of language, in critical discussion, is *validity* (as distinct from *invalidity*). (*OK* 237)

The new functions of language 'have evolved and emerged together with man, and with human rationality.' There is an almost equally important distinction, between the evolution of organs and that of tools or machines, credited to Samuel Butler, whom Popper describes as 'one of the greatest of English philosophers' (*OK* 238):

Animal evolution proceeds largely, though not exclusively, by the modification of organs (or behaviour) or the emergence of new organs (or behaviour). *Human evolution* proceeds, largely, by developing new organs *outside our bodies or persons*: 'exosomatically', as biologists call it, or 'extra-personally'. These new organs are tools, or weapons, or machines, or houses. ... Instead of growing better memories and brains, we grow paper, pens, pencils, typewriters, dictaphones, the printing press and libraries ... The latest development (used mainly in support of our argumentative abilities) is the growth of computers. (*OK* 238–9)

This distinction between animal and human evolution helps explain the possibility of freedom in human affairs. We want to explain, Popper observes, 'how freedom is not just chance but, rather, the result of a subtle interplay between something almost random or haphazard and something like a restrictive or selective control – such as an aim or a standard – though certainly not a cast-iron control' (*OK* 232). Popper's solution to this problem is contained in his much neglected notion of 'plastic control,' or freedom plus control.

Arthur Holly Compton's problem had been to explain how 'such nonphysical things as purposes, deliberations, plans, decisions, theories, intentions, and values, can play a part in bringing about physical changes in the physical world' (*OK* 229). And Popper adds: 'That they do this seems to be obvious, *pace* Hume and Laplace and Schlick.' It is clearly untrue that 'all those tremendous physical changes brought about hourly by our pens, or pencils, or bulldozers, can be explained in purely physical terms, either by a deterministic physical theory, or (by a stochastic theory) as due to chance' (ibid). What we need for understanding rational human behaviour 'is something intermediate in character between perfect chance and perfect determinism – something intermediate between perfect clouds and perfect clocks' (*OK* 228).

As a personal example of the problem, Compton provided the following anecdote:

It was some time ago when I wrote to the secretary of Yale University agreeing to give a lecture on November 10 at 5 p.m. He had such faith in me that it was announced publicly that I should be there, and that audience had such confidence in his word that they came ... at the specified time. But consider the great physical improbability that their confidence was justified. In the meanwhile my work called me to the Rocky Mountains and across the ocean to sunny Italy. A phototropic organism [such as I happen to be, would not easily ...] tear himself away from there to go to chilly New Haven. (*OK* 229)

Given the fantastically small probability that he would deliver the lecture in question, Compton asks, why were his audience's and his sponsor's beliefs justified? 'They knew my purpose, and it was my purpose [that] determined that I should be there.'[33]

This and this alone, Popper contends, should be reason enough for us to realize that mere indeterminism is not enough to sustain the belief in human freedom and rationality.[34] 'Hardly anybody will believe that what I am reading to you is the result of nothing but chance – just a random sample of English words, or perhaps letters, put together without any purpose, deliberation, plan or intention' (*OK* 227). And if physical determinism were true, the belief that Compton and Popper in preparing their lectures used their brains to create something new would be a mere illusion – a prospect Popper repeatedly describes as both a nightmare and an absurdity (*OK* 222–9). A commentator observes, 'Determinism means there is no freedom, only absolute control,' while indeterminism 'allows freedom, but only in the sense that control is no longer absolute, because there is an element of sheer chance ... whereas the kind of freedom that a satisfactory solution must allow for is one that is, in typical instances, subject to control.'[35]

Popper outlines the attributes of plasticity that embody 'the idea of combining freedom and control' (*OK* 232). Given his evolutionism, it is important for Popper (as Hannay notes) 'to locate the phenomenon of plastic control in the non-mental, in fact preferably in the inorganic world.'[36] Accordingly, Popper proposes a 'simple physical model,' a soap-bubble, to illustrate the process (*OK* 249–50). A soapy film that encloses the bubble accommodates itself to fluctuations in the air it encloses.

Such accommodation or 'openness' should not be confused with leak-iness or seepage, as might occur in a 'cast-iron control' that was to some extent left 'open.' Rather, the bubble 'consists of two subsystems which are both clouds and which control each other: without air, the soapy film would collapse, and we should have only a drop of soapy water. Without the soapy film, the air would be uncontrolled: it would diffuse, ceasing to exist as a system. Thus the control is mutual; it is plastic, and of a feed-back character. Yet it is possible to make a distinction between the controlled system (the air) and the controlling system (the film)' (*OK* 249).

The soap-bubble exemplifies responsiveness, two-way dependence between 'higher' controlling centres and 'lower' structural units, and constant feedback between subsystems. What he had sought was 'a simple physical model of Peircean indeterminism; a purely physical system resembling a very cloudy cloud in heat motion, controlled by some other cloudy clouds – though by somewhat less cloudy ones' (*OK* 248).

By a 'cloud,' Popper means to suggest systems which, like gases, are highly irregular, disorderly, and more or less unpredictable,' and by 'less cloudy,' 'exhibiting less such irregularity' (*OK* 207). Of course, in Pop-per's view, all systems (whether physical, biological, or social) are some-what cloudy: 'To some degree all clocks are clouds' (*OK* 213). Thus a very cloudy cloud should not be seen as a system teetering on the edge of collapse or disaster. There simply is no logical connection, he main-tains, between instability at the macro-level and irregularity at the micro-level of such systems. Rather, such systems are best understood as 'fairly stable and enduring' entities, whose parts 'behave in a highly irregular fashion – like children during playtime at school.'[37]

Popper offers other illustrations of plasticity. Take a cluster of gnats, for instance. Though each individual gnat 'does exactly what he likes, in a lawless or random manner,' the cluster as a whole 'does not dissolve or diffuse, but ... keeps together fairly well' (*OK* 208–9). The cluster, it seems, has devised an analogue to the gravitational forces known to operate in sufficiently large gas clouds (like our atmosphere, or the sun). So, though the gnats 'fly quite irregularly in all directions, those that find they are getting away from the crowd turn back towards that part which is the densest' (*OK* 209). Popper finds similar controls in social interaction, such as a picnicking family – 'parents with a few children and a dog – roaming the woods for hours, but never straying far from the family car (which acts like a centre of attraction, as it were). This system may be said to be even more cloudy – that is, less regular in the movement of its parts – than our cloud of gnats' (*OK* 210).

Popper's notion of freedom and autonomy as plastic control thus rests on a certain view of evolution as a growing hierarchical system of plastic controls and 'a certain view of organisms as incorporating – or ... evolving exosomatically – this growing hierarchical system of plastic controls' (*OK* 242). With the emergence and critical selection or adoption of standards of rational criticism and objective truth, human knowledge becomes 'structurally different from its evolutionary antecedents' (*CR* 384). Thus, working from the thoroughly realistic and pragmatic assumption that 'the origin of *life* and the origin of *problems* coincide' (IA 142), Popper's thought has come to focus on critical analysis of 'the biological function of consciousness' and the survival value of alternative mental processes (cf *SB* 121–4).

In his 'Intellectual Autobiography' Popper observes: 'Fashions are stupid and blind, especially philosophical fashions; and that includes the belief that history will be our judge ... Truth is timeless (and so is falsity). Logical relations such as contradictoriness or compatibility are also timeless, and even more obviously so' (IA 129).

In 'Facing up to Intellectual Pluralism,' Judith N. Shklar notes that although 'science may have no answers to moral questions ... it has obviously made it impossible to deal with them in the traditional way.'[38] As we have seen, Kant's manifest greatness was to face directly this potential antagonism between validation and enchantment, never wavering in his faith and hope in the prospects of orderly growth in science and society alike. Ernest Gellner, in *Legitimation of Belief*, argues that Kant – 'the greatest thinker of them all' – explored this situation 'from the inside' better than any thinker before or since. His thought, Gellner notes, was 'simultaneously inspired by two fears which, superficially, one might expect to make each other redundant. The first fear is that the mechanical vision does not hold; the second fear is that it does. The first fear is for science, and the second for morality ... Either way, disaster. Kant never stooped to the silly supposition that accepting either one of the two disasters would evade the other. He attempted to prevent both.'[39]

Now, during far more problematic times, Popper similarly is determined to redeem the best in the tradition of the Enlightenment – the commitment to reasonableness and rationality, the Faustian quest to 'become better' and overcome 'lack of self-control' and, in so doing, to help us 'transcend our animal past' (cf *SB* 144, *CR* 383–4). Popper captured the point with the question, 'If humanism is concerned with the growth of the human mind, what then is the tradition of humanism if not a tradition of criticism and reasonableness?' (*CR* 384).

From a biological point of view, Popper notes in *The Self and Its Brain*, 'It is, especially in the case of the higher animals, the individual organism that is fighting for its existence; that is relaxing; that is acquiring new experiences and skills; that is suffering; and that is ultimately dying' (*SB* 127). Indeed, Popper's thought may fruitfully be understood as a species of scientific moralism. In *The Liberal Mind*, Kenneth Minogue points out that the main props of scientific moralism traditionally have been 'psychology, physiology, and biology in close alliance' and that its program is 'clearly utilitarian' and pragmatic in design: 'It is a technology for getting the largest quantity of preferred things which the condition of the world will allow.'[40] Their scientific studies have convinced such moralists 'to look deeper into the mind in search of the *function* of certain kinds of preference.'[41] Popper seems to agree: 'What may perhaps be identified with higher forms of life is a behaviouristically richer preference structure – one of greater scope' (IA 141).

Thus, Popper notes, though science may 'annihilate the importance of man, considered as part of the physical universe,' a proper understanding of the Kantian self – as citizen and builder of his own world – can raise 'immeasurably his value an an intelligent and responsible being' (*SB* 3). Such a determination to treat human beings as 'ends in themselves' is evident throughout all periods of Popper's career and is seldom far from the centre of his writings (save on the most technical subjects). Indeed, the heat of his vision might best be described as the type of morally inspired consequentialism this concern of his entails. For Popper, the choice before us in selecting among alternative theories and ideas is never 'simply an intellectual affair, or a matter of taste. It is a moral decision' (*OS* II 232). Time and time again, we see Popper insisting on the anti-humanitarian and authoritarian political implications of embracing the wrong sorts of approaches to a wide variety of subjects. 'My sense of social responsibility told me that taking such problems [as psychologism, idealism, positivism, phenomenalism, and solipsism] seriously was a kind of treason of the intellectuals – and a misuse of the time we ought to be spending on real problems' (IA 59). Similarly, in a lecture to the British Academy in January 1960, he contends that overly pessimistic accounts of our capacity to know and denials of our ability to learn about the world through controlled inquiry tend 'to lead to the demand for the establishment of powerful traditions and the entrenchment of powerful authority,' whereas overly optimistic accounts foster disillusionment because of the inevitable fallibility of our theories and observations. The overly optimistic search for untainted and certain 'foundations' to knowledge thus also 'begs for an authoritarian answer' (*CR* 6 and 25).

Popper states the alternative to such a foundationalist line of thinking as follows: 'Every solution to a problem raises new unsolved problems; the more so the deeper the original problem and the bolder its solution. The more we learn about the world, and the deeper our learning, the more conscious, specific, and articulate will be our knowledge of what we do not know, our knowledge of our ignorance. For this, indeed, is the main source of our ignorance – the fact that our knowledge can be only finite, while our ignorance must neessarily be infinite' (*CR* 28). But, despite fallibility, mind can still encompass more and more of the mysteries of nature and alleviate the sufferings of man. Echoing Kant's second *Critique* – wisdom 'is not less worthy of veneration in respect to what it denies us than in what it has granted' – Popper contends: 'It would be worth trying to learn something about the world even if in trying to do so we should merely learn that we do not know much. This state of learned ignorance might be a help in many of our troubles. It might be well for all of us to remember that, while differing widely in the various little bits we know, in our infinite ignorance we are all equal' (*CR* 29).

One of Popper's favourite metaphors for the rational (because criticizable) growth of scientific knowledge is explicitly juridical, like Kant's. For example, in *The Logic of Scientific Discovery*, Popper compares the acceptance of test statements by a scientific community with the verdict of a jury:

The verdict of the jury (*vere dictum* – spoken truly), like that of the experimenter, is an answer to a question of fact (*quid facti?*) which must be put to the jury in the sharpest, the most definite form. But what question is asked, and how it is put, will depend very largely on the legal situation, i.e., on the prevailing system of criminal law (corresponding to a system of theories). By its decision, the jury accepts, by agreement, a statement about a factual occurrence – a basic statement, as it were. The significance of this decision lies in the fact that from it, together with the universal statements of the system (of criminal law) certain consequences can be deduced ... But it is clear that the statement need not be true merely because the jury accepted it. This fact is acknowledged in the rule allowing a verdict to be ... revised. (*LSD* 109–10)

There is a tight link between the pursuit of truth and the consequences of certain rules and procedures we should adopt in order to live more rational lives: 'The situation is really very simple. The belief of a liberal – the belief in the possibility of a rule of law, of equal justice, of fundamental rights, and a free society – can easily survive the recognition that judges are not omniscient and may make mistakes about facts ... But this belief in the possibility of a rule of law, of justice, and of freedom, cannot well survive the acceptance of an epistemology which teaches that there are no objective facts' (*CR* 5).

For Popper, science and scientific method are not ends in themselves, but rather the very best examples of rational problem-solving, the undisputed paradigms of the systematic elimination of error and ignorance. At the beginning of his recently released Postscript to *The Logic of Scientific Discovery* (*Realism and the Aim of Science*), Popper states: 'As a rule, I begin my lectures on Scientific Method by telling my students that scientific method does not exist ... There are only problems, and the urge to solve them.'[42] Two of the more dangerous ideas of our time are 'the aping of physical science' and 'the authority of the specialist' (*P* 1 7–8).

Popper's interest in and use of science have always been admittedly 'heroic' (IA 977). His concern has never been to describe, à la Ranke, science 'as it really happened.' Rather, Popper believes that we can learn in general from science about living more securely and harmoniously. The dynamic interplay of logical deduction and successful problem-solving is what most impresses Popper about the history of science – hence, my view that logical pragmatism may be the most appropriate general characterization of his thought.

In 'The Rationality of Scientific Revolutions,' Popper claims that, by the logic of science, new theories should contradict their predecessors – should 'overthrow' them by predicting at least some conflicting results – and each 'must always be able to explain fully the success of its predecessor.'[43] These two criteria

allow us to decide of any new theory, even before it has been tested, whether it will be better than the old one, provided it stands up to tests ... This means that, in the field of science, we have something like a criterion for judging the quality of a theory as compared with its predecessor, and therefore a criterion of progress. And so it means that progress ... can be assessed rationally. This possibility explains why, in science, only progressive theories are regarded as interesting; and it thereby explains why, as a matter of historical fact, the history of science is, by and large, a history of progress. (*P* 1 83)

In short, science is the embodiment par excellence of orderly growth.

Obviously, for the future of liberal societies such an understanding and vindication of the possibility of progress are of paramount importance. In his autobiography, Popper expresses the connection as follows: 'One way of life may be incompatible with another way of life in almost the same sense in which a theory may be logically incompatible with another. These incompatibilities are there, objectively, even if we are unaware of them. And so our purposes and our aims, like our theories, may compete, and may be discussed critically' (IA 155–6).

More poignantly still, shortly after the defeat of Hitler, Popper wrote: 'I am today no less hopeful than I have ever been that violence can be defeated. It is our only hope; and long stretches in the history of Western as well as Eastern civilizations prove that it need not be a vain hope – that violence can be reduced, and brought under the control of reason ... I am a rationalist because I see in the attitude of reasonableness the only alternative to violence' (CR 355). Standing, as we do, on the edge of destruction through nuclear warfare and the ecological consequences of a less disciplined variety of progress, a great deal indeed – if not life itself – would seem to ride on the truth of this hope.

In *An Essay on Philosophical Method*, R.G. Collingwood described the ideal critic as 'a reader who agrees with his author's views up to a certain point, and on that limited agreement builds his case for refusing a complete agreement.'[44] Before turning to the implications of Popper's epistemology and methodology for the conduct of social inquiry, I should lay at least the foundations for a line of criticism that will become increasingly important as this study proceeds.

There is good reason to believe that Popper's intention – to conserve the intellectual foundations of progress and the liberal way of life – is not well served by his rigid bifurcation of logical and psychological (and sociological) levels of analysis, or by the increasing 'Darwinian' turn to his thought. Arguing that the validity of a theory depends on the existence of criteria of evidence and rules of inquiry that exist independently of *my* particular wishes and *yours* is one thing. But to insist that truth-claims and theories are best conceived of without any reference to 'knowing subjects' is absurd – especially for someone interested in the improvement of our cognitive and moral performance.

I will argue that improvement or progress in these respects presupposes a more concrete and situated (or 'embedded') notion of human agency and practical judgment – in the Aristotelian senses – than Popper's thought allows. I will argue also that neither of these uniquely human capacities is reducible to, or adequately illuminated by, the Kantian-inspired notions of morality and scientific progress as mere rule-following behaviour and a purely formal (or 'theoretical') characterization of rational determination as the subsumption of the 'contingent' and particular by the timeless and 'universal.' It is simply not adequate 'to deny knowledge in order to make room for faith' when it comes to the evaluation and improvement of human institutions and practices like science, the quality of moral life, or political arrangements. Progress there demands ongoing responsibility and deliberation in concrete contexts of association with diversely inclined individuals. As Oakeshott observes, 'The "social" character of conduct *inter homines* is its character in respect of agents being associated in terms of some specific and understood conditions of association.'[45]

Thus understood, cognitive and moral achievement – or rational conduct – becomes a function not of the mere application of formal rules of inquiry or human behaviour, but of the exercise of practical judgment and prudence in the specific cricumstances at hand. It presupposes Aristotle's *phronesis* rather than the Kantian (and Cartesian) 'methodism' that lies at the root of Popper's thought. *Phronesis* was originally formulated by Aristotle in Book VI of *Nichomachean Ethics* and was more recently illuminated by Arendt, Voegelin, Oakeshott, Gadamer, and to some extent Habermas. It is not simply one virtue among others, but our most important and comprehensive moral capacity – entailing not only the possession of 'theoretical' knowledge of the course of action appropriate in a specific context but also the ability and strength of character to act on that knowledge.[46] It is, above all else, our ability to move back and forth, from the universal (and criterial) to the particular case at hand, such that praiseworthy and virtuous moral and cognitive conduct can be discerned and adjudicated, preferred in practice vis-à-vis other forms of conduct.

Unfortunately, Popper – like Kant – dismisses such a line of thought and the underlying appreciation of prudence as a form of teleological 'essentialism.' However, much of substance and human significance is unnecessarily lost in his excessively abstract conception of the self and his retreat from the existential dimensions of human autonomy into a realm of 'propositions-in-themselves.'

I think that it can be shown that there are several levels of analysis at which the metaphysical foundations of Popper's thought are insufficient for the conservation, let alone renewal, of the liberal way of life. For now, I will explore this claim in three respects: (1) the unfortunately reductionistic implications of his evolutionary 'functionalization' of Bühler's theory of language; (2) the difficulties he creates for himself because of his inability, or unwillingness, to appreciate the positive need for inductive habits of thought in all practical activity, including science itself; and (3) the problems that consequently arise for his overall, 'heroic' conception of science and scientific progress.

As we have seen, Popper's understanding of science as the deductive search for and ruthless elimination of error is grounded in his transcendental critique of Bühler's Gestaltist psychology, especially his theory of language. For Bühler, the 'highest' function of language is descriptive. While even lower animals can express and communicate fear, only human beings seem able to describe the object of fear. And disputes about the merits of one particular description over another are conceived of as involving questions of complex judgments.

The corner-stone of Popper's thought is to be found in his contention that conceiving of arguments as complex judgments – the handiwork of mere 'sensibility' and 'understanding' in Kant's terminology – 'is a mistake from the point of view of modern logic' – the transcendental, a priori frame of pure reason itself. This basic logical mistake prevented Bühler from appreciating the all-important difference between judging and arguing and, more particularly, how the theories within which all our arguments are pressed and defined always 'explain deductively' (IA 61; cf P I, chapter 1, sections 1–6 and 11–12).

Popper's point may be illuminating for the strict or purely logical comparison of arguments that will allow for the sort of abstract symbolization and propositional formalization that modern logic requires. But it seems of dubious value in adjudicating disputes that arise in everyday life. Popper's error, it seems to me, consists in overgeneralizing the obvious superiority and explanatory power of deductive forms of demonstrative inference, far beyond the contexts in which they are useful – in fact, so far 'beyond' that he cannot promote the goals he cherishes most.

Let me return to Popper's criticism of Wittgenstein's view that theories are like maps. For Popper, maps are merely descriptive devices that help us get from where we are to where we plan to go; theories are deductive explanations of some problem that confronts us and demands a response. In recent years, Popper has suggested that the fundamental distinction between describing and arguing, understanding and explaining, justifies the 'somewhat daring' conjecture of 'the principle of transference': 'What is true in logic is true in psychology,' and, by extension, 'What is true in logic is true in scientific method and in the history of science' (*OK* 6).

For most practical purposes, however, maps and a host of similar 'inductive' and 'descriptive' aids are more conducive to successful human conduct than the mere invocation of purely logical considerations and the sort of inferences that can settle the dispute or dilemma at hand 'once and for all' (in the manner implied by Popper's language concerning the strictly propositional nature of falsification). The same is even truer of skills that can only be adequately described as 'communicative' rather than 'argumentative.' In other words, if freedom or 'autonomy' is ever to be realized and if the pursuit of knowledge in practice is ever to be improved along the lines that Popper proposes, we will need a far more substantial conception of the art and agency by which praiseworthy choices are made.

Let me sketch two of the unfortunate implications of Popper's inability to recognize the limited force and applicability of the strict rules of logical inference. First, if we follow Popper's own strict non-inductivist line of reasoning and believe, for example, that 'learning by observation' and past experience 'is a fiction,' then it seems difficult to see why it should be rational at all to prefer the best tested theory as a basis of acting and how we are able to decide even whether a theory is well tested. Popper agrees with Hume that there is no justification in empirical science for reasoning from instances we have experience of to others of which we have none. Suffice it to say, the typical defence of induction, which holds that such reasoning has worked in the past, simply will not do as a coherent response, since it assumes that what has occurred in the past is likely to happen again in the future, which is precisely what needs to be shown.

Popper's solution to this difficulty – the brunt of a number of detailed criticisms raised by O'Hear and several others with whom I concur – is to insist that all that the logic of science can suggest under such circumstances is which among a number of competing theories has been more highly corroborated than the alternatives in the past.[47] But the degree of corroboration itself, Popper concedes, 'says nothing whatever about future performance, or about the "reliability" of a theory' (*OK* 18). Thus all that the measure of corroboration can do is to help us discard or eliminate some of our previously false theories and indicate which among the survivors has done well up till now.

Given such an approach, the only way to establish the rational preferability of one theory to another and to decide if it has been well tested is to admit some determinate, inductive links between failed refutations (or provisional corroborations) and future reliability (or truth). Only if Popper concedes at least a 'whiff of inductivism' can he answer the major problematic facing all non-inductivists: 'Why is the past performance of a theory any good reason for adopting it in the future?'[48] Popper himself instructs scientists to scrutinize the 'background knowledge' of their particular problem in order to decide whether a theory has been well tested or should be retained when confronted with adverse evidence (cf *CR* 112, 235, 244, 247, 288). Had he not driven the wedge between logic and psychology so deep, Popper's advice could be explored and developed in ways more consistent with other parts of his philosophy.

Stephen Toulmin draws an important distinction between the 'idealised logic' of formal logicians and the 'working logic' found in jurisprudence.[49] This distinction, important for the social sciences, can illuminate another reductionistic implication of Popper's deductive and 'logical' conception of the growth of science. There is hardly a practising scientist who would support Popper's view that good, 'heroic' science should aim only at disconfirming bold hypotheses.[50]

The full range of legitimate (or systematic) paths to knowledge would include analogical thinking (Peirce's 'abduction'), induction (or the correlation of events), and 'puzzle-solving' research – all of which defy the formalization required of 'demonstrative,' deductive inference.[51] If 'logic' ceases to bear the 'idealized' (Platonic and Kantian) stamps of timelessness and strict implication, these and a host of other important dimensions to the growth of knowledge can fruitfully be studied. But Popper's excessively formal and transcendentalist line of argument renders them either 'mysterious' aspects of empirical psychology or 'irrational' 'fictions' or 'dogmas' – hardly a happy state for a self-professed 'problem-solver.'

As Toulmin observes:

The formal logician demands to be shown the statements, all the statements and nothing but the statements: looking down from his Olympian throne, he then sets himself to pronounce about the unchangeable relations between them. But taking this kind of God's-eye-view distracts one completely from the practical problems out of which the question of validity itself springs: whether we ought to accept, trust and rely on the man's predictions, his grounds for it being what they are, or alternatively whether we should reject and discard it – that is the question we express in practice by the words, 'Is this argument *sound*?', and by divorcing 'logical relations' from all possible contexts we deprive ourselves of the means of asking it.[52]

In the chapters that follow, I will return to the connection between sound arguments, on the one hand, and practical problems and 'possible contexts,' on the other, from several different vantage points, ranging from Popper's conception of social science as a 'piece-meal social technology' to his notion of freedom or 'autonomy' as 'plastic control.' The radical divorce in Popper's thought between logic and psychology and between prudence and a priori principles of reason and his almost obsessive deductivism have deprived his vision of plausible linkages, mediations, and ligatures – the existential bonds and communal foundations of human autonomy and rational conduct.[53]

Although one of Popper's favourite metaphors is, like Toulmin's, juridical, Popper invokes it only to defend the possibility of establishing 'objective facts' (CR 5), whereas Toulmin is concerned with the full range of considerations, dispositional as well as criterial or statutory. So, whereas Popper's thought focuses on the 'rules of evidence' and the rule-following nature and determination of truth and falsity, Toulmin, like Aristotle, draws our attention to particular dilemmas, only a few of which concern simply evidence and truth and most of which revolve around problems of interpretation and improvisation.

If 'the essence of belief is the establishment of a habit' (as Peirce argued),[54] Popper's overall project – to conserve the liberal way of life and the foundations of scientific progress in an increasingly hostile environment – requires reflective judgment and a richer, more substantial understanding of the self. The self is not reducible to our 'consciousness' of being nature's most gifted 'problem-solvers' but is a substantive personality, the result of what Oakeshott characterizes as 'a difficult achievement ... the outcome of an education, whose resources are collected in self-understanding' and which are deployed in an endless series of dramas and social practices, 'whose resources it has made its own.'[55] Popper's excessive formalism obscures far too many dimensions of such an achievement.

5

Critical rationalism and the logic of the social sciences

> The utility of moral and civil philosophy is to be
> estimated, not so much by the commodities we have
> by knowing these sciences, as by the calamities we
> receive from not knowing them.[1]
>
> Thomas Hobbes

> Every discovery of a mistake constitutes a real ad-
> vance in our knowledge. As Roger Martin du Gard
> says in *Jean Barois*, 'It is something if we know
> where truth is not to be found.'
>
> Popper, *The Open Society and Its Enemies* II 376

Popper's contribution to the social sciences originates in the conviction that 'the conflict between rationalism and irrationalism has become the more important intellectual, and perhaps even moral, issue of our times' (*OS* II 224). By rationalism, Popper means the opposite not of empiricism but of all varieties of irrationalism. Thus, in strict keeping with the outlook of the Enlightenment, he describes rationalism as 'an attitude that seeks to solve as many problems as possible by an appeal to reason, i.e., to clear thought and experience, rather than by an appeal to emotions and passions' (ibid). Given the admittedly vague nature of terms such as 'reason' and 'passion,' however, Popper adds that it may be more illuminating to explain rationalism in terms of our practical attitudes or behaviour. Thus, 'rationalism is an attitude of readiness to listen to critical arguments and to learn from experience. It is fundamentally an attitude of admitting that "*I may be wrong and you may be right, and by an effort, we may get nearer the truth*" ... In short, the rationalist attitude, or, as I may perhaps label it, the "attitude of reasonableness," is very similar to the scientific attitude, to the belief that in the search for truth we need co-operation, and that with the help of argument, we can in time attain something like objectivity' (*OS* II 225).

That Popper sees the stakes riding on the adoption of such a rationalist attitude in social and political matters to be extremely high is clear from the moral intensity of his critiques of its alternatives – irrationalism, mysticism, and pseudo-rationalism. For instance, in a sequel to his controversial exchange with T.W. Adorno and other members of the Frankfurt School in 1961 at a congress of the German Sociological Association, Popper declares: 'If the method of critical discussion should establish itself, then this will make the use of violence obsolete: [since] reason is the only alternative to violence so far discovered.'[2] It is the 'obvious duty' of all intellectuals to work for this revolution, 'for the replacement of the eliminative function of violence by the eliminative function of rational criticism' (ibid).

According to Popper, all forms of anti-rationalism are based ultimately on the assumption – originally of Platonic inspiration – that reason is a kind of 'faculty' that may vary greatly from one person to the next (*OS* II 226). Popper calls such a position 'pseudo-rationalism,' or 'authoritarian intellectualism,' with its belief in an infallible method of discovery. For Popper, rationality is not the intellectual gift or cleverness of 'genius,' but a product of 'the social character of reasonableness' (*OS* II 225). Thus, although an individual marooned in early childhood might be able to cope with a number of different problems, he could never invent language or the art of argumentation, for 'we owe our reason, like our language, to intercourse with other men' (ibid).

In contrast to the authoritarianism and 'pseudo-rationalism' of Plato, Popper offers the 'true rationalism' of Socrates, with its awareness of one's limitations, the intellectual modesty of those who know how often they err, and how much they depend on others even for this knowledge. It is the realization that we must not expect too much from reason, (*OS* II 227). Whereas all forms of authoritarianism are necessarily hostile to criticism, the rationalism of Socrates, 'with its rejection of any pretension to knowledge or wisdom,' embodies a faith in – indeed 'the very life of' – democracy (*CR* 16). Popper contends that Socrates courageously insisted on the political and, if you will, methodological implications of human fallibility.

Popper writes in *Conjectures and Refutations* that we are most indebted to Socrates for the *maieutic* art of criticism and counter-example. This consists essentially 'in asking questions designed to destroy prejudices; false beliefs which are often traditional or fashionable beliefs; [and] false answers, given in the spirit of cocksureness' (*CR* 12–13). As opposed to the intellectual intuititionism of Plato, Socrates did not 'pretend to know,' and his teaching accordingly sought to purge and cleanse the soul 'of its false beliefs, its seeming knowledge, its prejudices.' And this it achieved 'by teaching us to doubt our own convictions' (*CR* 13).

In *The Open Society and Its Enemies* Popper links this Socratic doctrine of fallibility with the Kantian belief in treating human beings as ends in themselves. The belief that there is nothing more important in our life than other individuals leads directly to 'the appeal to men to respect one another and themselves' (*OS* I 190). Socratic reason 'is aware of its limitations ... respects the other man and does not aspire to coerce him – not even into happiness' (*ibid* II 238–9).

Popper is adamant in his conviction that 'rationalism' in his and Socrates' sense is irreconcilable with all philosophical justifications of authoritarianism. Since we 'not only owe our reason to others, but ... can never excel others in a way that would establish a claim to authority,' we must do our very best to establish the necessary preconditions of such a 'rational unity of mankind' (*OS* II 226 and 225). This entails not only recognizing 'everybody with whom we communicate as a potential source of argument and of reasonable information' but, much more important, ' "planning" its growth' by developing institutions that will protect freedom of thought (*OS* II 225 and 227). Unfortunately, Popper's thought on liberal institutions seldom rises above programmatic and abstract analysis, once again offering little guidance on preserving our freedoms in tough, particular cases. I will return to this criticism later.

Popper distinguishes such a conception of rationalism and its institutional approach to science and freedom from three other trains of thought that have become increasingly fashionable: the 'collectivism' of Hegel and Hegelianism, all varieties of outright irrationalism, and 'uncritical' or 'comprehensive rationalism.' Popper's social and institutional conception of science and rationality differs from Hegel and his followers:

They argue that, since we owe our reason to 'society' – or to a certain society such as a nation – 'society' is everything and the individual nothing; or that whatever the individual possesses is derived from the collective, the real carrier of all values. As opposed to this, the position presented here does not assume the existence of collectives; if I say ... that we owe our reason to 'society', then I always mean that we owe it to certain concrete individuals. ... Therefore, in speaking of a 'social' theory of reason (or of scientific method), I mean more precisely that the theory is an *inter-personal* one, and never ... a collective theory. ... [Similarly] the term 'tradition' also has to be analysed into concrete personal relations. (*OS* II 226; cf *CR* 120–35).

Popper points out that open conflict between rationalism and irrationalism originally broke out during the Middle Ages and centred around the opposition between scholasticism and mysticism, though the issue separating them dates back to Greek antiquity (cf *OS* II 229). But the tide against rationalism began to turn only after Kant's death, with the establishment of 'oracular irrationalism.' In Popper's analysis the chief culprit in the emergence of such a doctrine is Hegel, whose dialectics – that 'mystery method' – he regards with 'a mixture of contempt and horror' (*OS* II 28). Hegel's success, Popper contends, marked the beginning of what Schopenhauer characterized as the age of 'dishonesty' and 'irresponsibility' (here Popper borrows from Konrad Heiden's portrait of modern totalitarianism). Because Hegelian philosophy 'does not argue' but decrees and constantly 'escapes into verbiage,' it represents one of the most irresponsible forms of dogmatism, the harbinger 'of a new age controlled by the magic of high-sounding words, and by the power of jargon' (*OS* II 243 and 28).

As for the irrationalist doctrines and mysticism to which Hegel's thought allegedly gave rise, Popper's strictures are no less severe. Irrationalists 'insist that "human nature" is in the main not rational' (*OS* II 228). For thinkers sharing this outlook – Popper cites Wilhelm Dilthey, A.N. Whitehead, A.J. Toynbee, Franz Kafka, and Ludwig Wittgenstein as representative figures – man is more and less than a rational animal: 'less,' because the majority of mankind 'will always have to be tackled by an appeal to their emotions and passions rather than by an appeal to their reason,' and 'more,' since 'all that really matters in life goes beyond reason' (ibid). To such irrationalists, the rationalist and the scientist 'are poor in spirit, pursuing soulless and largely mechanical activities, and completely unaware of the problem of human destiny' (*OS* II 229).

Popper stresses the morally repugnant aspects of such views: 'It is my firm conviction that this irrational emphasis upon emotion and passion leads to what I can only describe as crime' (*OS* II 234). Whether it manifests itself as mere resignation toward the irrational or, much worse, as outright scorn for human reason, this attitude, Popper argues, leads to the use of force to settle disputes. Even 'he who teaches that no reason but love should rule opens the way for those who rule by hate' (*OS* II

236). For dispute or open conflict indicates that 'the more constructive emotions and passions,' such as love, reverence, devotion to a common cause, have shown themselves incapable of solving it. 'But if this is so, then what is left to the irrationalist except the appeal to other and less constructive emotions and passions, to fear, hatred, envy, and ultimately, to violence?' (*OS* II 234).

Moreover, and adding insult to their already damaged case, Popper charges that, given their emphasis on emotions and passions, irrationalists inevitably must be against egalitarianism, since it is impossible to have the same emotions toward everyone. By not judging a thought on its own merits, we inevitably tend toward the belief that 'we think "with our blood", or "with our national heritage", or "with our class" ' (*OS* II 235). Popper asserts, 'I refuse, on moral grounds, to be impressed with these differences' (*OS* II 235–6). Ultimately, he continues, 'the adoption of an anti-equalitarian attitude in political life, i.e. in the field of problems concerned with power of man over man, is just what I should call criminal. For it offers a justification of the attitude that different categories of people have different rights ... Ultimately, it will be used, as in Plato, to justify murder' (*OS* II 236).

It is characteristic of Popper's thought that in the struggle between rationalism and irrationalism, he is 'entirely on the side of rationalism' (*OS* II 229). There are only two options in the resolution of conflict: 'One is the use of emotion, and ultimately of violence, and the other is the use of reason, of impartiality, of reasonable compromise' (*OS* II 236). Of course, this is not intended to suggest, he adds, that he does not appreciate the difference between love and hate, or that he thinks that 'life would be worth living without love,' but means simply 'that no emotion, not even love, can replace the rule of institutions controlled by reason' (ibid).

Against the 'intellectual irresponsibility of a mysticism which escapes into dreams and of an oracular philosophy which escapes into verbiage,' Popper notes that rationalism in general, modern science in particular, 'enforces upon our intellect the discipline of practical tests. Scientific theories can be tested by their practical consequences' (*OS* II 243). These are the crucial ingredients of Popper's combat-toughened conception of rationality. Though 'the "world" is not rational, it is the task to rationalize it.' Similarly, though our society may not be rational at this time, 'it is the task of the social engineer to rationalize it. (This does not mean, of course, that he should "direct" it, or that centralized or collectivist "planning" is desirable). Ordinary language is not rational, but it is our task to rationalize it, or at least to keep up its standards of clarity. The attitude here characterized could be described as "*pragmatic rationalism*" ... Pragmatic rationalism may recognize that the world is not rational, but demand that we submit or subject it to reason, as far as possible' (*OS* II 357 note 19).

The foregoing case against irrationalism constitutes one of Popper's most important reasons for adopting 'critical rationalism,' which he contrasts with 'uncritical or comprehensive rationalism,' – 'the attitude of the person who says "I am not prepared to accept anything that cannot be defended by means of argument or experience" ' (*OS* II 230). Such 'excessive rationalism' 'tends to undermine its own position' and thereby contributes to an irrational reaction – the analogue of the alleged consequences of Hume's inductivism on epistemology.

Popper's belief that uncritical rationalism is inconsistent follows from the simple insight that 'since all argument must proceed from assumptions, it is plainly impossible to demand that all assumptions should be based on argument' (*OS* II 230). This was precisely Kant's point about needing to 'deny knowledge in order to make room for faith' in human freedom and autonomy. Seen in this light, the demand that we discard assumptions that cannot be conclusively supported by argument or by experience is analogous to the paradox of the liar (that is, to a sentence that asserts its own falsity). 'Uncritical rationalism is therefore logically untenable; and since a purely logical argument can show this, uncritical rationalism can be defeated by its own chosen weapon, argument' (ibid).

Popper's main concern here seems to be with preventing us from 'expecting too much from reason' (*OS* II 227). Though the rationalist attitude is primarily characterized by the importance of reason and argument, 'neither logical argument nor experience can establish' such a position; 'only those who are ready to consider argument or experience, and who have therefore adopted this attitude already, will be impressed by them' (*OS* II 230). The critical rationalist must embrace and advocate 'a modest and self-critical rationalism,' which recognizes its own assumptions and limitations.

Rationalists must never think of reason as 'self-contained': 'The fundamental rationalist attitude results from an (at least tentative) act of faith – from faith in reason' (*OS* II 231). In short, the decision to embrace critical rationalism is thus not a scientific deduction but a profound moral choice. And, as we have seen, Popper's choice amid the chaos, carnage, and brutality of the two world wars was unhesitant: 'I am a rationalist because I see in the attitude of reasonableness the only alternative to violence' (*CR* 355).

Because arguments cannot determine such fundamental choices does not imply for Popper that 'our choice cannot be helped by any kind of argument whatever' (OS II 232).[3] On the contrary, 'whenever we are faced with a moral decision of a more abstract kind, it is most helpful to analyse carefully the consequences which are likely to result from the alternatives between which we have to choose' (ibid) – a position strikingly similar to Max Weber's 'ethic of responsibility.'

Weber worked from the assumption, which he, too, derived from Kant, that questions of factual investigation and those of ethical evaluation are 'entirely heterogeneous problems.' He repeatedly insisted that 'it can never be the task of an empirical science to provide binding norms and ideals from which directives for immediate practical activity can be derived.'[4] None the less, as Giddens notes, 'this does not mean to say that empirical knowledge is irrelevant to the pursuit of values.'[5] Empirical knowledge gained through scientific investigation can help us in adjudicating the appropriateness of a particular means to the achievement of a given end. Science can provide a basis for 'indirect criticism' of an end as, for instance, being 'impractical' or as entailing unforeseen consequences or hidden costs. Moreover, logically deductive analysis can also help people clarify the ends they actually hold by elaborating the hierarchy or axiology of their values relative to those of others.

However, Weber vehemently opposed those who claimed that empirical science could tell us what we should do. He believed that such a confusion between facts and standards or values was increasingly evident in the universities of his time and posed the gravest dangers to our ability to make clear-sighted and responsible choices of the normative criteria by which to live. Weber saw the confusion in both theories of natural right and Marxist theories of the rational progress of history. Whereas the former claimed that 'what was normatively right was identical ... with the immutably existent,' the latter held that the 'normatively right' course of action was to be found in 'the inevitably emergent.'[6]

Against both, Weber insisted: 'The fate of an epoch which has eaten of the tree of knowledge is that it must know that we cannot learn the *meaning* of the world from the results of its analysis, be it ever so perfect; it must rather be in a position to create this meaning itself ... General views of life can never be the products of increasing empirical knowledge, and ... the highest ideals, which move us most forcefully, are always formed only in the struggle with other ideals which are just as sacred to others as ours are to us.'[7]

In 'Politics as a Vocation' (1918), Weber argued that 'we must be clear about the fact that all ethically oriented conduct may be guided by one of two fundamentally differing and irreconcilably opposed maxims: conduct can be oriented to an "ethic of ultimate ends" or to an "ethic of responsibility".[8] And the decisive point in the contrast, for Weber, is that whereas the absolute ethic 'just does not *ask* for "consequences",' the maxim of an ethic of responsibility is that 'one has to give an account of the foreseeable results of one's action.'[9] As we shall see, such an ethic of responsibility, based on the 'dualism of facts and standards,' lies at the heart of Popper's views on the proper methodology of the social sciences as well as his interpretation of liberalism (cf *OS* II 383–93).

In chapter 5 of *The Open Society and Its Enemies*, Popper argues that the distinction between 'facts and decision' is absolutely 'indispensable for a reasonable understanding of our social environment' (*OS* I 67). The ethical and methodological dimensions of the dualism are deeply intertwined in a boldly sculpted defence of the possibility of progress in mind and society. Only by honouring and appreciating this distinction can we come gradually to provide a more adequate and secure basis for the liberal tradition, above all, by learning the most we can about the consequential analysis of society from the method of the natural sciences.

Thus, although it is impossible to 'prove the rightness of any ethical principle, or even to argue in just the manner in which we argue in favour of a scientific statement,' Popper reminds us: 'The rational and imaginative analysis of the consequences of a moral theory' possesses 'a certain analogy in scientific method' (*OS* II 238 and 233). In science, as in morals, 'we do not accept an abstract theory because it is convincing in itself; we rather decide to accept or reject it after we have investigated those concrete and practical consequences which can be more directly tested by experience' (*OS* II 233). But, in spite of the obvious benefits of the analogy, Popper stresses the 'fundamental difference' between scientific and moral theories. In deciding between rival scientific theories, our decision 'depends upon the result of experiments ... [In moral theories] we only confront ... [their] consequences with our conscience. And while the verdict of experiments does not depend upon ourselves, the verdict of our conscience does' (ibid).

Popper's methodological prescriptions for the social sciences keep in mind this typically Kantian tension between the potential benefits but limited nature of scientific method. Time and again, he rules out rival methodologies and social theories for failing to realize that although 'ethics is not a science ... [and that] there is no 'rational scientific basis' of ethics, there is an ethical basis of science, and of rationalism' (*OS* II 238) – a number of intimate connections between underlying ethical and moral concerns and the evaluation of rival method and theoretical positions in the social sciences.

First, without the critical 'dualism of facts and standards' or decisions, no liberal tradition can be sustained: 'An essential part of this tradition is the recognition of the injustice that does exist in this world, and the resolve to try to help those who are its victims. [But] this means that there is, or that there may be, a conflict, or at least a gap, between facts and standards: facts may fall short of right (or valid or true) standards – especially those social and political facts which consist in the actual acceptance and enforcement of some code of justice' (*OS* II 392). Thus Popper contends that all monisms – the tendency to reduce norms to facts – are dangerous as well as mistaken (cf *OS* I 73 and II 392–3). Time and again we find societies, particularly liberal ones, 'searching for ever better standards' with which to run their affairs. And monisms lead to 'the identification of standards with established might or with future right: it leads to a moral positivism or to a moral historicism' (*OS* II 393).

This conviction propels Popper's extreme hostility toward Hegel and all varieties of Hegelianism. Hegel's philosophy of identity could not help but play 'a major role in the downfall of the liberal movement in Germany' (*OS* II 395). In thus 'contributing to historicism, and to an identification of might and right, [Hegel] encouraged totalitarian modes of thought' and deserves nothing but the most scathing of rebukes.

Second, the dualism of facts and standards is an essential precondition for the emergence of social science itself. No more than there are such things as 'pure, untainted' observations or similar 'sources or foundations' to our knowledge, 'facts as such have no meaning; they can gain it only through our decision' (*OS* II 228–9). Thus, only by maintaining this distinction with responsibility and methical determination can 'a theoretical understanding of the difference between "nature" and "society" develop' (*OS* I 57).

Popper contends that we owe to the generation of Protagoras – 'the first of the great thinkers who called themselves "Sophists" ' – the decisive discovery and understanding of the distinction at hand. Protagoras and others of that 'Great Generation which lived in Athens just before, and during, the Peloponnesian war' were finally able to demystify the 'magical attitude of a primitive tribal or "closed" society' by formulating the doctrine that 'human institutions of language, custom, and law are not of the magical character of taboos but man-made, not natural but conventional, insisting at the same time, that we are responsible for them' (*OS* I 185). By emphasizing the 'need to distinguish between two elements in man's environment – his natural environment and his social environment,' the Sophists grasped the crucial distinction between natural laws, or laws of nature, and normative laws, or prohibitions and commandments (*OS* I 57–61).

Popper explains the distinction as follows: 'A natural law is a description of a strict, unvarying regularity which either in fact holds in nature ... or does not hold ... A law of nature is unalterable; there are no exceptions to it ... Since laws of nature are unalterable, they can be neither broken nor enforced. They are beyond human control although they may possibly be used ... for technological purposes, and ... we may get into trouble by not knowing them, or by ignoring them' (*OS* I 58). In contrast, a normative law is alterable and 'can be enforced by men ... It may be perhaps described as good or bad, right or wrong, acceptable or unacceptable; but only in the metaphorical sense can it be called "true" or "false", since it does not describe a fact, but lays down directions for our behaviour ... If a significant normative law is observed, then this is always due to human control – to human actions and decisions' (ibid). This is not to say that all 'social laws' are 'normative and man-imposed' (*OS* I 67); 'there are important natural laws of social life,' such as those formulated by modern economics into theories of international trade and the business cycle (ibid).

These, and other 'sociological laws,' are closely connected 'with the functioning of *social institutions*' (ibid: cf chapters 3 and 9). Such laws perform a role in social life 'corresponding to the role played in mechanical engineering by, say, the principle of the lever' (*OS* I 67). It is only through institutions that we can 'achieve anything which goes beyond the power of our muscles' and individual capacities: 'Like machines, institutions multiply our power, for good and evil. Like machines, they need intelligent supervision by someone who understands their way of functioning and most of all, their purposes ... [and of the] social regularities which impose limitations upon what can be achieved by institutions (*OS* I 67). For much of our social life, both normative laws and social regularities are present and so closely interwoven into the fabric of institutional existence that it is impossible systematically to improve their functioning without being able to distinguish between them. Most institutions have arisen as 'the undesigned results of human actions ... [and] the indirect results of purposive actions,' but 'their functioning depends, largely, on the observance of norms' (*OS* I 63).

Looking back over the historical development of Western thought, Popper underscores two main tendencies blocking adoption of scientific rationalism or critical dualism: 'a general tendency towards monism ... [i.e.] towards the reduction of norms to facts' (*OS* 1 73) and 'our fear of admitting to ourselves that responsibility for our ethical decisions is entirely ours and cannot be shifted to anybody else; neither to God, nor to nature, nor to society, nor to history' (ibid).

As seductive as we may find theories that promise to 'take the burden from us,' Popper insists 'we cannot shirk this responsibility.' For whatever norms and authority we live by, 'it is we who accept them.' It is sheer mystification and a dangerous self-delusion to think otherwise. But, just because 'the realm of ends goes largely beyond the power of scientific argument,' it does not go 'altogether beyond the power of rational criticism' (*CR* 359).

Between the naïve monism that Popper finds most characteristic of 'closed societies' and the critical dualism of the 'open society,' there are a number of intermediate stages. Naïve monism (the distinction between natural and normative laws has yet to be made) cannot differentiate the 'unpleasant experiences suffered in the natural environment' from those intentionally and unintentionally 'imposed by other men' as sanctions or consequences of social living. It leaves our adjustment to our environment completely random or ad hoc, and therefore irrational.

Within naïve monism, two sub-stages are worthy of note: naïve naturalism and (more important) naïve conventionalism. In the former 'only an abstract possibility which probably was never realized', regularities – whether natural or conventional – are believed to be beyond alteration (*OS* 1 60). In the latter, 'both natural and normative regularities are experienced as expressions of, and as dependent upon, the decisions of man-like Gods or demons ... It is understandable that those who think in this way may believe that even the natural laws are open to modifications, under certain exceptional circumstances; that with the help of magical practices man may sometimes influence them; and that natural regularities are upheld by sanctions, as if they were normative' (*OS* 1 60).

Popper's explanation of the breakdown of such 'magical tribalism' seems to equivocate, as befits a species of scientific moralism, between materialistic or sociological and ideational or subjective causes and between descriptive and prescriptive vocabularies and tones. The breakdown, Popper maintains, 'is closely connected with the realization that taboos are different in various tribes, that they are imposed and enforced by man, and that they may be broken without unpleasant repercussions if one can only escape the sanctions imposed by one's fellow-men. This realization is quickened when it is observed that laws are altered and made by human lawgivers' (ibid). But elsewhere he wrote: 'It is only after this magical "closed society" has actually broken down that a theoretical understanding of the difference between "nature" and "society" can develop' (OS 1 57).

This last distinction presupposes 'a *critical dualism*, or critical conventionalism.'[10]

Critical dualism ... asserts that norms and normative laws *can* be made and changed by man, more especially by a decision or convention to observe them or to alter them, and that it is therefore man who is morally responsible for them ... Norms are man-made in the sense that we must blame nobody but ourselves for them; neither nature, nor God. It is our business to improve them as much as we can, if we find that they are objectionable ... Nature consists of facts and of regularities, and is in itself neither moral nor immoral. It is we who impose our standards upon nature, and who in this way introduce morals into the natural world, in spite of the fact that we are part of this world ... Responsibility, decisions, enter the world of nature only through us. (OS 1 61)

Popper goes to great lengths to distinguish his variety of critical conventionalism or 'pragmatic rationalism' from the 'fundamental misapprehension ... that "convention" implies "arbitrariness"; that if we are free to choose any system of norms we like, then one system is just as good as any other' (OS 1 64–5).

Popper claims that nothing could be further from the truth than such relativism and conceptual anarchism. A commitment to rationalism implies

a common medium of communication, a common language of reason; it establishes something like a moral obligation towards that language, the obligation to keep up its standards of clarity and to use it in such a way that it can retain its function as a vehicle of argument ... ; to use it as an instrument of rational communication, of significant information, rather than as a means of 'self-expression' ... And it implies the recognition that mankind is united by the fact that our different mother tongues, in so far as they are rational, can be translated into one another. It recognizes the unity of human reason. (OS 11 239)

As we shall see in chapter 7, the political implications of this egalitarian conception of reason take us to the heart of Popper's liberalism; for now, however, let us trace its ramifications through his proposals for the methodology of the social sciences and the study of society.

In *The Poverty of Historicism*, Popper reminds the would-be student of scientific method that 'there can be no doubt that, from the standpoint of history although not of logic, methodologies are usually by-products of philosophical views' (*PH* 54). It seems doubtful to me that *The Poverty of Historicism* deserves to 'stand alongside Durkheim's *Rules of Sociological Method* or Weber's *Methodology of the Social Sciences.*'[11] In terms of structure and content, *The Poverty* lacks balance, rigour, and consistency in comparison with Durkheim and Weber. But of all the many facets of his thought, Popper's views on the logic of the social sciences have been neglected the most.

This neglect mirrors the scholarly response to several of the major problems of *The Poverty* itself. If, as Jarvie recently has argued, 'it has become an anticlassic: read but not praised; diffused by not read; influential but disparaged,'[12] this in no small measure is the book's or, more correctly, Popper's own fault. Much to his credit, Popper grants as much. In his autobiography, for example, he writes: '*The Poverty of Historicism* is, I think, one of my stodgiest pieces of writing. Besides, after I had written the ten sections which form the first chapter, my whole plan broke down: section 10, on essentialism, turned out to puzzle my friends so much that I began to elaborate it; and out of this elaboration ... there grew, or exploded, without any plan and against all plans, a truly unintended consequence, *The Open Society*. [Only] after it had begun to take shape I cut it out of *The Poverty* and reduced *The Poverty* to what was more or less its originally intended content' (IA 90–1).

Let us review the weaknesses that resulted from this 'broken plan.' First, unlike *Logik de Forschung*, *The Poverty* begins not with a problem but with a doctrine, historicism. Popper's eccentric construction of 'historicism' exacerbated the lack of a clearly stated problem. One has the impression of witnessing the summary court-martialling and conviction of an entire battalion of only vaguely related troops or ideas. As Popper originally intended the term, 'historicism' was every bit as much a 'struggle concept' as it had been for Friedrich Meinecke.[13] For Meinecke, 'historicism' represented a laudatory reaction against the excessively arid Cartesianism of eighteenth-century rationalism; for Popper, it 'inspired both Marxism and fascism' (IA 80).

Accepted usage had always seen the doctrine (whatever else it may have implied for particular writers) as the exact opposite of the position

Popper has portrayed. Popper saw historicism as the doctrine that there are historical laws of social development (in roughly the same sense that there are laws of nature). But most 'historicists' follow Wilhelm Dilthey and others in the tradition of the Geisteswissenschaften, distinguishing between natural science and the 'historical' or 'cultural' sciences – between causal 'explanation' and the systematic study of the 'understandings' and meaningful dimension of human actions and social practices.[14] Popper has recently tried to rebuild a bridge between his doctrine of the 'autonomous' and 'objective' nature of the third world and the 'hermeneutics' of Dilthey and Collingwood.[15] Had he been less 'whiggish' and cavalier in his use of labels and in drawing the initial (strained) terms of discourse and debate with other traditions of thought, such an important dialogue might have been launched much earlier.

Another problem with *The Poverty* lies in its structure – a problem raised but not explored by Popper's self-criticism. The work is divided into four parts. Part I (sections 1–10) outlines 'anti-naturalistic' objections to the extension of the logic and methods of the natural sciences to the social sciences. Part II (11–18) outlines some 'pro-naturalistic' parallels between the methods of the natural and the social sciences. Parts III (19–26) and IV (27–33), by their titles, look to be criticisms of the pro- and anti-naturalistic arguments presented in parts I and II, respectively.

But, as Jarvie reluctantly admits, 'the parallel one hopes for is not quite there in the text.'[16] See table I.[17] In part I, ten arguments are advanced as to why the social sciences cannot follow the methodological prescriptions of the natural sciences. But part III has only eight sections, few of which specifically address the claims and positions encountered in part I; two (19 and 20) contain the essence of Popper's own positive position on the logic of the social sciences; two (21 and 22) on utopianism have more to do with points raised in part II, sections 15–17; one (25) criticizes the arguments encountered in section 2, on experimental design; and one (26) criticizes the views concerning generalization raised in section 1. In short, the other sections, on, for example, novelty, complexity, and inexactitude, do not receive parallel sections of criticism. The same asymmetry and inconsistency is evident between parts II and IV as well.

Confronted with these and other structural problems in the book, Jarvie has proposed that we restructure *The Poverty* along 'the same lines as *Logik der Forschung*.'[18] What problem does the work address? Jarvie replies: 'What are the methods of the social sciences?' More specifically, 'How, if at all, do the methods of the social sciences differ from the

TABLE 1
Parts and chapters of *The Poverty of Historicism*

Part I Anti-Naturalistic Doctrines of Historicism	Part II Pro-Naturalistic Doctrines of Historicism	Part III Criticisms of Anti-Naturalistic Doctrines	Part IV Criticisms of Pro-Naturalistic Doctrines
1 Generalization [see 26]	11 Comparison with Astronomy. Long-term Forecasts and Large-scale Forecasts	19 Practical Aims of This Criticism	27 Is There a Law of Evolution? Laws and Trends [see 14]
2 Experiment [see 25]		20 The Technological Approach to Sociology	
3 Novelty			28 The Method of Reduction: Causal Explanation, Prediction and Prophecy [see 11]
4 Complexity	12 The Observational Basis	21 Piecemeal vs. Utopian Social Engineering [see 15 and 17]	
5 Inexactitude of Prediction	13 Social Dynamics		
6 Objectivity and Valuation	14 Historical Laws		
7 Holism	15 Historical Prophecy vs. Social Engineering	22 The Unholy Alliance with Utopianism [see 16]	29 The Unity of Method [see 12]
8 Intuitive Understanding	16 The Theory of Historical Development	23 Criticism of Holism [see 7]	30 Theoretical and Historical Sciences [see 14, 15, 16]
9 Quantitative Methods		24 The Holistic Theory of Social Experiments	
10 Essentialism vs. Nominalism	17 Interpreting vs. Planning Social Change	25 The variability of Experimental Conditions [see 2]	31 Situational Logic in History: Historical Interpretation
	18 Conclusion of Analysis	26 Are Generalizations Confined to Periods? [see 1]	32 The Institutional Theory of Progress [see 6]
			33 Conclusion: The Emotional Appeal of Historicism

methods of the natural sciences? [And] how do the answers to these questions bear on (then) current social problems, including war and post-war reconstruction?'[19]

In light of Popper's own recollections of the mid- and late 1930s, such a proposal seems on secure ground (see Popper's 'Historical Note' prefacing the book as well as section 24 of his autobiography). But Jarvie's effort to discover more consistency and rigour in the book by catching 'glimpses' of its 'subtext [evidenced] (in notes and asides) than on the surface'[20] is dubious and unnecessary. For Popper has elsewhere advanced his views on the logic and methodology of the social sciences with a great deal more clarity, consistency, and force. Several lectures and addresses are much more revealing about his philosophy of social science. Critics and proponents alike of his social theory have not appreciated this fact.

Popper's most systematic and detailed exposition of his thinking about the social sciences is to be found in 'Twenty-Seven Theses and a Few Thoughts on the Logic of the Social Sciences,' delivered to a 1961 meeting of the German Sociological Association in Tubingen. First (theses 1–3), and reflecting his primary commitments to both fallibilism and the dynamic growth of knowledge, Popper asserts that the logic of any inquiry must be able to clarify 'the relations between our remarkable and constantly increasing knowledge and our constantly increasing insight that we really know nothing' (LSS 88) – it 'has to discuss this tension between knowledge and ignorance'.

   With thesis 4, 'we have arrived at the heart of our topic': 'Knowledge does not start from perceptions or observations or the collection of data or facts, but it starts, rather, from problems ... No knowledge without problems; but also, no problems without knowledge. But his means that knowledge starts from the tension between knowledge and ignorance. Thus we might say not only, no problems without knowledge; but also, no problems without ignorance. For each problem arises from the discovery that something is not in order with our supposed knowledge' (ibid). Note the similarity with John Dewey's writings on cognition and scientific method, especially concerning the 'tensional' nature of knowledge and the evolutionary dimension of problem-solving activity.

   The emphasis in thesis 4 on the problems that life continually poses colours all of Popper's other theses. Bearing in mind that 'the origin of life and the origin of problems coincide' (IA 142), Popper states in thesis 5:

As in all other sciences, we are in the social sciences, either successful, interesting or dull, fruitful or unfruitful, in exact proportion to the significance or interest of the problems we are concerned with; and also, of course, in exact proportion to the honesty, directness, and simplicity with which we tackle these problems. In all this we are in no way confined to theoretical problems. ... [And] in all cases, without exception, it is the character and the quality of the problem – and also of course the boldness and originality of the suggested solution – which determine the value, or the lack of value, of a scientific achievement. (LSS 88–9)

Observation thus always 'plays a particular role,' that of creating (or, as he says in *Logik*, of 'motivating') a new problem by clashing with conscious or unconscious expectations we have about our environment.

Thesis 6 represents Popper's general demand for a unity of method in all scientific areas of inquiry – the rational or critical approach to problem-solving: 'The methodology of the social sciences, like that of the natural sciences, consists in trying out tentative solutions to certain problems ... Solutions are proposed and criticized. If a proposed solution is not open to pertinent criticism then it is excluded as unscientific, although perhaps only temporarily' (LSS 89). If an attempted solution to a problem withstands criticism, 'we accept it temporarily; and we accept it, above all, as worthy of being further discussed and criticized' (ibid). In short, the method of all bona fide science is 'one of tentative attempts to solve our problems; by conjectures which are controlled by severe criticism' (LSS 89–90). Herein lies the right blend of imagination and sensitivity to critical standards against which we can compare the 'survival value' of different sets of ideas and theories.

This conception of scientific method – an unending series of conjectures being controlled by severe criticism – takes us to the centre of Popper's thinking concerning objectivity in the social sciences, which lies in 'the objectivity of the critical method. This means, above all, that no theory is beyond attack by criticism; and further, that the main instrument of logical criticism – the logical contradiction – is objective' (LSS 90). In explicating the 'basic idea which lies behind my central thesis,' Popper again refers us to Kant. Elsewhere he has written: 'The critical rationalism (and also the critical empiricism) which I advocate merely puts the finishing touch to Kant's critical philosophy' (CR 27). Kant's thought, particularly his ethical and moral theory, has a systematic framework and paradigm for the critical search for error (CR 26). In realizing the ever-present tension between knowledge and ignorance and that our knowledge is always tentative, Kant paved the way for our own realization that, 'the only way of "justifying" our knowledge is itself merely provisional, for it consists in criticism or ... an appeal to the fact that *so far* our attempted solutions appear to withstand even our most severe attempts at criticism. There is no positive justification: no justification that goes beyond this' (LSS 90).

Popper contrasts such a methodological and ultimately institutional view of objectivity with a number of other viewpoints. Foremost among these is 'the misguided and erroneous methodological approach of naturalism or scientism' (ibid), which recommends that the social sciences imitate a pseudo-scientific methodology. Popper charges that naturalism and scientism are not only 'based on a misunderstanding of the methods of the natural sciences' – the major sin of 'naturalistic' varieties of historicism – but 'actually on the myth of the inductive character of the methods of the natural sciences, and of the character of the objectivity of the natural sciences' (LSS 91). 'Misguided naturalism' recommends that we 'begin with observations and measurements; this means, for instance, begin by collecting statistical data; proceed, next, by induction to generalizations and to the formation of theories. It is suggested that in this way you will approach the ideal of scientific objectivity ... For an objective science must be "value-free"; that is, independent of any value judgement' (LS 90–1).

In thesis 11, Popper rejects such an ideal of objectivity in the natural sciences. It is a serious mistake, he declares, 'to assume that the objectivity of a science depends upon the objectivity of the scientist. And it is a mistake to believe that the attitude of the natural scientist is more objective than that of the social scientist. The natural scientist is just as partisan as other people, and unless he belongs to the few who are constantly producing new ideas, he is, unfortunately, often very biased, favouring his pet ideas in a one-sided and partisan manner' (LSS 95).

In a more positive and constructive vein, Popper notes in thesis 12 that objectivity is not a 'matter of the individual scientists but rather the social result of their mutual criticism, of the friendly-hostile division of labour among scientists, of their competition. [And] for this reason, it depends, in part, upon a number of social and political circumstances which make this criticism possible' (ibid).

In both the 'Logic of the Social Sciences' and chapter 23 of volume II of *The Open Society and Its Enemies*, Popper contrasts such a conception of objectivity with the so-called sociology of knowledge. In thesis 13, for instance, Popper contends that proponents of the latter approach try 'to explain the objectivity of science by the attitude of impersonal detachment of individual scientists, and a lack of objectivity in terms of the social habitat of the scientist' (LSS 95–6), looking upon science or knowledge as a process in the mind or "consciousness" of the individual scientist' (OS II 217). Such an approach misses the 'decisive point,' that 'objectivity rests upon pertinent mutual criticism,' and 'also shows an astounding failure to understand precisely its main subject, the social aspects of knowledge, or rather, of scientific method' (ibid). For a number of reasons to be explored in the next chapter, I think Popper has seriously misrepresented the sociology of knowledge, at least as formulated by Karl Mannheim, the main target of his criticism. For the time being, however, let us complete the reconstruction and immanent critique of his more general views on the logic of the social sciences.

Over the years, Popper has emphasized different aspects of this social dimension of objectivity and scientific method, depending upon the task – or perceived dangers – at hand. In the 1960s, for instance, he argued that 'objectivity can only be explained in terms of social ideas such as competition (both of individual scientists and of various schools); tradition (mainly the critical tradition); social institutions (for instance, publication in various competing journals and ... publishers; discussion at congresses); the power of the state (its tolerance of free discussion)' (LSS 96).

Earlier, during the mid-1940s, when *The Open Society* appeared, Popper wanted to discredit the putative analogy with objectivity in the natural sciences, which he felt was being advanced incorrectly by sociologists of knowledge and many Marxists. Thus he observed: 'Scientific objectivity can be described as the inter-subjectivity of scientific method' (*OS* II 217). He singled out for particular attention two aspects of natural science which, taken together, 'constitute what I may term the "public character of scientific method" ' (*OS* II 218). First, 'there is something approaching *free* criticism ... The scientific attitude means criticizing everything; and they are little deterred even by authorities, (ibid). Second, 'scientists try to avoid talking at cross-purposes ... They try very seriously to speak one and the same language, even if they use different mother tongues' (ibid).

These criteria suggest to Popper a normative standard to evaluate and compare the performance of social science as a whole, as well as particular disciplines within it. In general, Popper remarks, 'the social sciences have not yet fully attained [the] publicity of method' characteristic of the natural sciences (*OS* II 221). In the latter, scientists avoid 'talking at cross-purposes,' above all else, 'by recognizing experience as the impartial arbiter of their controversies': 'When speaking of "experience" I have in mind experience of a "public" character, like observations and experiments, as opposed to experience in the sense of more "private" aesthetic or religious experience; and an experience is "public" if everybody who takes the trouble can repeat it. In order to avoid speaking at cross-purposes, scientists try to express their theories in such a form that they can be tested, i.e. refuted (or else corroborated) by such experience' (*OS* II 218).

The fact that particular judgments or individuals may be 'partial or even cranky' will not 'seriously disturb the working of various *social institutions* which have been designed to further scientific objectivity and criticism' (ibid). For Popper, this dimension 'shows what can be achieved by institutions designed to make public control possible, and by the open expression of public opinion, even if this is limited to a circle of specialists. Only political power, when it is used to suppress free criticism, or when it fails to protect it, can impair the functioning of these institutions, on which all progress, scientific, technological, and political, ultimately depends' (ibid).

Throughout Popper's career, such a view also has translated into a (traditionally positivist) hierarchy of different bodies of knowledge within the social sciences. For instance, in thesis 8, Popper laments what he believes to be the post-war reversal of the proper relationship between sociology and anthropology. Whereas before the Second World War, the former was 'regarded as a general theoretical social science, comparable, perhaps, with theoretical physics' and the latter 'as a very special kind of sociology – a descriptive sociology of primitive societies,' in the 1960s 'this relationship has been completely reversed' (LSS 91): 'Social anthropology has been promoted from an applied descriptive discipline to a key theoretical science and the anthropologist has been elevated from a modest and somewhat short-sighted descriptive fieldworker to a far-seeing and profound social theorist and depth-psychologist. The former theoretical sociologist ... must be happy to find employment as a fieldworker and a specialist' (LSS 92).

Popper insists that such a reversal is a prime example of the victory of pseudo-scientific method in the social sciences. It not only represents yet another triumph of the erroneous, ultimately behaviouristic ideal of scientific objectivity outlined above, but, more significant, it reflects the influence of a deep-seated and pernicious mixture of historical and sociological relativisms. Historical relativism represents the claim 'that there is no objective truth but instead merely truths for this or that age,' while sociological relativism 'teaches that there are truths of sciences for this or that class or group or profession, such as proletarian science and bourgeois science' (LSS 95).

There can be little doubt that, of the remaining social sciences, economics receives pride of place. Popper spent his youth at the University of Vienna, the citadel of Austrian 'marginalism.'[21] At least 'in a part of modern economics,' he notes in *The Open Society*, different researchers 'try very seriously to speak one and the same language, even if they use different mother tongues' (*OS* II 218). They thus come much closer to the 'publicity of method' characteristic of the natural sciences. In fact, Popper's thesis 25, on the 'logic of the social sciences,' begins with the proposition (to be discussed shortly) that 'The logical investigation of economics culminates in a result which can be applied to all social sciences' (LSS 102).

As for psychology (thesis 22), 'it is impossible to explain society exclusively in psychological terms, or to reduce it to psychology. Thus we cannot look upon psychology as the basis of the social sciences' (LSS 101). In *The Open Society*, Popper contrasts the views of J.S. Mill and Marx in terms of this issue. Mill believed that 'the study of society, in the last analysis, must be reducible to psychology; that the laws of historical development must be explicable in terms of *human nature*, of the "laws of the mind" and, in particular, of its progressiveness' (*OS* II 88). Although Mill's psychologism was not without its virtues – especially its opposition to holism and 'methodological collectivism' – Popper contends that it leads ultimately to the adoption of historicist methods: 'The attempt to reduce the facts of our social environment to psychological facts forces us into speculations about origins and developments' (*OS* II 92). Ultimately, psychologism is forced to operate, 'whether it likes it or not, ... with the idea of a beginning of society' and with the mythical, dogmatic idea of a pre-social human nature and psychology (*OS* II 93).

Popper claims that it was 'perhaps the greatest achievement of Marx as a sociologist' to have successfully challenged such psychologism. He cites the well-known preface to Marx's *A Contribution to a Critique of Political Economy* (1859): 'It is not the consciousness of man that determines his existence – rather, it is his social existence that determines his consciousness'; Popper argues that Marx rightly understood that 'if a reduction is to be attempted at all, it would be ... more hopeful to attempt a reduction or interpretation of psychology in terms of sociology than the other way around' (*OS* II 93). Of course, Popper concedes, our social environment is 'man-made in a certain sense; that its institutions and traditions are neither the work of God nor of nature; but the results of human actions and decision' (ibid). But this certainly does not mean 'that they are all consciously designed, and explicable in terms of needs, hopes or motive.' On the contrary, Popper exclaims, in the spirit of Adam Ferguson and John Millar, among others, 'Even those which arise as the result of conscious and intentional human actions are, as a rule, *the indirect, the unintended and often unwanted by-products of such actions*' (ibid). Indeed, the realization that this is the case constitutes what Popper repeatedly describes as the 'main task of the explanatory social sciences' (*OS* II 94). Before examining this claim in greater detail, let us first discuss Popper's conception of theories.

In theses 14–21 of his 1961 address to the German Sociological Association, Popper outlines the logical attributes of the critical approach to social scientific method seeking to illuminate his earlier claim that 'objectivity lies in the objectivity of the critical method' (LSS 90). Popper's point of departure is reminiscent of Weber's and Kant's: 'What is possible and what is important and what lends science its special character is not the elimination of extra-scientific interests but rather the differentiation between the interests which do not belong to the search for truth and the purely scientific interest in truth' (LSS 96). In a 'pertinent scientific discussion,' we must distinguish between the following sorts of questions: '(1) The question of the truth of an assertion; the question of its relevance, of its interest and of its significance relative to the problems in which we are interested. (2) The problem of its relevance and of its interest and of its significance for various *extra-scientific problems*, for example, problems of human welfare, or the quite differently structured problem of national defence' (ibid). Scientific criticism and truly scientific discussion ought 'to fight against the confusion of value-spheres and, in particular, to separate extra-scientific evaluations from *questions of truth* (LSS 97).

The task will not be easy. Not only are 'our motives and even our purely scientific ideals ... deeply anchored in extra-scientific and, in part, in religious evaluations,' but our commitments to objectivity and 'value-freedom' (or freedom from such attachments) 'are themselves *values*' (ibid). The air of paradox in all this 'disappears quite of its own accord,' provided we continue to 'point out confusions of value and to separate purely scientific value problems of truth, relevance, simplicity, and so forth, from extra-scientific problems' (LSS 97–8).

Deductive logic, which can discipline our passion and intellect, relating the consequences of what we know to that which we believe lies in the future, is central in Popper's methodological writings. Thesis 15, for example, states: 'The most important function of pure deductive logic is that of an organon of criticism' (LSS 98). It can guarantee that we learn systematically from our mistaken preconceptions and erroneous theories. Thesis 18 reads in part: 'deductive logic becomes the theory of rational criticism. For all rational criticism takes the form of an attempt to show that unacceptable conclusions can be derived from the assertion we are trying to criticize. If we are successful in deriving, logically, unacceptable conclusions from an assertion, then the assertion may be taken to be refuted' (LSS 98–9).

A brief digression on the nature of logical fallacies will be helpful in linking Popper's demand here (and in thesis 19) that scientists work with theories formulated as deductive systems and his general criterion of demarcation as falsifiability. Take the hypothetical syllogism, 'If A is true, then B is true; A is true, therefore B is true.' If we are to conclude, 'B is true,' we must be able to say that A, in fact, is true 'affirm the antecedent' of the major premiss – (modus ponens). Deductive logic is an abstract calculus, the logical truth of which in no way depends on the factual truth of either its major or minor premisses.

Now, if we modify the minor premiss to read, 'if A is true, then B is true; therefore A is true,' we are trying to 'affirm the consequent' – that is, arguing from the truth of the consequent to the truth of the antecedent. But this is a fallacious line of reasoning, because our conclusion need no longer follow. To illustrate concretely: if Williams is a trained philosopher, he knows how to use the rules of logic; Williams knows how to use the rules of logic; therefore, Williams is a trained philosopher (alas, not the case). In short, though it is logically correct to affirm the antecedent, it is a fallacy to affirm the consequent. However, it is always logically correct to 'deny the consequent' (modus tollens). For example, let us express the same hypothetical syllogism negatively: 'If A is true, then B is true; B is not true; therefore A is not true.' To wit: if Williams fails to use the rules of logic correctly, we are logically justified in concluding that he indeed is not a trained philosopher.[22]

Popper insists on the logical asymmetry between verification and falsification in the evaluation of scientific theories and deductive method in the pursuit of theoretical knowledge. From a logical point of view, we can never assert that a scientific hypothesis is necessarily true because it agrees with currently known (or inductively arrived at) facts; that is affirming the consequent. Popper exploits this fundamental asymmetry and the realization that 'you can never demonstrate that anything is materially true but you can demonstrate that some things are materially false.'[23] First, it obviously forms the basis for his demarcation of scientific from non- and pseudo-scientific theories. Second, it leads to his view that genuine explanations are predictive and technological in nature.

In thesis 20, Popper observes: 'The basic logical schema of every explanation consists of a (logical) deductive inference whose premises consist of a theory and some initial conditions and whose conclusion is the explicandum' (LSS 100). This formulation merely reiterates the theory of explanation initially advanced in *The Logic of Scientific Discovery* in slightly less technical terminology: 'To give a causal explanation of an event means to deduce a statement which describes it, using as premises of the deduction one or more universal laws, together with certain singular statements, the initial conditions' (*LSD* 59). On Popper's account, the explicandum (what is to be explained) must be deduced from the explanans (what explains it). Moreover, in addition to requiring a statement of the initial conditions within which the event to be explained originates, Popper requires that the explanans contain one or more universal laws. The first requirement is usually referred to as the 'deductive thesis,' and the second (following W.H. Dray, especially *Laws and Explanation in History*) the 'covering law thesis.'[24]

Alan Donagan points out that Popper's intention was to offer a theory not of explanation in general but only of the causal explanation of particular (or singular) events – 'with explanations which answer questions of the form, "why did the event E occur, rather than not occur?" '[25] And Popper insists that the causal explanation of a regularity described by a universal law must be distinguished from those of individual events. Although, 'at first sight, one might think that the case is analogous and that the law in question has to be deduced from (1) some more general laws, and (2) certain special conditions which correspond to the initial conditions but which are *not* singular, and refer to a certain *kind* of situation. This, however, is not the case here, for the special conditions (2) must be explicitly stated in the formulation of the law which we wish to explain; for otherwise this law would simply contradict (1)' (*PH* 124–5; cf *LSD* 71–2). Such a conception of explanation becomes crucial for Popper in both substance and method.

With its insistence that explanations state 'what we cannot do,' such a conception is ideal for Popper, for whom 'One of the most striking things about social life [is] that *nothing ever comes off exactly as intended ...* [Hence] the real task of the social sciences is to explain those things which nobody wants – such as, for example, a war, or a depression ... It is the task of social theory to explain how the unintended consequences of our intentions and actions arise, and what kind of consequences arise if people do this, that or the other in a certain social situation, (*CR* 124–5). Popper's major objection in *The Poverty of Historicism* to both anti-naturalistic and naturalistic historicism is their common inability to grasp the logical structure and implications of such a deductive theory of explanation for the study of social phenomena – both rest on serious misunderstandings of the methodology of the natural sciences.

Popper believes that 'all theoretical or generalizing sciences make use of the same method' (*PH* 130), 'offering deductive causal explanations, and ... testing them (by way of predictions). This has sometimes been called the hypothetical-deductive method, or more often the method of hypothesis, for it does not achieve absolute certainty ... Rather, these statements always retain the character of tentative hypotheses' (*PH* 131). There is thus 'no great difference between explanation, prediction, and testing' (ibid). The difference between these concerns is 'not one of logical structure, but rather one of emphasis; it depends on *what we consider to be our problem*' (ibid).

Popper readily concedes that 'historical sciences' (as distinct from 'generalizing' ones) are interested neither in bringing about future states of affairs (as in engineering), nor in discovering laws (physics and other 'theoretical' sciences). But Popper vehemently denies, against proponents of the Geisteswissenschaften, any fundamental difference in the subject-matters of the generalizing and theoretical sciences. There are historical or genetic sciences of physical nature, such as geological history, and theoretical sciences of individuals and societies, such as psychology and sociology (*OS* II 265; cf *PH* sections 30–1).

In essence, the theoretical errors of historicism are twofold. The first has to do with the so-called principle of holism (*PH* 17–19). Historicists insist that 'sociology, like all "biological" sciences that deal with living objects, should not proceed in an atomistic, but in what is now called a "holistic" manner ... The social group is *more* than the mere sum total of the merely personal relationships existing at any moment between any of its members ... A group has a *history* of its own and ... its structure depends to a great extent on its history' (*PH* 17). Popper finds such claims incompatible with the spirit of science. Holism – such as that allegedly advanced by Karl Mannheim in *Man and Society in an Age of Reconstruction* – depends on an equivocal use of the word 'whole,' using it to mean both the totality of the properties or aspects of a thing and the thing considered as an organized structure, as opposed to a 'mere heap' (*PH* 76). Historicists claim that naturalists or positivists refuse to study social relations in either of these senses.

With regard to the first sense, Popper says that historicists are right in fact but not in logic, for it is impossible to study anything construed as such a totality. 'Wholes in the sense of totalities cannot be made the object of scientific study ... As a rule, science is selective ... All knowledge, whether intuitive or discursive, must be of abstract aspects, and ... we can never grasp the "concrete structure of social reality itself"' (*PH* 78). And on the second sense, Popper contends that the historicists are simply wrong. Even atomic physics, presumably 'atomistic,' studies atoms not as 'mere heaps' of particles, but rather as systems which certainly are wholes (*PH* 82). In 'Prediction and Prophecy in the Social Sciences,' he said:

While there are, admittedly, such empirical objects as the crowd of people here assembled, it is quite untrue that names like 'middle-class' stand for any such empirical groups. What they stand for is a kind of ideal object whose existence depends upon theoretical assumptions. Accordingly, the belief in the empirical existence of social wholes or collectives, which may be described as *naive collectivism*, has to be replaced, by the demand that social phenomena, including collectives, should be analysed in terms of individuals and their actions and relations.' (*CR* 341).

Another major error of historicism stems from what Donagan calls the principle of radical novelty.[26] Historicists maintain, Popper writes, that 'in the world of physics nothing can happen that is truly and intrinsically new ... Newness in physics is merely the newness of arrangements or combinations. In direct opposition to this, social newness, like biological newness, is an intrinsic sort of newness ... It is real newness, irreducible to the novelty of arrangements ... Historicism claims that nothing is of greater moment than the emergence of a really new period' (*PH* 10). Popper's objections follow directly from his analysis of causal explanation. The claim that, unlike natural events, social situations are radically novel vis-à-vis antecedent events and that development accordingly must be 'periodized' confuses novelty of initial conditions with novelty of laws. Popper claims that 'laws' of historical development are not universal and hence not true laws at all. Further, 'periods' and 'novelties' are not entirely foreign to the behaviour and study of natural phenomena. Many regularities of climate, for instance, are only true for certain regions of the earth and for some geological periods (*PH* 99–100).

Whenever they need to explain novelties of natural phenomena, scientists proceed not by 'periodizing' their laws to certain contexts or 'stages' of development but by discovering the novelties in initial conditions. Here Popper's charge that 'the poverty of historicism ... is a poverty of imagination' seems apposite (*PH* 130). Historicists have not shown why novelties in social life should not be explained similarly in terms of changes in initial conditions. There seems 'no reason,' Popper asserts, 'why we should be unable to frame sociological theories which are important for all social periods' (*PH* 101). Even if human nature changes, we can try to explain such changes in terms of initial conditions, according to universal laws (*PH* 102).

Perhaps historicism's most serious error derives from a 'naturalistic' inference, most frequently encountered in Marxism, made from this principle of novelty. This is the claim that 'the only universally valid laws of society must be laws which link *up the successive periods*. They must be laws of historical development which determine the transition from one period to another' (*PH* 41; cf *CR* 338). Once again, Popper's critique follows directly from his analysis of causal explanation. First, Popper denies the empirical existence of such laws, because the development of society, no less than of life on earth, is an individual or unique process. Such a process may take place 'in accordance with all kinds of causal laws, for example, the laws of mechanics, of chemistry, of heredity ... Its description, however, is not a law, but only a singular historical statement' (*PH* 108).

Universal laws not only 'make assertions concerning some unvarying order' but 'must be *tested* by new instances before [they] can be taken seriously by science' (ibid). The observation of one unique process does not meet these demands, 'nor can the observation of one unique process help us to foresee its future development' (*PH* 109). Popper cites from H.A.L. Fisher's *History of Europe*: 'I can see only one emergency following upon another' (ibid). The perception of chaos – 'the play of the contingent and the unforeseen'[27] – severely constrains Popper's hope for a rationalization of history.

Popper concedes that historicists may avoid his objection by arguing that historical development is cyclical or repetitive or if non-repetitive, nevertheless reflects 'a trend or tendency of direction,' the statement of which 'we may formulate [as] a hypothesis' or law linking successive periods (*PH* 109). But Popper rejects both contentions because of their logical confusion of 'trends' and 'laws'. A statement concerning a trend (i.e. of an individual process following a specific pattern) can never constitute a law. Laws are unconditionally and timelessly true. '*Trends are not laws*. A statement asserting the existence of a trend is existential, not universal. (A universal law, on the other hand, does not assert existence; on the contrary ... it asserts the impossibility of something or other.) ... [And] the practical significance of this logical situation is considerable: while we may base scientific predictions on laws, we cannot (as every cautious statistician knows) base them merely on the existence of trends' (*PH* 115).

But however important it is to realize that 'laws and trends are radically different things,' the 'habit of confusing' them, 'together with the intuitive observation of trends (such as technical progress), inspired the central doctrines of evolutionism and historicism – the doctrines of the inexorable laws of biological evolution and of the irreversible laws of motion of society' (*PH* 115–16).

In 'Prediction and Prophecy in the Social Sciences,' Popper takes a slightly different line. Historicists cannot possibly derive historical prophecies from conditional scientific predictions because 'long-term prophecies can be derived from scientific conditions only if they apply to systems which can be described as well-isolated, stationary and recurrent' (*CR* 339). Not only are 'these systems very rare in nature [but] modern society is surely not one of them' (ibid). The most striking aspects of development 'are non-repetitive. Conditions are changing, and situations arise (for example, in consequence of new scientific discoveries) which are very different from anything that ever happened before. The fact that we can predict eclipses does not, therefore, provide a valid reason for expecting that we can predict revolutions' (*CR* 340).

Popper argues in thesis 25 that 'the logical investigation of economics culminates in a result which can be applied to all' other areas of social inquiry (LSS 102). We can now see why he believes this. Such an investigation reveals that 'there exists a *purely objective method*' – 'the method of *objective* understanding, or situational logic' (ibid). 'Its method consists in analysing the social *situation* of acting men sufficiently to explain the action with the help of the situation, without any further help from psychology ... In other words, the situation is analysed far enough for elements which initially appeared to be psychological (such as wishes, motives, memories, and associations) to be transformed into elements of the situation' (ibid). Thus, whereas 'psychological or characterological hypotheses are hardly ever criticizable by rational arguments,' the types of explanations found in economics are 'rational, empirically criticizable, and capable of improvement' (LSS 102).

In thesis 26, Popper explains that the explanations that he is advocating are 'rational, theoretical reconstructions.' They are admittedly 'oversimplified and overschematized and consequently in general *false*' (LSS 103). But they use an individualist method and 'in a strictly logical sense' can 'be good approximations to the truth' of deductively explained social action. Popper introduces this situational methodology of economics in section 29, 'The Unity of Method,' of *The Poverty of Historicism*. There he cites Karl Menger, the founder of Austrian marginalism,[28] and Friedrich Hayek, Menger's best-known contemporary follower. In 1882, Menger fired the opening salvo of the Methodenstreit (or methodological dispute) in Austrian economics against Gustav Schmoller (1838–1917), a Swabian historicist and founder of the historical school of economic analysis. Menger won the prestigious chair of economics at the University of Vienna in 1873, two years after the publication of his path-breaking *Grundsätze der Wolkswirthschaftlehre*. He devoted most of his later work to methodological polemics against the kind of thinking which, in Germany, 'had allowed a transition from nationalist conservatism to the interventionism of the *Katherdersozialisten*.'[29] During the 1880s, when liberalism was forced to a permanent defensive against socialism in Vienna, Eugen Bohm-Bawerk (1851–1914) turned the same type of polemic against Marx's economics. Ludwig von Mises and Friedrich A. Hayek continued to champion the outlook of Austrian laissez-faire liberalism.

Like other marginalists Menger maintained that value 'is a relation between an appraising mind and the object appraised, a manifestation of mental activity,' not an inherent property of commodities or the system of production and exchange.[30] Hence the subsequent neo-classicist emphasis on consumer expectations, wants, risk, and uncertainty. Hayek later remarked 'Every important advance in economic theory during the last hundred years was a further step in the consistent application of subjectivism.'[31] Theoretical economics should seek not empirical laws, by induction, but 'exact laws,' which would form a deductive system not corrigible by empirical testing or experience.

An indefatigable nominalist, Menger argued that so-called 'exact laws' were to be found by analysing a given aspect of reality into its simplest parts and then, through the 'composite method,' demonstrating how complex phenomena and their interaction were the result of these elements. Such laws follow logically from deductive axioms but yield knowledge of empirical facts. Since 'exact laws' are not corrigible by experience, their validity – like that of any other set of 'idealizing assumptions' – depends ultimately on whether the primitive terms and axioms from which they are derived correspond to basic elements and interactions in economic life. Thus Menger's marginalism presupposed introspective and interpretive psychology, since he took for granted that human beings were enough alike psychologically to communicate with one another in 'planning individual performances as consumers, entrepreneurs, etc.'[32] Implicitly, sociology – an inductive science studying social phenomena 'in their full empirical reality' (as classically outlined by John Stuart Mill in book VI of his *System of Logic* – could not aspire to the same 'theoretical' stature and legitimacy.

Popper recommends that we construct 'a model on the assumption of complete rationality (and perhaps also on the assumption of the possession of complete information) on the part of all the individuals concerned, and of estimating the deviation of the actual behaviour of people from the model behaviour, using the latter as a kind of zero-coordinate' (*PH* 141). Popper's faith in such causal modelling stems from his belief that 'concrete social situations are in general less complicated than concrete physical situations. For in most social situations, if not in all, there is an element of *'rationality'* (*PH* 140). Popper admits that 'human beings hardly ever act quite rationally (i.e. as they would if they could make optimal use of all available information for the attainment of whatever ends they may have), but they act, more or less rationally; and this makes it possible to construct comparatively simple models of their actions and interactions, and to use these models as approximations' (*PH* 140–1). Popper describes this rationality as 'perhaps *the most important difference* in [the] methods' between natural and social sciences, since the other differences, concerning experimental design and quantification, are 'of degree rather than kind' (*PH* 141).

Such an 'economic approach' to social and political analysis can produce some impressive, if disturbing, results – witness the massive literature on the logic of collective choice.[33] Whether such studies assist liberal democracy is a question best left to the last two chapters of this study. However, several other reservations about Popper's writings on the method of the social sciences merit serious consideration.

I think Popper's reasoning is far too blunt and reductionistic vis-à-vis the practice of social inquiry to sustain his claims of a single, unified 'logic' for the social sciences – a liberal social science of 'piecemeal technologies.' Let me illustrate this problem in connection with his conception of historical analysis.

Popper's approach to historical inquiry and his critique of historicism make several epistemological and methodological assumptions. Perhaps the most important are the unity of scientific method, that all scientific statements must be empirically corrigible or falsifiable, and an ontological dualism between facts and moral standards. I think it can be shown that the first and third assumptions are logically incompatible, *if* there are important differences between 'brute facts,' and our moral criteria and deliberations.

Popper concludes that his three principles preclude any 'meaning' *in* history, since we can find at most conditional 'trends.' What he means to deny is that we can ever find the meaning *of* history. Following W.H. Walsh and, more recently, B.T. Wilkins, a meaning in history is an explanation that renders a particular historical event intelligible.[34] There cannot help but be many such 'meanings' *in* history, surely the proper objects of historical research. To seek the meaning *of* history is to search for either a system of laws or some pattern governing the historical process as a whole or a goal that unifies it and endows it with moral significance and purposiveness. Historicism, Popper charges, leads us to believe that we can find both. I think he confused the two quite different senses of the question.

In *The Poverty of Historicism* and *The Open Society*, Popper argues that several inherent limitations to historical knowledge prevent discovery of the meaning of history. First, whereas history is concerned with explaining singular events, the generalizing or truly 'theoretical' sciences seek universal laws. Second, although events can be explained by deducing them from universal laws, there are no distinctively historical laws; historians' laws are typically derived from other sciences and in any case, Popper argues, are usually trivial. Third, the historian usually employs theoretical concepts not consciously, as a natural scientist would, but unreflectively, leaving them unstated. Finally, historical research is necessarily selective, the outcome of preconceived, unfalsifiable points of view.

Popper seems profoundly insensitive to the real diversity of interests among historians and their theories.[35] Even if some historians do employ trivial laws, or rely on untestable hypotheses and tacit theories, this need not be the case. Popper has not shown that selectivity and reliance on preconceived interpretations are any more central to the practice of history than he himself already has shown them to be in scientific change. Ironically, Popper reverts to the sort of historical relativism that he opposes in his epistemology and philosophy of science. And, once again, the gap between Popper's epistemology and concrete human practices is to be found in Kant's influence on his thought; that human history, at best, is an object of hope, not knowledge, is difficult to reconcile with the drive to 'rationalize' our social existence. I will return to this problem in the chapers 6, 7, and 8. Had Popper been concerned more with historical practice than with using history to resolve disputes about the 'ideal' logic of the social sciences, no such scepticism would have been needed. This, of course, would presuppose that, *pace* Popper, we highlight the similarities, rather than the differences, between historical and scientific theories.

In Popper's writings on historical analysis and, more generally, on the conduct of social research, we see the logical incompatibility of the unity of scientific method and the dualism of facts and moral standards. If we conclude that historical analysis and natural science are methodologically identical, the difference between facts and decisions does not explain the distinctiveness of history. Then we see as did Vico some three centuries ago, that the two types of inquiry must be distinguished by subject-matter, not method.[36]

Vico's dictum, 'verum factum' – that we can know only truths made by man – underscores an essential difference between the natural sciences and historical analysis, or any social science. Unlike in science, in history and all but the most manipulated and contrived of social situations, creation and discovery of meaning are inseparable. The historian, or sociologist or student of politics, can reconstruct meanings of the past because they are already there. Popper's assumption – Kantian in origin and logical positivist more recently – of an absolute gulf between the context or logic of cognitive justification and the logic or context of the discovery of an idea or problem works an unnecessary hardship on, and distorts the practice of, all those forms of inquiry that address questions of morality, value-formation, conflicts of taste, and contingent choice.

Popper himself would probably admit as much qua moralist were he not as determined, indeed driven, by a priori logical and methodological ideals presented as being beyond dispute, beyond the immature 'Babel of words,' and (after Kant) the 'blind, fumbling guesswork' of non-scientific modes of reasoning. Such commitments render Popper's thought unfortunately reductionistic toward the most significant dimensions of social inquiry – the deliberative, communicative, and hermeneutical nature of human activity.[37] Although parts of Popper's thought, such as the 'logic of the situation,' could address these dimensions, he cannot reconcile them with the unity of method and the 'covering law' model of explanation. For him predictive and self-professed 'technological' interests split irrevocably the creation and the discovery (and explanation) of meaning and value in human affairs.

A related problem concerns Popper's conception of objectivity in social science. As we have seen, especially in the concluding section to the last chapter, Popper predictably follows Kant in driving a wedge between logic and psychology, between the ideal 'form' and the content of knowledge. Consequently, Popper tends to dismiss our effort to 'be objective' as an unwanted concession to 'psychologism' and related 'subjectivist' doctrines, denying much more than is advisable if we hope to cultivate and produce the kinds of scholars and researchers who will honour the values of rationality.

Popper argues that because bias is virtually universal, we should never link the objectivity of our inquiries to the attempt to become more impartial or detached from the sources of cognitive distortion. Hence, his notorious hostility toward the sociology of knowledge. But how then do some individuals nevertheless cultivate the scholarly predilections and habits of research necessary to achieve the 'publicity of method,' intersubjectivity, and other ingredients of intellectual criticism and progress? Were Popper less preoccupied with denying the contributions of psychological and sociological inquiries, he would realize that individual efforts to 'become more objective' can help eradicate bias and the abuse of data and increase methodological 'self-consciousness.'[38]

Scholarly traditions and scientific disciplines can begin to steer their collective destinies and clarify their objectives – or 'rationalize' – only through systematic, theoretically sophisticated approach to the sociology and psychology sustaining their particular bodies of knowledge. Moreover, given the many explanatory frameworks within even a single discipline, it seems extremely doubtful that a phenomenologically rich and detailed account will lend itself to purely 'causal' formalization. Contemporary political science, for example, uses several types of explanatory practices, diverse in intent and logic: functional, genetic, ideographic, and redescriptive explanations; 'law-like' and other types of generalizations; practical inferences; and so on. Each type forms a loosely knit family, extended and non-nuclear. But they do not conform in any sense to a single logical form, and their doing so in the manner that Popper suggests seems unlikely and unnecessary.

Popper gives pride of place and paradigmatic status to neo-classical economics. He see its investigators trying to 'speak one and the same language, even if they use different mother tongues' (*OS* II 218). According to Popper, its logic proceeds until the situations that human beings find themselves in are 'analysed far enough for elements which initially appeared to be psychological ... [to be] transformed into elements of the situation' (*LSS* 102). However, the alembic-like 'transformation' in question has not produced an objective and predictively cumulative body of falsified propositions. Indeed, something close to the opposite has occurred, with 'crisis' talk now as frequent in economics as in political theory.[39]

The most plausible explanation for this lack of performance is its excessively 'thin' conception of rationality or human agency and the self. A.K. Sen has expressed this inadequacy poignantly:

A person is given *one* preference ordering, and as and when the need arises this is supposed to reflect his interests, represent his welfare, summarise his idea of what should be done, and describe his actual choices and behavior. Can one preference ordering do all these things? A person thus described may be 'rational' in the limited sense of revealing no inconsistencies in his choice behaviour, but if he has no use for these distinctions between quite different concepts, he must be a bit of a fool. The *purely* economic man is indeed close to being a social moron. Economic theory has been much preoccupied with this rational fool decked in the glory of his *one* all-purpose preference ordering. To make room for the different concepts related to his behaviour we need a more elaborate structure.'[40]

Implicit in this image of 'economic man' is an even more problematic notion of society and of human need. The society envisaged by many economists has no structural complexity: it is nothing more than a mere agglomeration of atomized 'consumers'; 'goods are divisible like peanut butter (and not like babies)';[41] individuals are so similar in wants, needs, and goals that their differences do not affect questions of value and all are accorded an inordinate consistency, clairvoyancy, and stability – indeed, homogeneity – in ordering preferences and in virtually all other matters of the mind.

Perhaps most revealing is Popper's characterization of situational logic and its assumptions about 'complete rationality' and information and his view that rationality renders human situations less complicated than purely physical ones. Both claims seem wrong, each the product of an excessively abstract and formal portrayal of the self and human agency. Let me end this part of the discussion by clarifying the basis of this charge, to which I will return in the final chapters 7 and 8.

The transactional and socially embedded quality of our selves leads Norbert Elias to observe, in volume II of *The Civilising Process*, that as societies have become more 'rationalised' and as individualism has been elevated to an unquestioned premiss in philosophical and social analysis, 'the conveyor belts running through [one's] existence grow longer and more complex.'[42] As the individual exercises more 'self-control,' 'he is now less a prisoner of his passions than before.' But, as his life is increasingly bound by a host of functional dependencies, he also 'is much more restricted in his conduct, in his chances of directly satisfying his drives and passions. Life becomes in a sense less dangerous but also less emotional or pleasurable, at least as far as the direct release of pleasure is concerned. And for what is lacking in everyday life a substitute is created in dreams, books and pictures.'[43] Evidence from the analysis of dreams, modern literature, films, and social-psychological research and speculation suggests that the drives and passionate effects that no longer manifest themselves directly between people nevertheless struggle no less violently within and between different 'colonies' of our selves.[44]

These 'colonies' of our selves come strongly into play even in our conduct as 'economic' beings in ways scarcely contemplated by mainstream economists, sociologists, and political scientists. The various formalisms that these disciplines have adopted in recent decades – whether utilitarian or Kantian, Marxist or functionalist – demand that the researcher eschew as much of the reality and vocabulary of the 'self' and its subject-related qualities and constitutive practices as possible.[45] But the constitutive experiences of subjectivity, those peaks and valleys of our interior geography, and their effect on our conduct and character, stubbornly continue to impress themselves upon students of society. A number of economic studies have shown that many forms of commitment, status awareness, altruism, and welfare (or 'other-regarding') considerations, and a constant readjusting of expectations and preferences, occur regularly in markets and seriously violate the neo-classical desiderata of individually maximizing and instrumentally rational action.[46]

These and many related forms of conduct and identity are 'subjective' phenomena, irreducible to mere 'means / ends' efficiency calculations and seldom, if ever, simply the product of objective circumstances. A far more complicated chain of influences and considerations, as well as a different 'logic,' will be needed to explain our social rationality than the one offered by orthodox economists and, by extension, Popper.

Perhaps there is an alternative starting-point to the purely instrumental account of rationality. Herbert Simon has suggested that we abandon the quest for substantive rationality – always minimizing costs and maximizing profits given some specified goal – for the study of procedurally rational behaviour, which is 'the outcome of appropriate deliberation' in many different contexts.[47] Such an approach would allow us to understand different types of problem-solving more in terms of their own 'working logics' than on the basis of an overarching logical 'ideal.' The studies of Simon and others suggest that, even as 'maximisers,' we may actually be more appropriately conceived of as 'satisficers.' We are also 'dramatisers' and 'moralisers' as well![48]

Pace Popper, contemporary social inquiry and any philosophy hoping to illuminate its practice needs a sustained dialogue with psychoanalysis, the sociology of knowledge, and other forms of interpretive analysis that attempt to understand the psychological and cultural roots of our reason. These roots are in no way to be confused with their intellectual fruits or results. In spite of Popper's protestations, using such approaches, and jettisoning parts of the ideal of a unified 'logic' of social inquiry are essential if we are to enlarge the sphere of human autonomy and responsible activity. The next chapter expands on this line of criticism with respect to Popper's influential critique of Mannheim's sociology of knowledge.

6

Fallibilism and the sociology of knowledge: Popper on Mannheim

Meeting a friend in a corridor, Wittgenstein said:
'Tell me, why do people always say it was *natural* for
men to assume that the sun went round the earth,
rather than the earth was rotating?' His friend
said, 'Well, obviously because it just *looks* as if the
sun is going round the earth.' To which the philosopher replied, 'Well, what would it have looked
like if it had looked as if the earth was rotating?'

Tom Stoppard, *Jumpers*

No sooner had Karl Mannheim and others begun to outline the objectives
and philosophical presuppositions of the sociology of knowledge than
the advocates of formal logic started hounding the whole enterprise from
serious intellectual discourse. Critics – Gustav Bergmann, Talcott Parsons, and Hans Speier, among others – cited the enormous logical difficulties in attempting to understand 'the relationship between knowledge
and existence' and 'to trace the forms which this relationship has taken
in the intellectual development of mankind.' The alleged difficulties ran
the gamut from vicious circularity to self-referentiality.[1] Popper, more
than anyone, has been responsible for the philosophical hostility and
misunderstanding of Mannheim and the sociology of knowledge. Since
at least the Second World War, he has claimed repeatedly that Mannheim's thought embodies some of the worst philosophical sins of our
time: historicism, a 'romantic and even mystical Utopianism or holism,'
psychologism, and, worst of all, irrationalism. I believe that each of these
charges is largely mistaken, and the aim of this chapter is to question
and correct these errors.

Popper's views on the subject have had an immense impact. For instance, his critique of Mannheim and the sociology of knowledge in *The Open Society and Its Enemies* has been reproduced almost in its entirety, and, significantly, without any rebuttal whatsoever, in one of the most comprehensive readers on the subject.[2] Others have simply implied that Popper's arguments against the sociology of knowledge, as in his slaying of 'positivism,' have 'killed' the field of inquiry altogether.[3] Further, there has yet to appear in English, so far as I am aware, a single systematic defence against Popper's misleading and unjustifiable claims – a remarkable lacuna given the speed with which similar replies were made to Popper by classicists on behalf of Plato, Aristotle, and the Pre-Socratics and by others in defence of Marx and Hegel.[4]

This chapter makes three claims. First, Popper's presentation and criticisms of the sociology of knowledge as formulated by Mannheim rest on deep misunderstandings of the claims and arguments actually made on its behalf. Second, if the first claim is correct, several of the alleged differences between Popper's thought and Mannheim's begin to disappear – especially if one emphasizes the key role that effective communication and public discussion play in *both* thinkers' conceptions of social science and 'rationalization.' Third, this potential rapproachment between Popper's fallibilism and 'situational logic' and Mannheim's relationalism and sociology of knowledge lets us appreciate the unique role and problematic of language and communication in social and political analysis.

Charles Peirce wrote in 'What Is Science?':

Let us look upon science – the science of today – as a living thing. What characterizes it generally from this point of view, is that the thoroughly established truths are labelled and put upon shelves of each scientists' mind, where they can be at hand when there is occasion to use things – arranged, therefore, to suit his special convenience – while science itself, the living process, is busied mainly with conjectures, which are either getting framed or getting tested. When that systematized knowledge on the shelves is used, it is used almost exactly as a manufacturer or practicing physician might use it; that is ... it is merely applied. If it ever becomes the object of science, the moment has come when it must undergo a process of purification or of transformation.

In questioning Popper's characterization of Mannheim and the sociology of knowledge, my primary purpose is to pull down one of the boxes of 'established truth' and transform the neglect of Mannheim's project into insight and future dialogue.[5] However critical of Popper as historian of ideas this project leads me to be, it seems to me completely in the spirit of his own – and Peirce's – life-long insistence that we criticize ruthlessly theories blocking future inquiries. Misunderstanding and neglect of the sociology of knowledge present just such an unnecessary blockage to the future growth of knowledge and understanding in a number of areas of research.

Popper rejects the sociology of knowledge because of his belief that it represents a pernicious form of irrationalism – 'the Marxist doctrine that our opinions, including our moral and scientific opinions, are determined by class interest, and more generally by the social and historical situation of our time. Under the name of "sociology of knowledge" or "sociologism," this doctrine has been developed recently (especially by M. Scheler and K. Mannheim) as a theory of the social determination of scientific knowledge' (*OS* II 213). Both of Popper's major claims in this passage about the sociology of knowledge – at least as propounded by Scheler and Mannheim – are extremely misleading. First, although Scheler held that the selection of the objects of our inquiry is ultimately determined by social interests, he insisted that the content and validity of our knowledge are not so 'determined.' Similarly, though Mannheim at times was ambivalent about the status of natural science, at no point does he doubt the transcendental validity (or absolute autonomy) of logic and mathematics, and in general he also exempted natural science from sociological analysis.[6] Thus in an essay written in 1922, 'Structural Analysis of Epistemology,' about the subject of his doctoral dissertation in philosophy, Mannheim went to great lengths (citing E. Husserl, H. Rickert, E. Spranger, and E. Lask) to argue that all theorizing presupposes a timeless sphere of validity: 'Any systematization whatever can in the end permit but a single correct ordering of its elements ... All concrete acts of thinking are searching for this sequence, and even if it cannot be found in this way, it is still the indispensable presupposition of meaning for any and every act of thinking.'[7]

Second, Popper's claim that sociological analysis seeks to explain scientific knowledge deterministically is also wide of the mark, at least for Mannheim. Time and again, Mannheim reminds us that the sociology of knowledge intentionally limits itself to 'existence-related thought' (Seinsverbundene) – thought in which, 'to use Dilthey's phrase,' the 'whole man thinks.'[8] Such a concern with 'existentiality' (Seinsverbundenheit), or the 'relativity to existence' (Seinsrelativitat), Mannheim continues, simply means that 'certain qualitative features of an object encountered in the living process of history are accessible only to certain historico-social structures of consciousness.'[9]

Throughout his career, but perhaps most explicitly prior to publication of *Ideology and Utopia* in 1929 (translated into English in 1936), Mannheim used a similar distinction between exact, because noncontingent, and existentially bound knowledge. For example, in a recently translated essay, written in 1924, 'A Sociological Theory of Culture and Its Knowability: Conjunctive and Communicative Thought,' Mannheim drew the contrast between general scientific explanation (communicative knowledge) and understanding based on the interpretation of human meanings (conjunctive knowledge). Conjunctive knowledge, the principal object of Mannheim's concern (trained as he was in the classical tradition of the Geisteswissenschaften), corresponds to the products of 'moral-philosophic' thought, and accordingly its vocabulary can never 'aspire to univocality; [because it is] precisely the richness of their associations [that] gives them their vitality.'[10] Similarly, on page 1 of *Ideology and Utopia (IU)*, Mannheim concedes that he is not concerned with scientific knowledge or 'how thinking appears in textbooks on logic' but instead 'with the problem of how men actually think' and with how thinking 'really functions in public life and in politics as an instrument of collective action' (*IU* 1).

Traditionally, Mannheim points out, philosophers, especially philosophers of science, have ignored the type of existentially contingent knowledge that his analyses are intended to explore. The 'pure intellectualism' of the modern scientific or analytic approach 'would not tolerate a science which is so intimately tied up with practice' and the debate over qualitative matters and 'knowledge of societies as a whole' (*IU* 164 and 166). But the fact that politics 'as a process of becoming' does not 'fit into the existing framework of science ... and that it is in contradiction with our present-day conception of science does not mean that politics is at fault. Rather it should be a stimulus to the revision of our conception of science as a whole' (*IU* 164; cf 290).

Given the failure of others, particularly the positivists of his day, to deal with the problem of such 'tendencies and strivings in a constant state of flux,' Mannheim distinguishes between the 'exact' sciences and the 'so-called prescientific inexact modes of thought,' for which logic must be supplemented by a structural analysis of historical genesis and social rootedness.[11]

Acting men, for better or for worse, proceeded to develop a variety of methods for the experiential and intellectual penetration of the world in which we live, which have never been analysed with the same precision as the so-called exact modes of knowing. When, however, any human activity continues over a long period without being subjected to intellectual controls of criticism, it tends to get out of hand ... This so-called pre-scientific inexact mode of thought, however (which, paradoxically, the logicians and philosophers also use when they have to make practical decisions), is not to be understood solely by the use of logical analysis. It constitutes a complex which cannot be readily detached either from the psychological roots of the emotional and vital impulses which underlie it or from the situation in which it arises and which it seeks to solve.

It is the most essential task of this book to work out a suitable method for the description and analysis of this type of thought and its changes ... The method which we will seek to present is that of the sociology of knowledge. (*IU* 1–2)

Thus, rather than trying to deny or sociologically 'reduce' the formal logic of natural science, as Popper charges, Mannheim's explicit concern was with those propositions that are impregnated with value and meaning. Mannheim's thinking is reminiscent of Weber's demand that an adequate grasp of social phenomena include both a (causal) explanation of an event and an (interpretive) 'understanding' of it as an intellectual and spiritual phenomenon.[12] In such an inquiry, Mannheim notes, we find little guidance by focusing on

a few propositions in which the context is so formal and abstract (e.g. in mathematics, geometry, and pure economics) that in fact they seem to be completely detached from the thinking social individual. The battle is not about these propositions but about that greater wealth of factual determinations in which man concretely diagnoses his individual and social situation, in which happenings external to us are first correctly understood. The battle rages concerning those propositions in which every concept is meaningfully oriented from the first, in which we use words like conflict, breakdown, alienation, insurrection, resentment – words which do not reduce complex situations for the sake of an externalizing, formal description without ever being able to build them up again and which would lose their content if their orientation, their evaluative elements, were dropped out. (*IU* 43)

For Mannheim, then, as for Popper, the test of the separation of exact from inexact knowledge is whether the socio-historical genesis of an idea or phenomenon has any implications for its validity:

The historical and social genesis of an idea would be irrelevant to its ultimate validity if the temporal and social conditions of its emergence had no effect on its content and form. If this were the case, any two periods ... would only be distinguished from one another by the fact that in the earlier period certain things were still unknown and certain errors still existed which, through later knowledge, were completely corrected. This simple relationship between an earlier incomplete and later complete period of knowledge may to a large extent be appropriate for the exact sciences (although indeed to-day the notion of the stability of the categorical structure of the exact sciences is, compared with the logic of classical physics, considerably shaken). For the history of the cultural sciences, however, the earlier stages are not quite so simply superceded ... Every epoch has its fundamentally new approach and its characteristic point of view, and consequently sees the 'same' object from a new perspective. (*IU* 271)

Ironically, in light of Popper's charge of 'sociologism' and irrationalism, Mannheim's view is remarkably similar to Popper's distinction between the logical characteristics of scientific theories and general interpretations in historical analysis (*OS* II 265–9). And Popper acknowledges the significance and practical importance of general interpretations to historical knowledge. Since 'each generation has its own troubles and problems, and therefore its own interests and point of view, it follows that each generation has a right to look upon and reinterpret history in its own way' (*OS* II 267). Moreover, we must not let 'an inapplicable idea of objectivity' prevent us from providing such interpretations, even though they may be 'circular' or otherwise not strictly scientific (*OS* II 268).

Popper's use of 'social determination', it seems to me, unfairly portrays as reductionistic the sociology of knowledge. 'Social determination' is not an adequate rendering of *Seinverbundenheit*, more appropriately 'situational' or 'existential determination.' Even less misleading is 'existential boundedness,' 'connectedness to existence,' or 'existentiality.' Since Popper could grasp Mannheim's formulation, his narrower interpretation is particularly disturbing. In a footnote to the English version of *Ideology and Utopia* Mannheim writes: 'Here we do not mean by "determination" a mechanical cause-effect sequence: we leave the meaning of "determination" open, and only empirical investigation will show us how strict is the correlation between life-situation and thought-process, or what scope exists for variation in the correlation' (*IU* 267 note 1).

In *The Open Society*, 'the perennial revolt against reason' and 'historicism' become threats to rationality only under particular conditions, in periods of extreme and rapid social change. Popper's analyses of Plato,

Aristotle, Hegel, and Marx presuppose that their thought 'mirrored' the conflicts and traditions of their societies (cf *OS* II 210–11). Moreover, elsewhere Popper has written that everyone 'learned from Marx that the development of ideas cannot be fully understood if the history of ideas is treated (although such treatment may often have its great merits) without mentioning the conditions of their origin and the situation of their originators, among which the economic aspect is highly significant' (*CR* 332).

Popper is hostile not to 'contextual' analysis but to a mechanical type of it, which he identifies with Marx and transfers to Mannheim. 'I personally think that Marx's economism – his emphasis on the economic background as the ultimate basis of any sort of development – is mistaken and in fact untenable ... granted that it is at least as impossible to understand economic development without understanding the development of, for instance, scientific or religious ideas' (ibid).

Ironically, Popper concedes the need for precisely the sort of project that Mannheim proposed:

I do not deny that there are certain interesting sociological aspects of Beethoven's work. It is well known ... that the transition from a small to a large symphony orchestra is connected, in some way, with a socio-political development. Orchestras cease to be private hobbies of princes, and are at least partly supported by a middle class whose interest greatly increases. I am willing to appreciate any sociological 'explanation' of this sort, and I admit that such aspects may be worthy of scientific study. (After all, I myself have attempted similar things in this book, for instance, in my treatment of Plato.)

What then, more precisely, is the object of my attack? It is the exaggeration and generalization of any aspect of this kind. If we 'explain' Beethoven's symphony orchestra in the way hinted above, we have explained very little ... We cannot attempt to explain Beethoven's genius in this way, or in any way at all. (*OS* II 210–11)

Popper's reference to Beethoven's 'genius' indicates yet another misunderstanding of the sociological approach as advanced by Mannheim and as currently practised. The sociology of knowledge, in seeking to provide causal and / or functional types of explanations, is concerned with 'types' and structures of events rather than with unique aspects, idiosyncratic features, and 'exceptional' cases. As Mannheim proposed, sociology should – to borrow Sartre's notion – 'situate' such 'genius,' or historical aspects of it, within social structure – class relations, status groupings, new forms of technology, patterns of institutionalization, and the like.[13] Such factors can help explain a type of event, but Mannheim does not suggest that they explain the unique features of a specific historical phenomenon or individual.

Mannheim presupposes methodological distinction between, and the ultimate complementarity of, causal and interpretive explanatory practices. And as few commentators have realized, the sociology of knowledge need not threaten the crucial distinction between (1) the norms that establish criteria and determine validating procedures, (2) the act or practice of research and validation itself, and (3) the validity of a proposition thereby provisionally established.[14] Its raison d'être, in fact, is precisely to 'rationalize' and render more intelligible the nature of and relation between each level of reality. Kurt Wolff notes that the closing two sentences of Mannheim's essay 'Competition as a Cultural Phenomenon' (1928) summarize much of his work. Sociological interpretation does not imply

that mind and thought are nothing but the expression and reflex of various 'locations' in the social fabric, and that there exist only quantitatively determinable functional correlations and no potentiality of 'freedom' grounded in mind; it merely means that even with the sphere of the intellectual, there are processes amenable to rational analysis, and that it would be an ill-advised mysticism which would shroud things in romantic obscurity at a point where rational cognition is still practicable. Anyone who wants to drag in the irrational where lucidity and activity of reason still must rule by right merely shows that he is afraid to face the mystery at its legitimate place.[15]

In 'Science as a Vocation,' Max Weber declared that 'to take a practical and political stand is one thing, and to analyze political structures and party positions is another.'[16] 'Speaking in a meeting about democracy' has to be absolutely – that is, ontologically – distinguished from 'scientific analysis' in the academy and scientific laboratories. Working from virtually the same assumption – that 'political discussion possesses a character *fundamentally different* from academic discussion' – Mannheim argued, however, that such an analytic bifurcation between 'science' and 'politics' deprives any prospective science of politics and society of its necessary 'existential foundation.'[17]

Mannheim thus proceeded to argue for a revised model of rational discussion. Instead of basing our model of substantive (as opposed to technical) rationality on the necessarily abstract – and therefore limited – criteria of scientific journals, academic conferences, and well-designed philosophic dialogues, we must seek an empirically grounded body of knowledge. Its paradigms of communication and rational discussion should be trade union meetings, debates at party congresses, and discussions at mass political rallies.[18] For Mannheim, the growth of modern science has 'led to the growth of a technique of thought ... [which] has sought to construct a world of facts in which there will exist only measurable data.' Eventually, out of devotion 'to an ideal of narrow exactitude,' we will come to view virtually the whole of social existence as the mere expression of survey research and statistical data. In the 1930s Mannheim saw such 'mechanistic dehumanization' of social relations well under way in the Western world, aided and abetted by the objectivism of professional social scientists.[19] He never doubted that such a process – what Weber called the 'disenchantment' and de-magification of social life – posed the gravest of threats to a liberal society understood as a model of political discussion.

Mannheim points out that liberalism – 'bourgeois intellectualism' – has insistently 'acted as if real conflicts could be settled by discussion' (*IU* 150). Parliamentary democracy increasingly functions like 'a debating society in which truth is sought by theoretical methods' (*IU* 124). Ashcraft observes: 'Mannheim did not approach the crisis of liberalism from the standpoint of supplying a defense of individual rights or private property. *Property, rights*, or *the individual*, are not key terms in Mannheim's conception of liberalism. Rather, his emphasis is upon the *social exchange of ideas* and the systematic factors which provide support for this exchange. Liberalism, in other words, is defined by Mannheim *not in terms of interests*, but *as an activity*, namely, discussion.'[20] Note the similarities with Popper's 'open society' (cf *OS* II chapter 10; and *PH* section 32).

Yet Popper (and others) insist on obscuring Mannheim's overwhelmingly liberal and rationalist commitments. At least part of the reason lies in Mannheim's disquieting analysis of the twentieth-century crisis in liberalism. Here, the influences of Lukác's *History and Class Consciousness* and Marx and Hegel profoundly affected Mannheim's thinking. Working from the assumption, common to all three thinkers, that we 'discover the world in an intellectual sense' only in 'the context of collective action,' Mannheim argued that isolating 'the thinking social individual' from his or her particular group associations could pose the gravest danger to a rationalizing society, the success of which depends in large measure on whether 'the discussion' becomes more direct and democratic.[21] And yet such abstract individualism was precisely 'the chief source of error[s]' attributable to liberal political thought and the objectifying methodology of the social sciences (*IU* 168–9).

Take, for example, liberalism's response to the class struggle. Mannheim observed that it sought 'a formal rationalization of the political conflict but not a solution of it' (*IU* 122). Characteristically, it transformed 'the conflict of interests into a conflict of ideas,' thereby giving precedence to the 'spiritual goals' of liberalism over all rival objectives. Mannheim contended that if 'the bourgeois-liberal mode of thought' directed its attention, changed its 'perspective,' toward 'the factors of property and class position, its own inner antagonisms, for instance the antagonisms of capitalism itself, might become visible' (*IU* 278). For Mannheim, such conflicts and antagonisms are systematically distorted by a social science (and political theory) that insist on 'the fiction of isolated and self-sufficient individual[s]' as the social ontological limit beyond which the discussion can never trespass.[22] Almost as if with Popper's criticism in mind, Mannheim notes:

The loose play with the word 'sociologism' by the opponents of sociology gradually gets to be unbearable, for it always comes up when they can no longer meet sociology with objective arguments and thereupon treat the most decisive problems of the modern situation of thought as if they were problems of foreign policy, problems of border crossings between countries, or problems of departmental competence in a bureaucracy. They act as if a higher authority had issued directives concerning these matters, as if the distribution of the competencies of the individual disciplines were regulated *a priori*, and as if one had to guard against transgressions like a border policy.[23]

Popper quotes a passage from *Ideology and Utopia*: 'There is an increasing tendency towards making conscious the factors by which we have so far been unconsciously ruled ... Those who fear that our increasing knowledge of determining factors may paralyse our decisions and threaten "freedom" should put their minds at rest. For only he is truly determined who does not know the most essential determining factors but act immediately under the pressure of determinants unknown to him' (*OS* II 223; cf *IU* 180). Popper characteristically maintains that 'this is clearly just a repetition of a pet idea of Hegel's which Engels naively repeated when he said: "Freedom is the appreciation of necessity." And it is a reactionary prejudice. For are those who act under the pressure of well-known determinants, for example of political tyranny, made free by their knowledge?' (*OS* II 223).

Mannheim's next sentence reads: 'Whenever we become aware of a determinant which has dominated us, we remove it from the realm of unconscious motivation into that of controllable, calculable, and objectified. Choice and decision are thereby not eliminated; on the contrary, motives which previously dominated us become subject to our domination' (*IU* 189–90). Popper's charge that Mannheim's sociology of knowledge succumbs to a 'reactionary prejudice' and exemplifies Hegelian quietism (or 'moral historicism') – that 'freedom is the appreciation of necessity' – is thus completely untenable; Mannheim simply held no such view. In fact, he believed just the reverse.

Indeed, underlying virtually everything Mannheim wrote was the Kantian type of commitment to increasing human automony that one finds so often in Popper's own work. This was especially true of Mannheim's later work in educational reform and 'planning for the planners' – a theme central to Popper's political thought. In Mannheim's hands, a sociological approach to intellectual phenomena was simply another stage on the path toward 'enlightenment' – the abolition of dogma and what Kant called 'self-incurred immaturity of mankind.' According to Mannheim, 'the man of to-day has far more freedom in the determination of his destiny than the unsociological ethics of the past would have us believe ... Rightly understood, recent tendencies towards a mass society, and our ever increasing awareness of the determinism of sociological factors do not release us from responsibility for the future: responsibility increases with every advance in the course of history, and has never been greater than it is to-day.'[24]

In short, Mannheim, no less than Popper, continues the quest to 'rationalize' hitherto irrational forces of 'social competition and struggle' which all too frequently still 'decide the place and function of the individual in society' (*IU* 115). This commitment to the ideals of 'enlightment' they share with Jürgen Habermas's 'critical theory' of society (though *not* with Michel Foucault, Hans-Georg Gadamer, and several other advocates of linguistically based models of social science).[25]

Mannheim is guilty, according to Popper, of subscribing to an individualistic epistemology which assumes that impartiality is the foundation of objectivity. Thus, Popper writes in *The Open Society*, the sociology of knowledge fails to grasp the true nature of science

and shows an astounding failure to understand precisely its main subject, the social aspects of knowledge, or rather, of scientific method. It looks upon science or knowledge as a process in the mind or 'consciousness' of the individual scientist, or perhaps as the product of such a process. If considered in this way, what we call scientific objectivity must indeed become completely ununderstandable, or even impossible; and not only in the social or political sciences, where class interests and similar hidden motives may play a part, but just as much in the natural sciences ... If scientific objectivity were founded, as the sociological theory of knowledge naively assumes, upon the individual scientists, impartiality or objectivity, then we should have to say good-bye to it. (*OS* II 217)

Such a portrait profoundly distorts and misrepresents Mannheim's position. Mannheim explicitly denies the view attributed to him by Popper. For example, in analysing the emergence and interaction of the epistemological, psychological, and sociological points of view after the collapse of the medieval vision, he writes: 'The fiction of the isolated and self-sufficient individual underlies in various forms the individualistic espistemology and genetic psychology ... It is much more correct to say that knowledge is from the very beginning a co-operative process of group life, in which everyone unfolds his knowledge within the framework of a common fate, a common activity, and the overcoming of difficulties' (*IU* 28–9). Mannheim denies neither the significance of scientific testing procedures nor the social and institutional basis of scientific creativity and practice – in fact, the exact opposite.

At the centre of Mannheim's thought, seemingly lost on Popper, is his profound insight that the 'merit of the sociological point of view [is] that it *set alongside the individual* genesis of meaning, the genesis from *the context of group life*' (*IU* 28). Time and again, Mannheim emphasizes that the sociology of knowledge is not intended to be a substitute for direct empirical research or an alternative to epistemology; for example: 'The mere delimitation of the perspectives is by no means a substitute for the immediate and direct discussion between the divergent points of view or for the direct examination of the facts ... [Accordingly,] epistemology is not supplanted by the sociology of knowledge but a new kind of epistemology is called for which will reckon with the facts brought to light by the sociology of knowledge' (*IU* 284–5 and 289). For Mannheim, 'in the social sciences, as elsewhere, the ultimate criterion of truth or falsity is to be found in the investigation of the object, and the sociology of knowledge is no substitute for this.'[26] But for Mannheim, merely accepting all this in principle was not enough; we must realize and practise these formal requirements of reason. However, the examination of the object is not an isolated act; it takes place in a context which is coloured by values and collective-unconscious volitional impulses. In the social sciences it is this intellectual interest, oriented in the matrix of collective activity, which provides not only the general questions, but the concrete hypotheses for research and the thought-models for ordering experience. Only as we succeed in bringing into areas of conscious and explicit observation the various points of departure and of approach to the facts ... can we hope ... to control the unconscious motivations and presuppositions which, in the last analysis, have brought these modes of thought into existence' (*IU* 5).

Popper challenges the allegedly self-contradictory view of objectivity being proposed. He writes:

The sociology of knowledge believes that the highest degree of objectivity can be reached by the freely poised intelligence analyzing the various hidden ideologies and their anchorage in the unconscious. The way to true knowledge appears to be the unveiling of unconscious assumptions, a kind of psycho-therapy, as it were, or if I may say so a socio-therapy. Only he who has been socio-analyzed or who has socio-analyzed himself, and who is freed from his social complex, i.e. from his social ideology, can attain to the highest synthesis of objective knowledge. (*OS* II 215)

Skilled logician that he is, however, Popper notes that this method, like psychoanalysis, can be turned against its practitioner: 'For is not their description of an intelligentsia which is only loosely anchored in tradition a very neat description of their own social group? ... Is it not, therefore, to be expected ... that those who hold it will unconsciously deceive themselves by producing an amendment to the theory in order to establish the objectivity of their own views? Can we then take seriously their claim that by their sociological self-analysis they have reached a higher degree of objectivity; and their claim that socio-analysis can cast out total ideology?' (*OS* II 216).
This charge largely falsifies Mannheim's explicit view of objectivity and of his striving for a synthesis of perspectives amid increasingly polarized 'party-based' schools of thought. Throughout, Popper assumes that Mannheim equates social 'determination' with falsity, when perhaps the most pioneering aspect of his work was to have underscored the fact that all thought is socially conditioned, including the realm of valid propositions. In *Ideology and Utopia*, Mannheim expresses the point as

follows: 'We need not regard it as a source of error that all thought is so rooted. Just as the individual who participates in a complex of vital social relations with other men thereby enjoys a chance of obtaining a more precise and penetrating insight into his fellows, so a given point of view and a given set of concepts, because they are bound up with and grew out of a certain social reality, offer, through intimate contact with this reality, a greater chance of revealing their meaning' (*IU* 80). This passage does not hint whatsoever at Mannheim's alleged 'sociological self-analysis'. However difficult such a project, Kettler, Meja, and Stehr describe Mannheim's 'most original and brilliant contribution' as 'the suggestion that "ideologies" may approximate to the structures of practical social knowledge by virtue of the very features which make them radically inadequate as scientific theories and which make them comprehensible only in the context of their social functions.'[27] Mannheim's 'great and constitutive question' 'was whether sociology can provide the integral and comprehensive practical knowledge which liberalism requires in order to master the disruptive irrationalities first projected by the critics of liberalism and then brutally real in the events of the twentieth century.'[28]

There are interesting parallels between Habermas's 'critical social science' and the image of Mannheim's sociology of knowledge drawn in this chapter. Habermas insists that psychoanalytic encounters – or his idealized version of them – offer 'the only tangible example of a science incorporating methodical self-reflection.'[29] Habermas sees psychoanalysis as above all an interpretive exercise: the analyst attempts to understand the verbalizations and symbolizations of the analysand through an explication of their (hidden) meaning, an aim achieved exclusively through dialogue.[30] But psychoanalysis cannot remain at the hermeneutic level of reflection, since the encounter must delve below the descriptions of experiences so as to explain causally the symptoms of neurosis or depression.[31] Giddens expresses the point as follows:

In the process of psychoanalytic therapy, the analysis moves constantly from one level, or frame of reference, to the other, thus 'explaining' what lies behind the distorted self-understanding of the patient. In Freud's original writings, this necessary 'tacking' between the hermeneutic and the nomological was not explicitly recognized as such: hence the confusion of terms such as 'energy', used on analogy with physical forces, with those ('symbol', etc.) which refer to 'meaningful' categories. What ties together and yet also balances the hermeneutic and nomological moments of the psychonalytic encounter, Habermas says, is the emancipatory impulse which is its stimulus.[32]

Habermas and Mannheim thus both hope to rationalize 'the irrational' by developing more appropriate models of communication and discursive practice. For Mannheim, the sociology of knowledge was 'the first preparatory step leading to direct discussion of interests and problems in conflict.' Habermas has begun to press the psychoanalytic analogy further toward a theory of communicative competence and a model of progressively more perfect mutual comprehension. In his Postcript to *Knowledge and Human Interests*, Habermas explains that 'unrestrained consensus', – full and mutual understanding of the other, reached solely through rational examination of arguments – presupposes a notion of truth that does not guarantee the 'objectivity of experience' but inheres 'in the possibility of argumentative corroboration of a truth claim.'[33] 'Truth' depends on rational discourse in much the same sense that 'non-neurotic' and 'non-ideological' experiences depend on the removal of barriers to communication with and between self and other.

Let us end the present discussion with one final irony. In *Ideology and Utopia*, Mannheim notes that the liberal or 'bourgeois ideal of reason' always seeks to transcend the existing 'imperfection in things' by promulgating 'the belief that reality moves continuously towards an ever closer approximation to the rational' (*IU* 223; cf 224–5). Such a vision animates Popper's thought as much as Mannheim's and Habermas's. Had Popper more carefully examined the sociology of knowledge and Freud's thought, he would have found an image of the social realm quite consistent with his own stated views on objectivity, fallibilism, situational analysis, and the role of critical institutions and traditions in a 'free society.'

If fallibilism is primarily about cognitive agents and their liability to error, then any coherent epistemology must allow for, indeed encourage, precisely the systematic and empirical analysis into forms and conditions of distortion that Mannheim and Habermas have launched. The sociology of knowledge does not seek to replace epistemology, or to reduce the truth to a matter of social genesis, or to deny the need for objective, intersubjective criteria for evaluating alternative claims about the world and its affairs. Mannheim's conception of the sociology of knowledge underwent several significant changes during his complicated careers.[34] But social and historical conditioning constitutes a series of problems in the human studies of an order and magnitude unparalleled in the natural sciences and in formal logic, and students of each area may lose sight of this crucial difference. Popper's polemic against Mannheim and the sociology of knowledge has all too frequently led us to ignore these differences and complexities.

7

Conserving liberalism:
truth, hope, and power

> It has for some time seemed to me that a criticism
> which has at heart the interests of liberalism might
> find its most useful work not in confirming liberal-
> ism in its sense of general rightness but rather in
> putting under some pressure the liberal ideas and
> assumptions of the present time.[1]
>
> Lionel Trilling

Western political thought since the Second World War has been deeply
disillusioned – sometimes bordering on despair – with its inherited traditions of discourse. If earlier periods of crisis, as Wolin argues, awak-
ened in political philosophers an architectonic impulse toward mastery,[2]
the unprecedented brutalities of the war and the massive convulsions
and social reorganization that followed seem to have eroded the intellectual optimism that such creativity and political imagination require.

In the early 1950s, Judith Shklar observed: 'It is next to impossible
to believe strongly that the power of human reason expressing itself in
political action is capable of achieving its ends. The various theories of
historical determinism prevalent since the last century have long since
undermined this hope, and historical disaster has completed the process.'[3] The decline in hope and the eclipse of the 'urge to construct grand
designs for the political future of mankind' are especially troubling to
contemporary liberalism, for its 'primal act of imagination by which it
establishes its essence and existence ... [is] its vision of a general enlargement and freedom and rational direction of human life.'[4]

Popper is determined to retrieve the essence of this liberal vision – its
meliorism and faith in the powers of reason to enlarge human freedom.

But unlike the often caricatured optimism of older liberal visions, Popper's is more conservative and cautious. It represents a sustained interrogation of liberalism's typically utilitarian vocabulary of desiring and the reaffirmation of a sobered, combat-toughened conception of rationality and the 'ends' that it is rational to pursue.

With a sense of historic mission and a degree of moral intensity seldom encountered in our times, Popper proclaims that just as there is no reason to despair of the growth of knowledge and the progress of science, there is no reason to forsake the essence of liberalism, provided that we learn from our mistakes in the manner that he suggests is possible. Although history in and of itself 'has no meaning,' we can give it meaning if we learn to live within the limits of how little we know about its ultimate structure and the consequences of our actions (OS II 169 and 278).

In 'The History of Our Times: An Optimist's View,' Popper conceded that, although 'it is much easier for us to regress than to progress,' 'I think I may fairly describe myself as an optimist. For my optimism lies ... in my strongly appreciative view of our time ... No doubt there is much in our world about which we can rightly complain if only we give our mind to it; and no doubt it is sometimes most important to find out what is wrong with us. But I think that the other side of the story might also get a hearing' (CR 365).

Popper continues his lecture with a spirited defence of the 'strongly appreciative view of our time.' He challenges the view of fellow rationalists such as Bertrand Russell, 'that it is a mixture of cleverness and wickedness [that] lies at the root of our troubles' (ibid). He notes Russell's increasing fear that we have not achieved the moral and political maturity necessary to direct our tremendous intellectual achievements, including thermonuclear bombs. Popper proclaims just the opposite view: 'We are good, perhaps a little too good, but we are also a little stupid; and it is this mixture of goodness and stupidity which lies at the root of our troubles' (ibid). Wickedness, Popper notes, is more difficult to remedy and combat than stupidity, but it is surely more in keeping with an optimist's view that we are not 'hopelessly stupid.' As Samuel Butler understood so well in *Erewhon*, 'What is wrong with us is that we so easily mislead ourselves, and ... are so easily "led by the nose" by others,' particularly false prophets, irresponsible ideologues, and dictators. Popper observes:

The main trouble of our time – and I do not deny that we live in troubled times – is not due to our moral wickedness, but, on the contrary, to our often misguided moral enthusiasm: to our anxiety to better the world we live in. Our wars are fundamentally religious wars; they are wars between competing theories of how to establish a better world. And our moral enthusiasm is often misguided because we fail to realize that our moral principles, which are sure to be over-simple, are often difficult to apply to the complex human and political situations to which we feel bound to apply them. (*CR* 366)

For Popper – as for many other liberals – one of the gravest dangers to our freedom and humanity is an excess of moral fervour and certainty in politics. We must be on guard as to 'how dangerous goodness can be if too much of it is combined with too little rational criticism' (*CR* 367). That the attempt to 'make heaven on earth invariably produces hell' is one of the most important, though admittedly painful, lessons that liberalism must learn about its past and its enemies (*OS* II 237; cf I chapter 9). Such a lesson explains Popper's hostility to utopianism and all attempts at wholesale or revolutionary social reform, and his 'modification' of utilitarianism as well.

Popper begins by dissenting from Leibniz's view that ours is the best of all possible worlds. Popper asserts that this is simply not true. But, 'in spite of our great and serious troubles, and in spite of the fact that ours is not the best possible society, I assert that our own free world is by far the best society which has come into existence during the course of human history' (*CR* 369). Popper's standard of evaluation is again the Kantian demand that we treat human beings as individual 'ends in themselves': 'At no other time, and nowhere else, have men been more respected, as men, than in our society. Never before have their human rights, and their human dignity, been so respected, and never before have so many been ready to bring great sacrifices for others, especially for those less fortunate than themselves' (ibid).

Popper is not oblivious or indifferent to other facts and dangers relative to such ideals. 'Power still corrupts, even in our world.' 'Civil servants still behave like uncivil masters,' while 'pocket dictators still abound' (*CR* 369–70). But 'our own free world' has 'very nearly, if not completely, succeeded in abolishing the greatest evils which have hitherto beset the social life of man' (*CR* 370). Popper even proffers a list of 'some of the greatest of those evils which can be remedied, or relieved, by social cooperation': poverty, unemployment and some similar forms of social insecurity, sickness and pain, penal cruelty, slavery and other forms of serfdom, religious and racial discrimination, lack of educational opportunity, rigid class differences, and war.

Abject poverty, for example, 'has been practically abolished. Instead of being a mass phenomenon, the problem has become one of detecting the isolated cases which still persist' (*CR* 370). As opposed to earlier periods of widespread insecurity, Popper argues, 'we are now faced with new problems brought into being by the fact that the problem of mass-unemployment has largely been solved' (ibid). Similarly, 'class differences have diminished enormously everywhere' (*CR* 371): 'In Scandinavia, the United States, Canada, Australia, and New Zealand, we have ... something approaching classless societies' (ibid). And even though the problem of blocked educational opportunities is 'still very serious,' 'it is being tackled sincerely and with energy' (ibid).

Perhaps the most important item on his list is war. Popper feels it to be of sufficient gravity to merit yet another thesis. Since the time of the Boer War, he contends, 'none of the democratic governments of the free world has been in a position to wage a war of aggression. No democratic government would be united upon the issue ... Aggressive war has become almost a moral impossibility' (*CR* 371). Indeed, on Popper's account, it was largely the revulsion of feeling engendered by the Boer War 'amounting to a moral conversion in favour of peace,' that made Britain initially hesitate in resisting the Kaiser and ready 'to make allowances for Hitler' prior to 1939 (ibid). Only widespread outbursts of public indignation and outrage, as when Mussolini attacked Ethiopia finally convinced the government of the need to enter the war. Even 'preventive war' against the Soviet Union in 1950 or so – Popper (following Russell) suggests 'there were strong reasons in favour of it' – was out of the question. 'Even in these crucial circumstances, and with the then practical certainty of victory,' an aggressive war 'had become morally impossible' (*CR* 371). Thus, although the free world is ready to go to war in the face of unambiguous aggression, 'as far as the free world itself is concerned war has been conquered' (ibid).

Running throughout Popper's political thought is this 'appreciative' attitude toward our major institutions and practices, his sense of just how precious – like life itself – are these achievements. From such an attitude flows a profoundly conservative impulse to preserve the necessary beliefs and other intellectual preconditions for the continued growth of this kind of freedom and autonomy. For example, in *The Open Society*, Popper criticizes the tendency to equate individualism and egoism, on the one hand, and altruism and collectivism, on the other, for it 'bars the way even to a clear formulation of the main problem [of ethics], the problem of how to obtain a sane appreciation of one's own importance in relation to other individuals' (*OS* II 177). And in 'The History of Our Times,' he states:

I believe that it is most important to say what the free world has achieved. For we have become unduly sceptical about ourselves. We are suspicious of anything like self-righteousness, and we find self-praise unpalatable. One of the great things we have learned is not only to be tolerant of others, but to ask ourselves seriously whether the other fellow is not perhaps in the right ... We have learned the fundamental moral truth that nobody should be judge in his own cause. This, no doubt, is a symptom of a certain moral maturity; yet one may learn a lesson too well. Having discovered the sin of self-righteousness, we have fallen into its stereotyped inversion: into a stereotyped pose of self-depreciation, of inverted smugness. Having learned that one should not judge in one's own cause, we are tempted to become advocates for our opponents. Thus we become blind to our own achievements. But this tendency must be resisted. (*CR* 371)

One of our greatest achievements – for Popper, perhaps the greatest – is the 'possibility of fighting with words instead of fighting with swords' (*CR* 373). As a firm believer in the 'power of ideas, including the power of false and pernicious ideas,' Popper sees much – if not the survival of the human species, at least the fate of liberalism – riding on the 'war of ideas.' To see just how 'powerful ideas have become since the days of the Greeks,' 'we only need to remember that all religious wars are wars of ideas, and that all revolutions were revolutions of ideas. [And] although these ideas were more often false and pernicious than true and beneficial there is perhaps a certain tendency for some of the better ones to survive, provided they find sufficiently powerful and intelligent support' (ibid).

Whereas lower organisms and those individuals who remain on a dogmatic or 'pre-scientific' level of problem-solving are often destroyed and eliminated, with their false theories and conjectures, those who have mastered the critical method of error elimination and have come to respect the views of others can let their false theories die in their stead (cf CKP 96–7). Largely because of their potential effects on, and contributions to, the quality of life, Popper proposes another thesis: 'The power of ideas, and especially of moral and religious ideas, is at least as important as that of physical resources' (*CR* 373).

If we ask ourselves, à la Kant, 'In what kind of world is political theory in principle possible?' the answer must be, as Isaiah Berlin reminds us, 'Only in a world where ends collide.'[6] Popper accordingly seeks to formulate the means to protect the clash of ends inherent in an individualistic and pluralistic universe. In 'Utopia and Violence' (1947), Popper distinguishes utopians, who 'dream about distant ideals' and who are willing to fight over 'blueprints for a new world and a new man,' and those people, like himself, 'who believe in man as he is, and who have therefore not given up the hope of defeating violence and unreason, [and who] must demand instead that every man should be given the right to arrange his life himself so far as this is compatible with the equal rights of others' (*CR* 363).

As attractive as utopianism may seem, Popper insists that it is dangerous and pernicious in its consequences, and self-defeating as well. Because the utopian method 'chooses an ideal state of society as the aim which all our political actions should serve,' it cannot tolerate, let alone rationally adjudicate, differences of opinion, which invariably arise as to what ends the ideal state should pursue (*CR* 360). Given the impossibility of ever determining ends scientifically and given that 'the rationality of his political action demands constancy of aim for a long time ahead,' the utopianist cannot help but try to 'win over, or else crush, his ... competitors' and 'as far as possible stamps out all memory of them' (*CR* 359–60). Thus, however benevolent its ends, utopianism must stand condemned as a self-defeating doctrine: 'It does not bring happiness, but only the familiar misery of being condemned to live under a tyrannical government' (*CR* 360).

Popper argues that, far from being an accidental result or a contingent feature of periods of radical social change, the problems outlined above – and pressed at great length against Plato, Marx, and Mannheim in *The Open Society* – are inherent in the utopian project. For whereas 'evils' are concrete, 'ideal goods' are not: 'These we know only from our dreams and from the dreams of our poets and prophets. They cannot be discussed, only proclaimed ... They do not call for the rational attitude of the impartial judge, but for the emotional attitude of the impassioned preacher' (*CR* 361). Ultimately, Popper contends, utopianism is another expression of the 'false rationalism' outlined in chapter 5, a claim to power 'on the basis of one's superior intellectual gifts.' Of all political ideals, he writes in *The Open Society*, 'that of making the people happy is perhaps the most dangerous one. It leads invariably to the attempt to impose our scale of "higher" values upon others, in order to make them realize what seems to us of greatest importance for their happiness ... It leads to intolerance. It leads to religious wars, and to saving souls through the inquisition. And it is, I believe, based upon a complete misunderstanding of our moral duties' (*OS* II 237).

In the final thesis Popper advances in 'The History of Our Time,' the cautious nature of his optimism becomes most evident. The liberalism and rationalism of the eighteenth and nineteenth centuries, he notes, believed not only in the power of ideas but also in the mistaken doctrine that 'truth, once put forward, would always be recognized.' Their error was to believe that 'truth is manifest – that it cannot be missed once the powers which are interested in its suppression and perversion are destroyed' (*CR* 373). This 'is one form of optimism which I cannot support. I am convinced that it is mistaken, and that, on the contrary, truth is hard, and often painful, to come by' (ibid).

Popper concedes that the naïve and mistaken view that truth is manifest – 'That it is an open book, there to be read by anybody of good will' – has contributed much of value to modern civilization. It inspired the advancement of learning and the birth of modern science and technology but also led to 'the doctrines of individual moral and intellectual responsibility and freedom,' thereby making 'the spiritual authority of the Church and its interpretation of the truth superfluous, and even pernicious' (*CR* 374). A less optimistic, more sceptical attitude towards the truth, Popper argues, invariably 'leads to an emphasis upon the authority of the church, and to other forms of authoritarianism. For if truth is not manifest, then you cannot leave it to each individual to interpret it; for this would of necessity lead to chaos, to social disintegration, to religious schisms, and to religious wars' (ibid).

Typical of his dichotomous style of thought, Popper sums up the conflict simplistically, as 'one between individualistic rationalism and authoritarianism.' For Popper, 'the issue between rationalism and authoritarian traditionalism is best described as that between, on the one hand, faith in man, in human goodness as well as human reason, and, on the other hand, distrust of man, of his goodness and of his reason' (*CR* 374). Popper leaves no doubt as to where his sympathies lie: 'My feelings are all on the side of the naive liberal optimists, even though my reason tells me that their epistemology was all wrong, and that truth is in fact hard to come by' (ibid).

The epistemology of those who hold that 'truth is manifest' is 'all wrong not just because truth is often hard to come by' but because 'once found it may be easily lost again' (*CR* 8). Erroneous beliefs, Popper continues in 'On the Sources of Knowledge and Ignorance,' 'may have an astonishing power to survive, for thousands of years, in defiance of experience, and without the aid of any conspiracy. The history of science, and especially of medicine, could furnish us with a number of good examples' (ibid).

Disastrous consequences follow from adopting such a doctrine. First, we feel the need to explain only falsehood. Such a view leaves much to be desired if 'the central problem of epistemology ... is the problem of the growth of knowledge' (*LSD* 15). Second, 'how can we ever fall into error if truth is manifest?' (ibid). Only, Popper believes, 'through our own sinful refusal to see the manifest truth; or because our minds harbour prejudices inculcated by education and tradition, or other evil influences which have perverted our originally pure and innocent minds. Ignorance may be the work of powers conspiring to keep us in ignorance, to poison our minds by filling them with falsehood' (ibid).

Thus, whatever form this doctrine assumes – his favourite targets are the Marxist 'conspiracy theory' of the capitalist press and 'big business' and Plato's attitude toward religion as nothing but a 'noble lie' and his 'myth of the metals' in man (cf *OS* I chapter 8, section ii, and II 94–5, 101 and 133) – Popper insists that the view that 'truth is manifest' breeds fanaticism and, ultimately, authoritarianism (*CR* 8–9).

Popper's cautious, indeed Burkean, variety of optimism appears in his contrast between the 'critical form' of his own rationalism and the excessively optimistic – indeed 'false' – rationalism of the French and Russian revolutionaries. He is 'repelled by the idea of keeping men under tutelage and authority' but finds himself forced to admit 'that the pessimists who feared the decline of authority and tradition were wise men' (*CR* 374), as proved by 'the terrible experience of the great religious wars, and of the French and Russian revolutions' (ibid). But, 'although these wars and revolutions' prove that the cautious pessimists were wise, they do not prove them right,' for there 'were other revolutions, the Glorious Revolution, and the American Revolution. And there is our present free world, our Atlantic Community' (*CR* 374 and 375). The parallel with Burke's account is striking indeed.

As a consequence of the Reformation, 'the society of our free world' has 'seen a decline of authority without parallel in any other epoch' (*CR* 375). Indeed, it is a society without authority, 'or, as one might call it, a fatherless society.' Given the Reformation's emphasis on the conscience of the individual, we have 'dethroned God as the responsible ruler of Man's World ... The responsibility for the world is mine and yours: this is the Protestant faith' (ibid). Authoritarians and traditionalists were convinced that such a 'fatherless' society 'must spell the destruction of all

human values,' but Popper maintains that they were wrong. For a 'fatherless' society, 'ruled by the interplay of our own individual conscience,'
is, 'as I have tried to convince you, ... the best society that has ever existed'
(ibid).

Popper sees 'three elements of our free world which have successfully
replaced the dethroned authority' (ibid). First, there is our respect for
the authority of truth: of an impersonal, interpersonal objective truth
which it is our task to find, and which it is not in our power to change,
or to interpret to our liking' (ibid). This belief in objective truth 'is
indispensable for a free society based on mutual respect' (ibid), for it
constitutes the necessary precondition of fallibility and the tolerance
implied in the liberal notion that we can learn from our mistakes. For
example, in *The Open Society*, Popper argues at length that the notion of
truth as a progressively closer approximation to the facts of whatever
we are investigating is essential to the liberal tradition, which holds that
particular facts 'may fall short of right (or valid or true) standards,
especially in the field of politics and of legislation' (*OS* II 392). Similarly,
in 'On the Sources of Knowledge and Ignorance,' he argues that the
'very idea of error or human fallibility involves another one – the idea
of *objective truth*: the standard which we may fall short of' (*CR* 16). This
doctrine of an essential fallibility was made the basis of the doctrine of
tolerance by Nicolas of Cusa, Erasmus of Rotterdam, Montaigne, Locke,
Voltaire, John Stuart Mill, and Bertrand Russell, among others, and
more recently the basis of political freedom by Hayek in *The Constitution
of Liberty* (cf *CR* 16–17).

Second, there is 'a lesson learnt in the religious wars' (*CR* 375):

> We learnt that religious faith and other convictions can only be of value when
> they are freely and sincerely held, and that the attempt to force men to conform
> was pointless because those who resisted were the best, and indeed the only ones
> whose assent was worth having. Thus we learnt not only to tolerate beliefs that
> differ from ours, but to respect them and the men who sincerely held them ...
> And we learnt that we must not draw authoritarian conclusions from this great
> truth [that truth is not manifest] but, on the contrary, suspect all those who claim
> that they are authorized to teach the truth. (Ibid)

Third, we have learned from our past mistakes, 'though in social and
political fields this seems a rare and difficult thing,' that 'by listening to
one another, and by criticizing one another, we may get nearer to the
truth' (ibid). The 'critical approach' he advocates thus 'makes room, at

the same time, for a reconciliation between rationalism and tradition-alism. The critical rationalist can appreciate traditions, for although he believes in truth, he does not believe that he himself is in certain pos-session of it. He can appreciate every step, every approach towards it, as valuable, indeed as invaluable; and he can see that our traditions often help to encourage such steps, and also that without an intellectual tra-dition the individual could hardly take a single step toward the truth (*CR* 376).

Such a compromise between rationalism and scepticism, between 'the respect for traditions, and at the same time the recognition of the need to reform them, has been the basis of the British middle way' for a long time (ibid) – a fitting tribute from someone born and raised in war-torn Vienna. Indeed, Popper hit upon the notion of an 'open society' as a result of his first visits to Britain in the mid-1930s: 'I now found that I could at last breathe freely. It was as if windows had been flung open. The term "open society" ... derives from this experience.'7

Popper's conception of the 'open society' is at once a powerful rhetorical, moral, and methodological defence of individualism and liberal democ-racy against some of the best-known justifications of collectivism and utopianism in the Western tradition – those of Plato, Hegel, and Marx. Though the terms 'open society' and 'closed society' apparently were first used by Henri Bergson in *Two Sources of Morality and Religion*, Pop-per's usage is quite different.8 Bergson intended to capture the drama of the opening of the soul through love, philosophic reflection, and revelation to the world-wide community of man – like Eric Voegelin's 'leap in being' in *Order in History*.9 Popper's is a thoroughly secular and rationalist distinction: 'The closed society is characterized by the belief in magical taboos, while the open society is one in which men have learned to be to some extent critical of taboos and to base decisions on the authority of their own intelligence (after discussion)' (*OS* I 202). Thus, in terms of the vocabulary introduced in chapter 5, proponents of the 'closed society' are 'monists' of one stripe or another.

In *The Open Society*, Popper explains that he uses 'closed society' to capture the main element of 'the magical or tribal or collectivist society' – 'the lack of distinction between customary or conventional regularities of social life and the regularities found in "nature"; and this often goes together with the belief that both are enforced by a supernatural will. The rigidity of social customs is probably ... only another aspect of the same attitude' (*OS* I 172). It is not so much that 'no changes can occur in the tribal ways of life', but, that rather, the 'comparatively infrequent changes' that do occur 'have the character of religious conversions or revulsions, or the introduction of new magical taboos. They are not based upon a rational attempt to improve social conditions' (ibid). By contrast, the open society – 'the society in which individuals are confronted with personal decisions' – is increasingly able to free itself from such tabooism and 'make rational decisions concerning the desirability or otherwise of new legislation, and of other institutional changes ... decisions based upon an estimate of possible consequences, and upon a conscious preference for some of them. We recognize rational personal responsibility' (*OS* 1 173).

In the open society there 'is the possibility of rational reflection' about personal and political destinies (ibid). Popper invokes Kant as an exemplar of 'the possibility of rational reflection' and hope in ethics and politics. In his principle of autonomy, Kant realized that 'we must not accept the command of an authority, however exalted, as the basis of ethics. For whenever we are faced with a command by an authority, it is for us to judge, critically, whether it is moral or immoral to obey ... If we have the physical power of choice, then the ultimate responsibility remains with us' (*CR* 26). On a number of occasions, Popper has drawn political lessons from this legacy of Kant's 'critical rationalism.' Popper believes that critical rationalism suggests a radically different approach to the problems of politics than has been proposed. If we follow Plato and the mainstream of Western political thought in believing that the fundamental problem of political theory is 'Who should rule?' 'it is hard to avoid some such reply as "the best" or "the wisest" or "the born ruler" or "he who masters the art of ruling" (or, perhaps, "The General Will" or "The Master Race" or "The Industrial Workers" or "The People")' (*OS* 1 120). All these responses assume 'that political power is "essentially" unchecked ... They assume that political power is, essentially, sovereign' (*OS* 1 121). From Popper's point of view, not only is the question wrongly put, but the answers it elicits are paradoxical. Such an approach precludes the rational analysis that a non-authoritarian and 'open' society requires.

Popper points out that even those who share Plato's assumption are forced to admit that rulers are not always – indeed, if ever – sufficiently 'good' or 'wise' and 'that it is not at all easy to get a government on whose goodness and wisdom one can implicitly rely' (ibid). If this is granted, 'then we must ask whether political thought should not face from the beginning the possibility of bad government; whether we should not prepare for the worst leaders, and hope for the best' (ibid). This in turn leads to a new approach, 'for it forces us to replace the question: Who should rule? by the new question: How can we so organize political institutions that bad or incompetent rulers can be prevented from doing too much damage?' (ibid). It is only thus 'by changing our question in this way, that we can hope to proceed towards a reasonable theory of political institutions' (*CR* 135). Only then will we be in a position to learn from our mistakes and eliminate peacefully some of their known causes.

The traditional question of political theory produces paradoxical results. Popper credits Plato in the *Republic* (562b–565e) with suggesting that a free man may exercise his absolute freedom 'first by defying laws and ultimately by defying freedom itself and by clamouring for a tyrant' (*CR* 123). Popper believes that '*all theories of sovereignty are* [similarly] *paradoxical*' (*CR* 124). We may choose 'the wisest' or 'the best' to be our ruler, 'but "the wisest" in his wisdom may find that not he but "the best" should rule, and "the best" in his goodness may perhaps decide that "the majority" should rule ... Even that form of the theory of sovereignty which demands the "Kingship of Law" is open to the same objection ... [For] as Heraclitus' remark shows: "This law can demand, too, that the will of One Man must be obeyed" ' (ibid).

Such choices are 'not just far-fetched,' 'but [have] happened a number of times.' Every time they have, it has put 'all those democrats who adopt, as the ultimate basis of their political creed, the principle of sovereignty' in an absolutely 'hopeless intellectual position' (*CR* 123). And worse still, the 'inconsistency of their theory must ... paralyse their actions' (ibid). Ultimately, democrats who demand the 'institutional control of the rulers by the ruled' must find better grounds for their demand than the empirically and logically weak ones advanced in naïvely optimistic accounts of liberalism, democracy, and majority rule.

Popper wishes to demonstrate that a 'theory of democratic control can be developed which is free of the paradox of sovereignty.' Rather than proceed 'from a doctrine of the intrinsic goodness or righteousness of a majority rule,' we should build our political arrangements around the Kantian-inspired assumption 'of the baseness of tyranny; or more precisely ... upon the decision, or upon the adoption of the proposal, to avoid and to resist tyranny' (*CR* 124). This more cautious goal leads to other important distinctions. First, 'there are only two kinds of governmental institutions, those that provide for change of government without bloodshed, and those which do not' (*CR* 344). In societies of the latter type, the government 'cannot, in most cases, be removed at all'; in societies of the former type, 'the social institutions provide the means by which the rulers may be dismissed by the ruled, and social traditions ensure that these institutions will not easily be destroyed by those who are in power' (*OS* 1 124). Further, once we realize that '*all long-term politics are institutional*,' we can begin to develop a rational and systematic appreciation of what can and cannot be achieved in the pursuit of collective goals in a liberal society (*OS* 1 126).

In 'Towards a Rational Theory of Tradition,' Popper argues that institutions and the traditions that mediate and sustain them can 'give people a clear idea of what to expect and how to proceed' (*CR* 130). By so doing, they furnish perhaps the most important antidote – excepting eternal vigilance – to the appeal of totalitarianism, which promises to relieve us from the 'strain created by the effort which life in an open and partially abstract society continually demands from us – by the endeavour to be rational, to forgo at least some of our emotional social needs, to look after ourselves, and to accept responsibilities' (*OS* 1 176). By thus bringing some order and rational predictability into the social world, traditions and institutions give rationalists and reformers such as Popper 'something upon which we can operate; something we can criticize and change' responsibly and humanely (*CR* 131).

The distinction between personal and institutional approaches to politics prevents us from burdening democracy with tasks that it cannot, and should not attempt to, meet in a liberal society. Opponents of democracy, for example, frequently criticize its institutions for not preventing a policy or state 'from falling short of some moral standard or of some political demands which may be urgent as well as admirable' (*OS* 1 126). Such detractors do 'not understand what democratic institutions may be expected to do' and fail to realize the alternatives (ibid). Democracy, Popper writes,

provides the institutional framework for the reform of political institutions. It makes possible the reform of institutions without using violence, and thereby the use of reason in designing new institutions and the adjusting of old ones. [But] it cannot provide reason. The question of the intellectual and moral standard of its citizens is to a large degree a personal problem ... It is quite wrong to blame democracy for the political shortcomings of a democratic state. We should rather blame ourselves ... Those who criticize democracy on any 'moral' grounds fail to distinguish between personal and institutional problems. It rests with us to improve matters. The democratic institutions cannot improve themselves ... If we want improvements, we must make clear which *institutions* we want to improve. (*OS* I 126–7)

Popper here emphasizes the need to develop the critical pedagogy of the liberal tradition. Time and again he reminds us, 'Institutions alone are never sufficient if not tempered by traditions' (*CR* 351) that promote a humanitarian and egalitarian ethic. There are three cardinal principles of that ethic:

(1) Tolerance towards all who are not intolerant and who do not propagate intolerance ... This implies, especially, that the moral decisions of others should be treated with respect, as long as such decisions do not conflict with the principle of tolerance.

(2) The recognition that all moral urgency has its basis in the urgency of suffering or pain. I suggest ... to replace the utilitarian formula 'aim at the greatest amount of happiness for the greatest number' ... by the formula 'the least amount of avoidable suffering for all', or briefly, 'Minimize suffering' ... We should realize that from the moral point of view suffering and happiness must not be treated as symmetrical ... The promotion of happiness is in any case much less urgent than the rendering of help to those who suffer, and the attempt to prevent suffering. (The latter task has little to do with 'matters of taste', the former much.)

(3) The fight against tyranny; or ... the attempt to safeguard the other principles by institutional means of legislation rather than by the benevolence of persons in power. (*OS* I 235 note 6).

With regard to the first principle – tolerance – Popper's combat-toughened approach avoids the sort of paradox to which other, more optimistic and excessively naïve theories of liberal democracy have succumbed. If we grant unlimited tolerance 'even to those who are intolerant,' and 'if we are not prepared to defend a tolerant society against the onslaught of the intolerant, then the tolerant will be destroyed and tolerance with them' (*OS* I 265). Of course, we should do everything in our power to refute the intolerant by rational argument and to hold them at bay through the mobilization of public opinion, but frequently the intolerant may be unwilling to meet us on the level of rational argument and instead 'begin by denouncing all argument.' At such a point, the very life-blood of a free and 'open' society is in jeopardy. The only way to avoid such a threatening state of affairs is to 'claim, in the name of tolerance, the right not to tolerate the intolerant. We should claim that any movement preaching intolerance places itself outside the law, and we should consider incitement to intolerance and persecution as criminal, in the same way as we should consider incitement to murder, or to kidnapping, or to the revival of the slave trade, as criminal' (ibid).

The second principle – a humanitarian and egalitarian ethic – suggests a profound modification of the traditional utilitarian justification of liberal democracy. Here the imprint of Kant and Peirce is evident. Like Popper, Peirce believed that the essentially conditional and fallible nature of human cognition had far-reaching moral and ethical consequences, not the least of which was his ideal of progress, as 'giving a hand toward rendering the world more reasonable whenever ... it is "up to us" to do so.'[10] Such an ideal of 'concrete reasonableness' anticipates Popper's hostility to utopian radicalism as well as his critique of utilitarianism's vocabulary of desiring as inappropriate for an 'open' society. In 'Prediction and Prophecy in the Social Sciences,' Popper notes that 'since absolute freedom is impossible, we must, with Kant, demand in its stead equality with respect to those limitations of freedom which are unavoidable consequences of social life; and that, on the other hand, the pursuit of equality, especially in its economic sense, much as it is desirable in itself, may become a threat to freedom' (CR 345). 'The greatest happiness principle' of the utilitarians can 'easily be made an excuse for a benevolent dictatorship' (ibid).

Other important considerations, many already noted, also suggest the inadvisability of pursuing ever-increasing happiness through political action. Not only are evils concrete and tangible in a way that 'ideal goods' such as happiness are not, but policies that 'attempt to make heaven on earth invariably produces hell' (OS II 237). Further, whereas new ideas of promoting happiness 'are theoretical, unreal things, about which it may be difficult to form an opinion' or informed consensus, misery 'is with us, here and now, and it will be with us for a long time to come. We all know it from experience' (CR 346).

The goal of alleviating misery and suffering could 'lead much more easily to agreement on social reform' than more abstract objectives (ibid). As pedagogue for the future well-being of liberal societies, Popper exhorts: 'Let us make it our task to impress on public opinion the simple thought that it is wise to combat the most urgent and real social evils one by one, here and now, instead of sacrificing generations for a distant and perhaps forever unrealizable greatest good' (ibid). In short, public policy – in any society that respects the individuality and freedom of its citizens – should be oriented toward 'the more modest and more realistic' goal of fighting avoidable misery, 'while the increase of happiness should be left, in the main, to private initiative' (*CR* 345). Caring for the happiness of others

must be considered a privilege confined to the close circle of their friends ... But the use of political means for imposing our scale of values upon others is a very different matter. Pain, suffering, injustice, and their prevention, these are the eternal problems of public morals, the 'agenda' of public policy ... The 'higher' values should very largely be considered as 'non-agenda', and should be left to the realm of *laissez-faire*. (*OS* II 237)

Popper's third principle – a humanitarian and egalitarian social order – concerns 'the attempt to safeguard the other principles by institutional means.' The state is the most powerful of these means. In 'Public Opinion and Liberal Principles,' Popper advanced a group of theses, the first of which he called 'Liberal Razor': 'The state is a necessary evil: its powers are not to be multiplied beyond what is necessary' (*CR* 350). The state is necessary, even if we reject the pessimistic Hobbesian view of human nature and instead assume gentleness or angelic goodness as the dominant characteristic of man. 'There would still be weaker and stronger men,' and, in the absence of a state, 'the weaker ones would have *no legal right* to be tolerated by the stronger ones' (ibid). 'Anyone who finds such a state of affairs unsatisfactory, and who think[s] that every person should have a *right* to live, and ... a *legal claim* to be protected against the power of the strong,' will thus concur that 'we need a state that protects the rights of all' (ibid).

The state 'must be a constant danger, or ... an evil,' albeit a necessary one. Even if we assume the benevolence and good intentions of rulers, 'if the state is to fulfill its function, it must have more power at any rate than any single private citizen or public corporation' (ibid). These awesome powers can always be misused. While human beings 'will always have to pay for the protection of the state' in one form or another – for example, in taxes or the insensitivity of bureaucrats – 'the thing is not pay too heavily for it' (ibid). However, 'governments live from hand to mouth, and discretionary powers belong to this style of living – quite apart from the fact that rulers are inclined to love those powers for their own sake' (*OS* II 133). Thus, although unlimited freedom is paradoxical – it 'defeats itself, if it is unlimited' – Popper repeatedly insists on the need to design institutions that minimize the danger inherent in the power of the 'protectionist' state (cf *OS* I 124 and 111–13).

It is common in discussions of liberalism to emphasize what Wolin has characterized as its 'anti-political quality.' This was perhaps evident first in Locke, pervasive in the classical economists of the eighteenth century, and dominant in the writings of d'Holbach, Bentham, Mill, and Spencer. In this view, liberalism focuses on economic action, describes social life in terms of the spontaneity, self-adjustment, and lack of authority in the market-place, and eliminates reference to the most characteristic element of political action, the resort to power.[11] Similarly, in *The Liberal Mind*, Kenneth Minogue observes that 'liberalism cherishes the hope that one day politics will fade away, and the era of "power-mad politicians" (Lord Russell's phrase) will come to an end ... Liberals are rather like ingenious accountants ... They have, over the years, transferred many issues from "politics" into a variety of other columns.'[12]

So strong, in fact, has the hostility toward politics and the 'hankering after a non-political condition' become, that it gained support among utopian socialists such as Fourier and Owen, futuristic technocrats like Saint-Simon and his followers, virtually the whole of the Marxist-Leninist tradition, with its dream of the 'withering away of the state' and its replacement by the mere 'administration of things,' and most modern pluralists. Except for perhaps the odd eighteenth-century radical like Mably, or some rare moments in the struggles of nineteenth-century socialism, 'the older themes of political theory as a saving form of knowledge and action as a means of regeneration were ... lost to the Western tradition' of political thought with the ascendancy of liberalism.[13]

However accurate such an account may be for previous liberal thinkers, and however appropriate for contemporary figures such as Hayek and Nozick, it fails to do justice to Popper's thought, not least to his defence of the autonomy of politics and his belief that political theory can be a 'saving form of knowledge.' He never suggests that politics – the perpetual clash of ends and the possible invocation of power – should or will ever 'fade away.'

Just as freedom of action must be limited, 'so that everybody's freedom is protected by law,' Popper argues that unlimited economic freedom must be similarly constrained. 'Even if the state protects its citizens from being bullied by physical violence (as it does, in principle, under the system of unrestrained capitalism), it may defeat our ends by its failure to protect them from the misuse of economic power' (*OS* II 124). In the absence of some state control over the economy, the economically strong can 'bully one who is economically weak, and to rob him of his freedom' (ibid).

Marx witnessed precisely this type of 'shameless and cruel exploitation' and came to believe that parliamentary democracy represented 'nothing but a veiled dictatorship of the bourgeoisie' (*OS* II 122). Popper concedes: 'Using the slogan "equal and free competition for all", the unrestrained capitalism of this period resisted successfully all labour legislation until the year 1833, and its practical execution for many years more. The consequence was a life of desolation and misery which can hardly be imagined in our century' (ibid). Popper's appreciation of Marx's 'keen sociological insight' into such conditions and of his 'invincible humanitarianism and sense of justice' has frequently been ignored by critics on the left, who portray Popper as a leading member of that 'white emigration' which has sought to rejuvenate a reactionary and moribund political culture in post-war Britain.[14] In light of the conditions of the working class even as late as 1863, when *Capital* was being written, Popper notes that Marx's 'burning protest against these crimes which were then tolerated, and sometimes even defended not only by professional economists but also by church-men, will secure him forever a place among the liberators of mankind' (*OS* II 122).

Marx failed to realize, however, the political remedies necessary and available 'for securing us that freedom which he considered to be the aim of the historical development of mankind' (*OS* II 124). Marx's disparaging attitude toward politics derives from his view that mere 'formal or legal freedom' is insufficient, if not impotent, vis-à-vis the underlying infrastructure of economic determination. As he observed in *Capital*, politics can do no more than 'shorten and lessen the birth pangs' of a new or emergent order (quoted by Popper, *OS* II 125). Popper traces this 'extremely poor political programme' to Marx's theory that 'real power lies in the evolution of machinery; next in importance is the system of economic class-relationships; and the least important influence is that of politics' (*OS* II 126).

Popper disputes two consequences of this view. First, Marx's attitude toward political power prevented him from developing 'a theory of the most important potential means of bettering the lot of the economically weak' (ibid). Second, perhaps more important, 'he neglects the greatest potential danger to human freedom,' the paradoxical nature of freedom and the necessary function of, and limitations on, state power 'in the service of freedom and humanity' (ibid).

With regard to the first criticism:

We must construct social institutions, enforced by the power of the state, for the protection of the economically weak from the economically strong. The state must see to it that nobody need enter into an inequitable arrangement out of fear of starvation, or economic ruin.

This, of course, means that the principle of non-intervention, of an unrestrained economic system, has to be given up; if we wish freedom to be safeguarded, then we must demand that the policy of unlimited economic freedom be replaced by the planned economic intervention of the state. We must demand that unrestricted *capitalism* give way to an *economic intervention*. And this is precisely what has happened. The economic system described and criticized by Marx has everywhere ceased to exist. (*OS* II 125)

And to opponents of state intervention, Popper later adds that the very idea of a 'free market' is paradoxical: 'If the state does not interfere, then other semi-political organizations, such as monopolies, trusts, unions, etc. may interfere,' reducing freedom of the market to a fiction (*OS* II 348 note 26; cf, 330 note 20). From Popper's essentially neo-classical point of view, the 'only rational purpose' of an economic system is 'to satisfy the demands of the consumer:' 'If the consumer cannot choose; if he must take what the producer offers; if the producer, whether a private producer or the state or a marketing department, is master of the market, instead of the consumer; then the situation must arise that the consumer serves, ultimately, as a kind of money-supply and rubbish-remover for the producer, instead of the producer serving the needs and desires of the consumer' (ibid).

Thus, Marx failed to realize that political power can control economic power, that we could pass laws that have severely curtailed the exploitation characteristic of the period of unrestrained capitalism: laws, for example, that limit the work-day, that insure workers – 'or better still, all citizens' – against disability, unemployment and old age, and the like. By so doing, we have been able to 'make impossible such forms of exploitations as are based upon the helpless economic position of a worker who must yield to anything in order not to starve. And when we are able by law to guarantee a livelihood to everybody willing to work, and there is no reason why we should not achieve that, then the protection of the freedom of the citizen from economic fear ... and intimidation will approach completeness. From this point of view ... political power and its control [are] everything' (*OS* II 126).

Marx's expectation that in a classless society 'state power would lose its function, and "wither away"' indicates to Popper that he never understood the potential abuse of power and the paradox of freedom (*OS* II

127–8). For Popper, to the contrary, ' "mere formal freedom" becomes the basis of everything else' (*OS* II 127) – 'the only guarantee of a democratic economic policy' (ibid). Democracy, or 'the right of the people to judge and to dismiss their government, is the only known device by which we can try to protect ourselves against the misuse of political power; it is the control of the rulers by the ruled ... Without democratic control there can be no earthly reason why any government should not use its political and economic power for purposes very different from the protection of the freedom of its citizens' (ibid). We must think 'in even more materialist terms, as it were,' than Marx, for 'we must realize that the control of physical power and of physical exploitation remains the central political problem' (*OS* II 128). Against the Marxist dogma that 'economic power is at the root of all evil,' we must understand 'the dangers of *any* form of uncontrolled power' (ibid).

Once one fully appreciates that 'the most fundamental problem of all politics [is] the control of the controller, of the dangerous accumulation of power represented in the state,' the merits of democracy relative to more radical and utopian methods of social planning will be clear (*OS* II 129). Indeed, Popper refers to his criticism of the Marxist doctrine of the impotence of politics and to his own defence of the view that 'political power and its control [are] everything' as 'the most central point in [his] analysis' of historicism and its effect on public policy (*OS* II 125). In spite of his well-founded conviction that 'liberalism and state-interference are not opposed to each other,' since for reasons given above 'there is no freedom if it is not secured by the state,' Popper continually reminds us that such intervention is 'extremely dangerous' (*OS* I iii and II 130).

Whereas Marx and his followers assume that state power in and of itself presents no important problem, 'and that it is bad only if it is in the hands of the bourgeoisie,' Popper cautions us to realize that even the 'piecemeal' method of social planning he advocates will run up against the '*paradox of state planning*' (*OS* II 129). 'If we plan too much, if we give too much power to the state, then freedom will be lost, and that will be the end of planning' (*OS* II 130). We need not completely resist it; the costs in terms of human misery and suffering would be far too high for that. 'But it should be a warning that if we relax our watchfulness, if we do not strengthen our democratic institutions while giving more power to the state by "interventionist" "planning", then we may lose our freedom. And if freedom is lost, everything is lost, including "planning". For why should plans for the welfare of the people be carried out if the people have no power to enforce them. Only freedom can make security secure' (ibid). Thus, the most important challenge for social engineering in an 'open society' is to control the market 'in such a way that the control does not impede the free choice of the consumer and that ... does not remove the need for producers to compete for the favour of the consumer. Economic "planning" which does not plan for economic freedom in this sense will lead dangerously close to totalitarianism' (OS II 348 note 26).

In a passage reminiscent of Mill's *On Liberty*, Popper reminds us that 'there will always be borderline cases ... [and] these must be welcomed, for without the stimulus of political problems and political struggles of this kind, the citizens' readiness to fight for their freedom would soon disappear' (OS II 111). These considerations, Popper notes, lead us back to his demand 'that measures should be planned to fight concrete evils rather than to establish some ideal good.' Such a demand specifies the empirical and methodological pre-conditions of liberal democracy, similar to Schumpeter's aim in *Capitalism, Socialism and Democracy*.[15] Yet, unlike those who have claimed that the nature and value of democracy are but relative – unable to claim any superior moral virtue or elevated 'cognitive' status vis-à-vis other ways of life[16] – Popper professes unflagging commitment to the rationality, indeed objective basis, and potential problem-solving capability of liberal democracy relative to all alternative social orders. Never does he doubt that 'we can learn from our mistakes' (CR vii); we do so (systematically) only to the extent that we formulate our theories and couch our political demands in a cautious and melioristic fashion.

Since Kant, philosophy has sought to prevent reason from exceeding the limits of experience and to watch over power in political relations. Earlier, I characterized this preoccupation as a metaphysic of orderly growth. Indicative of this concern for order and growth is Popper's belief that 'state intervention should be limited to what is really necessary for the protection of freedom' (OS II 130). Similarly, Popper has characterized his brand of 'critical rationalism' as entailing 'belief in the authority of objective truth' and 'reconciliation between rationalism and traditionalism' (CR 375–6) – that is, hope in the orderly growth of mind and society. And we have just seen his moral commitment to conserving what he takes to be the empirical and methodological pre-conditions of an 'open society,' both individualist and humanitarian. His thought represents an impressive – though not unproblematic – response to the twentieth-century convergence of the decline in the optimism of the

Enlightenment and the unprecedented expansion of hitherto 'limited' state activity.

Popper has been one of the first to propose formal requirements and policy guide-lines for problem-solving in the liberal societies of today. Herein lies much of the force and appeal of his powerful synthesis of Neo-Kantianism and pragmatism. Popper realizes that in light of the many potential paradoxes of political action – particularly those surrounding public power and the debilitating effect of such problems on the citizen – 'it is not enough to say that our solution should be a minimum solution; that we should be watchful; and that we should not give more power to the state than is necessary for the protection of freedom' (*OS* II 130). In social and political affairs '*nothing ever comes off exactly as intended*' (*CR* 124). Thus a social science worthy of an 'open society' must 'explain those things which nobody wants' (*CR* 125). This is a tremendously important lesson for liberalism during a century of escalating violence, shrill ideological combat, and profound ignorance about what the future holds.

One of the most neglected aspects of Popper's political thought is his theory of critical institutionalism. For him, life in society is 'not only a trial of strength between opposing groups: it is action within a more or less resilient or brittle framework of institutions and traditions, and it creates – apart from any conscious counter-action – many unforeseen reactions in this framework, some of them perhaps even unforeseeable' (*OS* II 95). Thus, though our primary concern should be 'to find conditions of progress,' we must 'try to imagine conditions under which progress would be arrested' (*PH* 154).

Popper finds that the greatest obstacles to progress are primarily political and institutional. How could we arrest scientific and industrial progress?

By closing down, or by controlling, laboratories for research, by suppressing or controlling scientific periodicals and other means of discussion ... All these things which indeed might be suppressed or controlled are social institutions. Language is a social institution without which scientific progress is unthinkable ... Writing is a social institution, and so are ... all the other institutional instruments of scientific method. Scientific method itself has social aspects. Science, and more especially scientific progress, are the results not of isolated efforts but of the *free competition of thought*. For science needs ever more competition between hypotheses and ever more rigorous tests. And the competing hypotheses need personal representation, as it were: they need advocates, they need a jury, and even a public. This personal representation must be institutionally organized if we wish to insure that it works ... Ultimately, progress depends very largely on political factors; on political institutions that safeguard the freedom of thought; on democracy. (PH 154–55)

Popper's method of piecemeal social engineering represents 'the kind of experiment from which we can learn [the] most' about our constantly changing social environment (OS 1 163). It involves 'the alteration of one social institution at a time,' for only in this way 'can we learn how to fit institutions into the framework of other institutions, and how to adjust them so that they work according to our intentions. And only in this way can we make mistakes, and learn from our mistakes, without risking repercussions of a gravity that must endanger the will to future reforms' (OS 1 163). Unlike the piecemeal social technologist, who 'knows, like Socrates, how little he knows,' the holistic or utopian social engineer 'aims at remodelling the "whole of society" in accordance with a definite plan or blueprint' (PH 67). The holistic approach is 'incompatible with a truly scientific attitude,' since it denies independent testing of the plan at hand: 'While the piecemeal engineer can attack his problem with an open mind as to the scope of the reform, the holist cannot do this; for he has decided beforehand that a complete reconstruction is possible and necessary' (PH 69). And all too frequently the utopian 'substitutes for his demand that we build a new society, fit for men and women to live in, the demand that we "mould" these men and women to fit into his new society' (PH 70).

Once again, Popper's determination to treat individuals as 'ends in themselves' leads him to denounce the 'aestheticist' impulse and radicalism of utopian schemes. 'I do not believe that human lives may be made the means for satisfying an artist's desire for self-expression' (OS 1 165). Although aestheticism – 'the desire to build a world which is not only a little better and more rational than ours, but which is free from all its ugliness' – is understandable, it can be valuable 'only if it is bridled by reason, by a feeling of responsibility, and by a humanitarian urge to help' (ibid). We must demand 'that every man should be given, if he wishes, the right to model his life himself, as far as this does not interfere too much with others' (ibid). All dreams of beauty or perfection in politics must 'submit to the necessity of helping men in distress, and men who suffer injustice; and to the necessity of constructing institutions to serve such purposes' (OS 1 165). 'At present, the sociological knowledge necessary for large-scale engineering is simply non-existent' (ibid).

In *The Liberal Imagination*, Lionel Trilling notes that criticism 'which has at heart the interests of liberalism takes into account the value and necessity of its organizational impulse.'[17] Popper's institutionalism is a most notable contribution to such a discourse and to addressing the problems it encounters in contemplating the future well-being of liberal democracies. By focusing on the institutional element in political and social relations, Popper hopes to lay the foundation upon which 'we may get over the very greatest practical difficulty of all reasonable political reform, namely the use of reason, instead of passion and violence, in executing [a particular] programme' (*OS* 1 159). Institutions are 'inevitably the result of compromise with circumstances, interests, etc.' (ibid). Learning to conduct our affairs and social scientific inquiry according to their logic and limitations, Popper contends, holds the key to rational public policy in an 'open society.' Therein lies the greatest hope for the preservation and 'rational' enlargement of what Weber and Dahrendorf have described as our 'life chances.'[18]

Popper has never ceased being a keen student of liberal psychology, particularly its vulnerability to habits of thought hostile to freedom of the individual and to the autonomy of the mind and of political activity. Even the very best institutions 'can never be foolproof,' he characteristically observes (*PH* 157). 'Institutions are like fortresses. They must be well-designed and properly manned' (ibid). But because the 'human or personal factor' remains 'the irrational element in most social theories,' it becomes essential for the conservation of liberalism to realize 'that what we need is not so much good men as good institutions' (*CR* 344) – and the right kind of critical traditions: 'Institutions alone are never sufficient if not tempered by traditions. Institutions are always ambivalent in the sense that, in the absence of a strong tradition, they may serve the opposite purpose to the one intended' (*CR* 351). Popper illustrates this 'ambivalence': a system of opposition 'is, roughly speaking, supposed to prevent the majority from stealing the taxpayer's money,' but he 'well remember[s] an affair in a south-eastern European country' where such a system was undermined.

Only a systematic understanding of the situational logic and ambivalence of our traditions and institutions can give us a sane appreciation of our place in the universe and as members of society. In his autobiography he observes,

One way of life may be incompatible with another way of life in almost the same sense in which a theory may be logically incompatible with another. These incompatibilities are there, objectively, even if we are unaware of them. And so our purposes and our aims, like our theories, may compete, and may be discussed critically ... Everything depends upon the give-and-take between ourselves and our task, our work, our problems ... It is through the attempt to see objectively the work we have done – that is to see it critically – and to attempt to do it better, through the interaction between our actions and their objective results, that we can transcend our talents, and ourselves. (IA 156)

And more poignant still is Popper's closing reflection to volume II of *The Open Society*:

To progress is to move towards some kind of end, towards an end which exists for us as human beings. 'History' cannot do that; only we, as individuals, can do it; we can do it by defending and strengthening those democratic institutions upon which freedom, and with it progress, depends. And we shall do it better as we become more fully aware of the fact that progress is with us, with our watchfulness, with our efforts, with the clarity of the conception of our ends, and with the realism of their choice.

  Instead of posing as prophets we must become the makers of our fate ... [and] when we have given up worrying whether or not history will justify us, then one day perhaps we may succeed in getting power under control. In this way we may even justify history, in our turn. It badly needs justification. (*OS* II 280)

Liberalism's long-standing connection with the Faustian vision – a life of self-mastery, self-expression, active pursuit of knowledge, and un-hesitating acceptance of moral responsibility – has seldom found a more spirited, intellectually gifted, or eloquent advocate. But Popper's attempt to thus define and further 'rationalize' the relation between the demands of truth, the realities of politics and power in our time, and the traditional foundations of liberal optimism and hope concerning the rational progress of mankind is certainly not without its problems. Let me end this discussion of Popper's political thought by raising the more important of these problems – each of which can be traced to the legacy of Kant.

As we have seen, there is in Kant's thought a yawning gap between the demands of truth and objective (or 'theoretical') knowledge and a variety of human practices and concrete ('practical') judgments. In his aesthetic theory, 'a judgment of taste is not a cognitive judgment,' and in his moral theory, where he found it 'necessary to deny knowledge in order to make room for faith,' Kant's thought, as Merleau-Ponty has observed, left 'the two spheres of knowledge and practice juxtaposed without any relations,' reducing history to 'a sort of malefactor.'[19] Similarly, in his political writings, Kant pulled 'basic rights' and 'moral duty' – each 'immediately accessible to the a priori voice of reason – so far from mere (because 'uncertain') calculations of happiness and prudential deliberations, that he could purchase universalism and democratic virtues in this world only by recourse to divine providence and an instrumentalism incompatible with self-determination and real autonomy.[20]

But the mere juxtaposition of the ideal and formal requirements of natural scientific knowledge, let alone 'rational' politics, and the empirical realm of contingency, choice, and human need cannot bring this world into closer conformity with such principles. For the improvement of mankind's 'self-incurred immaturity' – the achievement of cumulative progress in our scientific, moral, and political affairs – is not a logical but a social-psychological and cultural matter, a matter of conduct rather than mere blueprints or correct inferences. Principles of conduct, and blueprints for institutions, should be objects of criticism and rational scrutiny. But to perform regularly any specific activity in a praiseworthy fashion is different from merely having read a book, an instruction manual, or some other rulebook. As Norbert Elias observes, 'People living in the example-setting circle do not need books in order to know how "one" behaves. This is obvious; it is therefore important to ascertain with what intentions and for which public these precepts are written and printed'[21]

Unlike most thinkers who have consciously followed in Kant's metaphysical footsteps, Popper has realized the need for more effective mechanisms to protect the interests of 'enlightenment' and the prospects of progress in intellectual and political affairs. Thus an acute awareness of the importance of promoting the right, 'critical' institutions and traditions lies at the centre of both Popper's conception of scientific progress and the 'open society.' But Kant's path creates serious difficulties in this regard, which must be remedied if human autonomy is to be realized. Let me return to a point raised in chapter 5: once history becomes fundamentally an object of hope and not knowledge, serious tensions arise for those hoping to 'rationalize' its future and to justify particular policy preferences on the basis of the superior rationality or epistemological credibility of their principles and criteria for action. At this point thinkers caught in this predicament adopt a variety of ad hoc and purely instrumental political measures, while leaving a vast range of the world's problems and irrationalities up to isolated individuals to confront and the vagaries of chance to remedy.

Several telling pieces of evidence submitted above point to Popper's inability to escape from these sorts of problems. First, in spite of the surface optimism of his thought and his 'highly appreciative attitude' toward the 'open societies' of our time, for Popper, history remains fundamentally 'non-repetitive,' indeed 'chaotic.' However much we may 'hope' for the best, Popper's political theory insists that we must 'prepare for the worst.' Darwinian necessities here begin to displace Kant's lofty goals. In this context Popper repeatedly insists that 'political power and its control is *everything*.' This general perception of history clashes with his belief that rationality renders social life less complicated than most situations found in nature. Perhaps more important, Popper's thought in this regard lacks sympathy and the vocabulary for articulating the experience of the passage from the reality of the isolated ego or 'I' to the 'we'[22] – a prerequisite, I would argue, of sustained improvement or 'enlightenment' of public life in even the most liberal and individualistic of societies.

Like Kant, Popper is so deeply committed to a form of reductive and atomic individualism – refusing to grant even the existence, let alone the importance, of all forms of 'collective' behaviour – that he is unable to provide anything but the 'thinnest' or most mechanical and instrumental – 'technological' – interpretations of the institutions and traditions upon which the future of liberal societies depends. Thus he lacks an appreciation of the concrete links, or ligatures, or mediations between human beings and the 'ideal' or theoretical standards of conduct he advocates. The standards of a democratic citizenry are 'to a large degree personal,' as though groups and collectivities – families and churches, corporations, schools and universities, and sprawling bureaucracies – play no role in this critical area.

Lucien Goldmann observed that Kant's was essentially a 'tragic vision,' for nowhere is community 'so absolutely necessary as in *action*.'[23] By leaving the whole sphere of duties toward other human beings completely up to the individual's isolated decision, Kant and his followers, like Popper, provide us with no assurance whatsoever about the possibilities of progress. In Goldmann's words, 'the proposition *I ought* is not in the future tense, but – as is too often forgotten – in the present; the real future would be an *I shall*. In the critical philosophy, where man's limitations and the problem of his destiny predominate, only secondary importance is ultimately accorded to the philosophy of history; there is only *present, duty,* and an *eternity, religion,* but no *future, no history.*'²⁴ And, I would add, no culture, or appreciation of the 'embedded' and mediated nature of human practices.

Popper talks as though 'creating' the institutions of an 'open society' and having them 'properly manned' are relatively straightforward incremental exercises in socioeconomic and political engineering. Unfortunately, Popper's discussion of this process fails to recognize that the relation between certain practices and activities and the criteria for their evaluation and performance demand much more than the instrumental and mechanical sensibility of social engineers. Oakeshott has remarked: 'We do not first decide that certain behaviour is right or desirable and then express our approval of it in an institution; our knowledge of how to behave well is, at this point, the institution. And it is because we are not always as clear about this as we should be that we sometimes make the mistake of supposing that institutions (particularly political institutions) can be moved around from place to place as if they were pieces of machinery instead of idioms of conduct.'²⁵ Popper's political thought, it seems to me, proceeds all too uncritically on the reverse, erroneous assumption that our desires and moral capacities somehow exist and can be discussed meaningfully, independent or autonomous of practices and institutions.

The problematic nature of Popper's conception of the relation between theory and practice, between knowledge and culture, was raised by Ralf Dahrendorf, on Sir Karl's seventy-fifth birthday. Popper had reportedly told Dahrendorf how delighted he was to receive messages of congratulations from both the chancellor and the leader of the opposition in West Germany and in Austria. Dahrendorf asked Popper if he were worried because the same theories 'seem to attract opposition and government in very similar ways.' Dahrendorf continued: 'Do you not believe that your theories should above all be accepted and used and believed in by those whose political predilections you share?' Popper replied: 'No, not at all. I could not care less. I know what I believe and make it clear, and that is good enough.'²⁶ But in light of the enormous obstacles now confronting the 'open societies' of the Atlantic community, as well as Popper's determination to promote the interests of 'enlightenment' and a politics of reasonableness, we can only wonder if his stoical reiteration of Weber's 'ethic of responsibility' here is really 'good enough.' Popper's position, as Dahrendorf worries, leaves more of the world's 'political practice to unargued, unreasoned, and possibly unreasonable decisions'²⁷ than is compatible with the liberal and Enlightenment dream.

One obvious difficulty that Popper's thought encounters in 'rationally' addressing developments in the real world arises in his 'Reason or Revolution?' There, Popper criticizes the growth of what Kuhn calls 'normal science,' which 'is linked to the growth of "big" science.' According to Popper – the advocate of 'heroism' in such matters – the continued growth of such 'big science' is likely to prevent if not destroy the 'growth of great science' upon which our civilization rests: 'If the many, the specialists, gain the day, it will be the end of science as we know it – of great science. It will be a spiritual catastrophe comparable in its consequences to nuclear armament' (RR 258–9). Popper leaves it far from clear how he would go about reversing the trend toward specialization in science, when it has constituted the predominant principle for the division of all social labour, manual and intellectual alike, for about two hundred years. How can such an advocate of progress and the ideals of the Enlightenment consistently so argue, since most such thinkers have taken for granted the 'progressive' nature of the division of labour?

Popper's unwillingness to discuss political ends – except in terms of his misleading insistence that 'the only alternative to violence' is his particular story of the 'open society' and its 'enemies' – and 'collective' and structural phenomena seems symptomatic of his failure to appreciate the ideal of the good life in a free and egalitarian society. In his autobiography, Popper tells us that he has been most happy in life 'finding new problems, in wrestling with them, and in making some progress.' This 'is the best life, ... a completely restless' and 'highly self-contained' existence (IA 100). Such an ideal is singularly unilluminating for political activity and debate and the mobilization of resources and support for myriad collective goals. Popper himself notes the affinities between his notion of the good life and the '*autark* in Plato's sense.' Such determined self-sufficiency, restlessness, and isolation confront, rather than measure, the success of today's liberal democracies.

As they struggle to survive in an increasingly hostile international context, as well as confront their own domestic conflicts and potentialities, the liberal democracies must collectively redefine and revivify their traditional ideals in a culturally relevant and sensitive manner. The degree of cosmopolitanism and universalism presupposed in Popper's atomic or near-autarkic individualism flies in the face of powerful forms of self-consciously communal politics – the politics of ethnicity and of caste, regionalism, religious communalism, and a host of varieties of separatism, to name only the most explosive.[28] Parts of Popper's political theory place liberal democracies at a severe disadvantage in trying to understand

and come to grips with the different social logics at play in these sorts of conflicts and leaves to future scholars the perhaps more important task of giving new meaning and life to their collective identities. In this respect, there is little 'new' in Popper's political theory, at least of a positive vein, compared with Mill's *On Liberty*. Popper's contribution lies in his dramatic renewal of our sense of the urgency and need to conserve the gains and hope of the past as we set about that other order of affairs. This is indeed an important task, given the nature of our times, but one best pursued by abandoning Popper's Kantian conception of truth.

8

The limits of Popper's liberalism

In a modern state the actual ruler is necessarily and unavoidably the bureaucracy ...

Bureaucratic administration always tends to exclude the public, to hide its knowledge ... The treasury officials of the Persian Shah have made a secret science of their budgetary art and even use a secret script.[1]

Max Weber

In *The Ramparts We Guard*, R.M. MacIver writes: 'Every social order, like every living thing, has forces working against it, threatening to destroy it.'[2] One challenge for those confronting such hostility is to identify the perceived threats and to articulate the necessary conditions for the survival of the endangered society. This study has sought to document and analyse Karl Popper's contribution to contemporary liberal democracies in their struggle against a host of threats. Popper's project is 'conservative' in the Social Darwinian sense, except that his focus is on liberal culture as a whole rather than the 'fitness' and 'survival value' of this or that particular group or interest.[3]

I have tried to situate Popper's formidable defence of the 'open society' within a comprehensive philosophical outlook derived from Kant. Like Kant's, Popper's political theory is embedded in a systematic understanding of our pursuit of knowledge about ourselves and the problems we face, our freedom of thought and action, our rationality, and the reasonableness of our hope in the possibility of a more humane and tolerant future. I have woven these concerns into a largely sympathetic account of how the problems of truth, hope, and power are interrelated, and at times in tension, in Popper's thought.

As indicated in the preface, this work reflects my considered judgment about the kind of caring scholarship and the type of study of Popper's thought that needs to be done in light of the reception that his work has enjoyed to date. There has yet to be published in English a single (!) study of Popper's political thought. Under such circumstances, the primary obligation of the intellectual historian and social theorist alike is Rankean: to present what Popper says and means to say as accurately and coherently as possible, given the sources.

Thus far the reception to Popper's thought has been polarized. Dutifully attendant 'masons in the cathedral' (his own favourite metaphor for the growth of knowledge) labour on Popper's thought, while other people are so at odds with his moral commitments and/or 'scientific' style of philosophizing that they systematically indict Popper for intellectual sins he has not committed. The former group seems determined to canonize his achievement into a strict code of scientific rectitude and 'good practice'; the latter has caricatured and otherwise so misrepresented Popper's views that their contribution to a scholarly and informed understanding of his thought and the problems it addresses is negligible at best. In attempting to portray the unity and power of Popper's philosophy in the context of his intellectual development and the main traditions within which it should be understood, I sought to avoid both these tendencies; my reconstruction of his thought has led me to be equally critical of acolytes and vilifiers. In this chapter, I would like to probe as immanently as possible several remaining tensions and ambiguities in Popper's thought as they bear upon 'open societies' of the Western world.

Another consideration has also affected my emphasis on the unity of Popper's thought. The division of intellectual labour tends to fragment complex problems and comprehensive systems of thought into but vaguely related specialisms – an insight shared by Weber, Durkheim, and Marx alike. Indeed, under the increasing bureaucratization of scholarship in today's universities, the more a thinker's thought defies such fragmentation, the more his or her work will be divided and compartmentalized by, and among, a plethora of often mutually estranged faculties and disciplines. Popper is a truly polymathic, integrative thinker and has suffered this fate.

Popper has sought to unify disparate aspects of our intellectual culture

– physics and biology, music (and other forms of art) and science, natural scientific thought and the concerns of the humanist – and to provide coherence for an increasingly disenchanting assortment of specialized bodies of knowledge. Like a classical positivist, Popper is determined to unify the sciences by applying the same problem-solving method to the full range of human experience. Popper constantly polemicizes and moralizes on behalf of such an undertaking, of continuing the centuries-old cultivation of the liberal conscience, or retooling the discourse of liberalism to meet unprecedented challenges, from both within and without – in short, of promoting orderly growth in mind and society alike. And yet, except for Bryan Magee's brief introduction to Popper, the secondary literature on Popper ignores these dimensions to his thought.[4] A sympathetic method and approach to Popper's thought seemed the most suitable way to deal with this state of affairs.

In my immanent critique, I hoped to suggest a line of criticism and a series of problems that flow from within Popper's own attempt to secure the autonomy of the individual through the progressive elaboration and application of an evolutionary naturalism inspired by Darwin. The political and moral ends he wants to promote may not always be compatible with the means and methodological prescriptions he suggests toward their attainment. Thus such a critique reveals that his own faith in the power and progress of scientific rationality is frequently at odds with the maintenance and survival, let alone enhancement, of the individual's freedom and autonomy.

The culmination – both logical and chronological – of Popper's thought is his elaboration and improvement upon the 'metaphysical research programme' of Darwinism (IA 133–43, OK chapters 6–7). While a theory of the growth of knowledge and scientific advance could be found as early as Logik der Forschung, Popper's argument and analysis were devoted to the philosophical foundations of Einstein's theories of relativity and their implications for contemporary physics and with their impact and paradigmatic status vis-à-vis the future growth and progress of knowledge.

Beginning in the early 1960s, Popper added a new focus and concern to his still-keen interest in physics, that of the theory of evolution. The new focus is at the centre of some of Popper's most important lectures and writings from this period (many appeared in Objective Knowledge in 1972). However, as early as The Poverty of Historicism, Popper proposed 'detailed and significant comments about evolutionary biology.'[5] A brief overview and recapitulation of his most recent writings on evolutionism are a helpful means of approaching the first problem I will be raising, his excessively abstract and formalistic, or 'thin' conception of the self.

As might be expected from someone determined to deny laws of human destiny, in *The Poverty* Popper argues that there are no – nor indeed can there ever be – such laws of evolution (*PH* 117). Whereas true laws require repeatability, the evolution of life on earth, like that of human society, 'is a unique historical process' (*PH* 108); evolutionary biology thus lacks the necessary logical structure of a properly testable body of theoretical knowledge. Popper has presented his own recent reflections on the subject as an examination and enrichment of the 'metaphysical' structure of Darwinism. This naturalistic metaphysics is relevant to Popper's conception of freedom or autonomy. Although biologists may find Popper's metaphysical speculations both unwelcome and unnecessary, students of politics and society may find that they show how his project of a comprehensive evolutionary naturalism and, more generally, his scientific style of philosophizing may be incompatible with his Neo-Kantian moral theory.

Working from the assumption that 'the origin of life and the origin of problems coincide,' Popper believes that by reconstructing Darwinism as a paradigm case of successful trial-and-error elimination or 'applied situational logic,' we can explain evolution toward 'higher' forms of life. In spite of a good deal of expert opinion and practice to the contrary,[6] Popper contends that Darwinism as usually presented fails to address this problem, since at best it can 'explain something like an improvement in the degree of adaptation' but not the actual mechanisms, structures, or rates of evolutionary change (IA 141). In 'Evolution and the Tree of Knowledge' Popper argues that Darwinism cannot explain evolutionary developments that appear to be goal-directed, such as that of the eyes or our higher linguistic and symbolic capabilities (*OK* 270).

Indeed, the failure of physicalist or behaviourist reductions of language to do justice to the higher linguistic functions as initially outlined by Bühler (see chapter 4), led Popper to reject all such theories. Popper's evolutionary concerns and theory of language are schematized in Table 2. Those who insist that language is merely expression and communication will neglect that which distinguishes human from animal language – 'its ability to make true and false statements, and to produce valid and invalid arguments' (*SB* 59). And to the extent that this is true, there can be no means of explaining the difference between propaganda, verbal intimidation, and rational argument.

TABLE 2 Popper on evolution and language

		Linguistic functions	Values	
		(4) Argumentative function	Validity/invalidity	
		(3) Descriptive function	Falsity	Man
			Truth	
animals, and plants	perhaps bees	(2) Signal function	Efficiency/inefficiency	
		(1) Expressive Function	Revealing/not revealing	

SOURCE: *SB* 58

So, while in the most general of terms the process of problem-solving is always the same – 'from the amoeba to Einstein,' as Popper is fond of saying – profound differences emerge between human beings and lower organisms once traditions of scientific criticism institutionalize our argumentative and descriptive capacities.[7] In evolutionary terms, scientific theories make it possible for our theories to perish in our stead, 'eliminating our mistaken beliefs before such beliefs lead to our own elimination' (*OK* 261). Indeed, 'higher forms of life' are distinguished by their 'behaviouristically richer preference structure' (IA 141). Elaboration of the emergence of such a structure constitutes the corner-stone of Popper's self-described 'enrichment' of Darwinism.

Although external or environmental changes may lead an animal to adjust to a new situation without prior genetic change, such a purely behavioural change, Popper argues, will constitute the adoption, or discovery, of a new ecological niche. Those individuals whose genetic preferences (or 'aims') produce adequate changes in their 'skill-structure' will determine the individual's 'fit' with such a new niche. Only after such skills have changed will there be changes in the anatomical structure of a species. For Popper, most of the 'problems' that a species confronts are posed 'not so much by survival [itself], but by preferences, especially instinctual preferences,' which are constantly emerging with new problems (IA 142).

Construed thus, the primary function of human consciousness, or the self, is to help solve new problems and to integrate behaviour at a particular time relative to expectations about impending or future courses of action (SB 125–9). In reply to Hume's contention that there is no 'self' beyond the potentially chaotic stream of our experiences, Popper thus replies that our very success at coping with our always changing environment constitutes a prima facie case for the unity and continuity of the self. Popper also links this position with research findings from experimental neurophysiology (SB 128–9): 'Most organisms, if not all, are programmed to explore their environment, taking risks in so doing. But they do not take these risks consciously. Though they have an instinct for self-preservation, they are not aware of death. It is only man who may consciously face death in his search for knowledge ... Only a man can make an effort to become a better man: to master his fears, his laziness, his selfishness; to get over his lack of self-control' (SB 144).

That Popper sees his contribution to Darwinism as the ideal complement or counterpart to his ontology of the three worlds is clear from the context in which this passage occurs. Popper contends that as selves, as human beings, 'we are all products of World 3' (ibid). We are 'anchored' or oriented in space by means of world 3 models and theories, which Popper claims we have a 'disposition' to make conscious and explicit at will, thereby enhancing our chances for survival. Further, we are similarly 'anchored' in time through our disposition to recall the past and by the theoretical expectations and 'action programmes' we bring to bear upon the future. The basis of all this is human language, which alone lets us be 'not only subjects, centres of action, but also objects of our own critical thought, of our own critical judgment' (SB 144).

At this juncture, Popper's 'Darwinian turn' leads us back to Kant. Citing Kant's dictum that 'a person is a subject that is responsible for his actions,' Popper explains that – what Kant, Josiah Royce, and, most recently, John Rawls have described as – the need of moral agents for a developing plan of life 'gives unity to the person, and ... largely determines our moral character' (SB 145). For Popper, it is possession of such a changing life-plan, 'or set of theories and preferences, which makes us transcend ourselves – that is to say, transcend our instinctive desires and inclinations ("Neigungen", as Kant called them)' (SB 135). The overcoming of severe physical challenges like the heights of Mt Everest, and the life-plans of the great artists and scientists, disprove the strictly physicalist view of man. In all such cases, 'somehow the mind, the conscious self, has taken over' (*SB* 146). 'There is much heroism in human life: actions which are rational, but undertaken for aims which clash with our fears, our instincts for safety and security' (ibid). Perhaps our greatest challenge is to prevent such heroism from degenerating into an evolutionary nightmare or tragedy.

The most 'democratic' of aims or life-plans, Popper writes, is the personal task of providing for oneself and for one's dependents. Remove it, 'and you make life meaningless for many' (*SB* 145). As much as we may need the welfare state for those who do not succeed in this, Popper believes that it is even more important that such a state not create 'un-reasonable and insurmountable difficulties for those who try to make this most natural and democratic of tasks a major part of their aims in life' (*SB* 146).

If the poverty of historicism – as Popper presents it – is the failure of imagination, then the weakness of Popperianism lies in formalism and its effect upon his social and political thought. In Popper's concept of the self the conflict and antagonism between the demands of his natu-ralism and of his moral theory manifest themselves in striking relief.

Liberalism and naturalism have always shared an assumption about the continuity, consistency, and ultimate predictability of the self. Such a view emerges in Popper's characterization of the unity of the self as a necessary, evolutionary precondition for successful problem-solving and 'integrated' action over time. Our problem lies in what his account leaves out and/or asks us to deny. The alleged continuity, consistency, and universality of the self (or 'human nature') are misleading and unillu-minating for concrete questions of identity and transformations thereof – the hub of any coherent theory of political culture and social change.

Georg Simmel, perhaps the most neglected figure in modern social theory, pointed out that we are very cautious about – if not incapable of – showing anything but 'fragments' of our inner selves. Such frag-ments are never a 'representative selection' but 'a transformation of this inner reality, teleologically directed, reduced and composed.'[8] The 'ed-iting' of our selves is directed toward communication, toward creating 'the palatable and comprehensible.' But explicitly political considerations are also frequently involved: those who command part of what Simmel called our 'psychological-real whole,' who know the 'truth' about our motivations in this or that particular context, have power over us. And, conversely, the more we can reach into and command the 'inner self' of another by knowing their feelings and desires, or their emotions, the more we have control over their behaviour. 'By playing on these emotions you can regulate his receptivity to information and his capacity to see, examine, criticize, and test.'[9] Moreover, politics continually affects the specific 'editions' of our selves that we present: the repertoire of socially acceptable and prohibited roles through which we gain and struggle with our identity is the ongoing product of prior conflicts and legitimations of our society, especially as conveyed in the institutionalized rules and meanings of our culture or subculture. In other words, 'there are alternative structures of the self, just as there are alternative cultures.'[10] The complexities we must confront in such contexts are all the greater once we acknowledge that any one of our 'selves' – our 'moral' self, for example – contains a wide range of potentially available character ideals and relevant communities to which they refer.[11]

Even such a schematic characterization or phenomenology of the 'colony of our selves' suggests serious difficulties in Popper's account of human autonomy and the future of liberal societies. If, at any point in time, the 'self' is the socially mediated and negotiated summation of contending personae – tactical, divine, civic, moral, and frivolous selves, to name the most obvious – then Popper's view of the self – as the formal presupposition and possibility of successful problem-solving, or as the evolutionary means of overcoming our lack of self-control – is simply not a rich enough portrait of the deliberations and vocabularies we continually encounter in trying to understand and cope with the world.

Let me briefly reconsider Popper's theory of freedom as 'plastic control.' Popper proposes the notion in order to explain 'Compton's problem' how such abstract things as aims, purposes, rules, and agreements can influence and control our behaviour. For Popper, explanation of such control must also account for the possibility of freedom, since he rejects deterministic accounts of human action as 'absurd' and a 'nightmare.' Further, whereas determinism entails the unacceptable conclusion that freedom is an illusion, indeterminism can allow for freedom, but only in not guaranteeing control of future action, there being an element of sheer chance at play. Neither solution is acceptable to Popper, for whom an adequate solution must allow for freedom subject to control.

Popper's evolutionary naturalism initially leads him to locate 'plasticity' in the non-mental, thereby depriving him of the volitional and deliberative dimensions that our self-determination implies. There are profound, qualitative differences between the role of meanings and the ongoing reinterpretation and conflict of meanings in human affairs and the role of 'centres of gravity' for gnat clusters or the 'responsiveness, dependency, and feedback' of a soapy bubble vis-à-vis its surrounding environment. As Alistair Hannay has observed, 'Nothing that [Popper's hypothetical] picknickers do under the influence of meanings can be described as "free" in just the way that the hither and thither of gnats is free.'[12] Similarly, unlike the enclosed air in a soap bubble which entails the system's performance of its role or function as soapy film, the mere existence of the idea of validity in no way entails performance of the role of eliminating inconsistency. All tools – logical and technological alike – need to be used in order to achieve the purposes for which they were contrived. The same is true of any 'exosomatic control' or other 'regulative ideal' for human conduct.

Popper seems to feel that in talking about the evolutionary and biological functions of consciousness he need not address the question of what 'consciousness' *is*. From his Neo-Darwinian perspective, mind or self is simply another 'control stage' 'thrown up' by evolution, a richer preference structure, another source of trials and methods of error elimination. And ultimately, the mind, too, is subject to yet another level of controls: that of its own products, with which it interacts and by which it is controlled. In my view, such a theory confuses the scientific description of the processes and structures involved in the acquisition of knowledge and the philosophical analysis, criticism, and justification of the concepts we use to refer to these processes. In short, in proposing his enrichment of evolutionary theory, Popper has committed a new fallacy, biologism.

Biologism is perhaps best understood, as John Kekes suggests,[13] in contrast to two other fallacies which Popper has spent the greater part of his career trying to refute: psychologism and sociologism. Each in its own way represents the consequences of relativism, which Popper sees as a constant danger to our way of life. Psychologism seeks to justify rationality and objectivity in terms of the attributes of putatively rational and objective subjects, while sociologism seeks to explain them by social conditions or surrounding environment. In neither case, however, can the desired justification be found, for psychological and social conditions vary from one individual or context to another. As far as Popper is concerned, justification can be found only in the correspondence of our theories with the relevant facts, not in the conditions that give rise to them. Critics have continued to charge that there is no way of establishing this alleged correspondence with the facts and that the success or failure of a theory is dependent on psychological and social conditioning. Popper has, in rejoinder, proposed his three worlds doctrine: theories exist independent of subjects who discover and formulate them, and the critical attitude is the best means of achieving such a correspondence and thereby arriving at a truer picture of the world.

Although Popper's approach is based on a much firmer scientific base than psychologism or sociologism, it none the less represents a serious logical fallacy. Psychologism and sociologism seek to locate the source of rationality and objectivity in individuals or societies; biologism attempts to place them in the biological condition of the species. But, logically, the epistemic status of a belief or theory is independent of its biological origin and/or function – a point that Popper makes about the other two types of fallacy. A false belief or theory could aid the survival of the species more than a true one. For example, it could be argued that 'if we knew more about how to manipulate our gene-pool, we would cause irreparable damage to our species.'[14] Our ignorance has a survival-value without possessing any epistemic value whatsoever. Moreover, even if we grant that some theories are biologically valuable for the species, the one value is not logically dependent upon, let alone entailed by, the other.

I believe that the source of this surprising confusion on Popper's part is his excessively abstract and ultimately dualistic ontology. To be a person is an achievement of a human organism; it is not a kind of thing. But Popper's three worlds doctrine throws in doubt this qualitative distinction. World 2 is best thought of *not* as the realm of 'subjective' experience but as that of persons capable of self-determination. Similarly, world 1 is more appropriately understood as the natural world, as opposed to the 'physical.' Both modifications help us see, first, that the classes of living things, though subsets of the class of physical systems, are so organized as to show remarkable differences from other physical systems and, second, that while 'every normal human organism possesses by genetic endowment the capacity for becoming a person,'[15] no animal does. Wittgenstein remarked appositely: 'A dog can expect his master; but can he expect his master tomorrow?'[16]

World 3 is best thought of not as 'objective' in Popper's transcendental sense but as the social and cultural world. This world includes first and foremost languages, other symbol systems (religious, moral, artistic, and cognitive, among others), and the social, economic, and political institutions within which we become human beings. This world is indeed 'objective' – it surrounds and constrains us from birth just as surely as the natural environment does any organism. But this is a very different sort of objective reality from the one Popper introduces with talk of 'knowledge without knowing subjects' and the like. Far too much Platonism and Cartesianism can, I think, be seen in notions such as these.

Our position in the world is far more 'eccentric' (Helmut Plessner's apt phrase) than Popper's naturalism allows.[17] As 'unique' and 'irreplaceable' as Popper hopes to have shown human beings to be, he is compromised by a more all-encompassing commitment to a Neo-Darwinian and three worlds ontology that casts serious doubt on the nature of and interaction between different levels of our experience (or his three worlds). The relationship between worlds 2 and 3 is one not, as Popper implies, of external causality but of participation and expression. World 3 is communal and historical; it is the ongoing and cumulative outcome of various traditions through which human beings have defined themselves, as well as the basis upon which they will engage the future. World 3 is ultimately a prospective and projective endeavour through which cultures and subcultures constitute themselves. Though science itself is more appropriately understood as an endless series of conjectures and refutations, as Popper has claimed, he leaves the sources of those conjectures unexplained and denies that they can be analysed rationally. I believe that a more robust concept of the self and of the interaction between worlds 2 and 3 could remedy this state of affairs and add much-needed flesh and blood to Popper's schematic characterization of 'situational logic.'

Ironically, some dimensions of Popper's thought require exactly the sort of person or cognitive agency to which I am here referring. If fallibilism is taken to be a theory about cognitive agents and their liability to error, then any coherent fallibilist epistemology must make the knowing 'subject' central. Popper's *Logik der Forschung* seemed to offer a refreshingly bold and promising treatment of the problem. There, 'objectivity' was not construed as the transcendental precondition of ultimately true theories and evolutionary 'success' but was found in this world, in the best critical consensus of the research community, and in the institutionalized means whereby theories would be 'ruthlessly thrown overboard' if they failed the critical tests that scientists perform. From such a perspective, cognitive communities and the rules by which they agree to govern their conduct are rational or irrational, not the 'objective' contents of world 3 knowledge, in Popper's sense.

In *Logik* Popper concedes a far more active role to 'knowing subjects' than later, when his position has swung in the opposite direction. For example, in the formulation of the demarcation criterion, Popper refers to cognitive agents: their methodological decisions guarantee that theories will be subject to serious tests (in addition to the formal and propositional tests of deductive logic). Similarly, Popper's 'basic statements' require a decision to overcome the 'Babel of tongues' to which research all too frequently succumbs. And on his own account, logical relations hold only between propositions and not between propositions and perceptions; experience can 'motivate' but never logically ground or guarantee the acceptance or rejection of a particular 'basic statement' as refuting evidence in a critical test; only our prior agreement to have some specific statements so exposed can secure that result.

If Popper's overriding concern is with the growth of knowledge, the way we learn about the world, then his fallibilism requires formulations of and approaches to the acquisition of knowledge prohibited by his later writings on 'objective knowledge.' Popper sometimes concedes that the 'autonomy' of the contents of world 3 is only partial and that there is a significant 'feed-back effect' from world 3 to 2, but I believe that this sits poorly with his overall ontology, in which logical relationships (and certainly the propositions thereof) appear timeless and static. His 'principle of transference' – 'What is true in logic is true in psychology' (*OK* 6) – shows further how far Popper has moved from the critical conventionalism of his youth and the problems that logicism raises for his evolutionary fallibilism. In short, I agree, with some logicians, that this aspect of Popper's thought constitutes 'a serious ontological extravagance and hypostatization' and a 'marked conservatism toward logic.'[18]

The earlier approach to objectivity seems to me far more promising and more likely to square with a 'fuller,' more robust portrait of how our knowledge does in fact grow. Cognitive agents, not propositions, are partial or impartial. And there are no transcendentally secure means of eliminating or even guarding against partiality – only our continuing commitment to and belief in shared norms and criteria of critical inquiry. That 'ideas' and theories exist independent of my 'mind' and yours does not mean that they exist independent of 'other minds' altogether. In short, our social and cultural world represents an altogether different sort of reality from that of Frege's sun (which rises and sets whether or not we 'know' it or see it) or the 'inmates' of Popper's third world (who enjoy more 'autonomy' than we human agents possibly can, given the naturalistic foundations of our 'plasticity').

The problems with Popper's 'thin' concept of the self and human autonomy can be traced to their source, his negative and abstract conception of community. Our post-industrial societies are no longer 'culturally positive.'[19] – we have no guarantees of some sort of salvation and enchantment by virtue of membership and participation in a particular community. Western culture's endemic individualism has destroyed any conceivable foundation for such collective salvation. In place of 'an experience which transforms all personal relations by subordinating them to agreed communal purposes,'[20] our purely negative communities can promise only better data and more information, to help us manage the ever-increasing strains of living in a world of detached individualism.

This distinction between positive and negative communities is crucial for an overall assessment of Popper's contribution to Western social and political theory. On Popper's own analysis the 'strains' of living in an increasingly 'abstract society' best explain the 'perennial revolt against reason' and the appeal of totalitarianism, which he has done so much to combat. Unfortunately, there is a serious problem with his account and justifications of the liberal alternative – that is, of individually 'paying the costs ... for being human' (OS 1 176). The naturalistic foundations he provides for the 'open' self and society are themselves a large part of the very 'strain' in question. Natural science has been modernity's most 'disenchanting' force. Consequently, Popper is unable to understand the traditional cultural and psychological demand for meaning and salvation.

There are two main sources of social change: the push of problems and the pull of ideals. In Popper's thought, however, preoccupation with the former all but precludes the latter. His life-long revulsion against what he believes were the causes of the two world wars (an excessive longing for order) and the overwhelming preventative and prophylactic function he assigns to philosophy (which he inherited from Kant) lead Popper to see the pull of ideals as an obstacle to clear, sober thought and successful problem-solving. Popper's scientifically honed character-ideal is thus that of the vita negativa: eliminating errors, falsifying mistaken hunches, learning how not to perish with mistakes, etc. For a self-consciously conservative ethic and a defence-minded ideology, such an ideal undoubtedly holds much promise. For a full account of our human potential, particularly for a meliorist ideology such as liberalism, it leaves much to be desired.

This ideal fails to comprehend that for most of recorded history, the dynamic and 'compulsive' aspect of culture has been one variety or another of faith, the content, function, and enforcement of which have fallen to the community. Once we grant that the 'higher dividends' in life are 'essentially symbolic in nature'[21] and that the 'colonies of our selves' are integrated by the symbols that communal purpose generates, then Popper's diagnosis of, and prescriptions for, the evils of our time look regrettably 'thin.'

One should not lose sight of the historical development of the negative communities which Popper's thought addresses. Their immediate precipitant was the ascendancy of 'economic ideology' in the seventeenth, eighteenth, and early nineteenth centuries and its image of 'market man.' With the triumph of the putatively neutral market, the rational entrepreneur – secure in and driven by his asceticism, self-reliance, and sense of personal achievement – increasingly found medieval-style participation and membership in the church civilization suffocating and expendable. Thus, the West's last great positive community came to an end, progressively displaced by a more compelling set of rewards and punishments, interdictions and remissions. In short, the 'civilization of work' was born.[22]

From the end of the last century onward, however, the reality of 'psychological man' has undermined the assumptions of the neutral market. Chief among its revelations were the manipulated and frequently irrational nature of consumer preferences; the impossibility and/or arbitrariness of comparing individual utilities; the seemingly insurmountable difficulties in computing (and, therefore, in 'discounting' for) poor information, risk, and uncertainty in the market-place; and the socially irrational consequences of trying to provide collective goods on the basis of individual preferences and 'consumer sovereignty.' Psychological man has rendered the market mechanism a fiction, with its usefulness increasingly in doubt. The irrationality and potential destructiveness of liberal 'rationality' thus became a principal concern of those, like Popper, determined to conserve this abstract society of isolated individuals from the consequences of their own ignorance and appetites, as well as from its 'enemies' abroad.

Popper's 'modification of utilitarianism' and critique of utopianism should be understood in this context. 'It cannot be our duty to make others happy,' Popper proclaims, 'because we have no intersubjective criterion for establishing what happiness is or means to different individuals' (*OS* II 237). The attempt to do so is probably the most dangerous of all political ideals, since 'it leads invariably to the attempt to impose our scale of "higher" values upon others' (ibid). We should pursue the 'more modest and much more urgent' task of minimizing pain – the only ideal and policy goal that a rigorous consequentialism can sustain.

The problem with such a foundation for public policy in a liberal society is not unlike that encountered by H.L.A. Hart in *The Concept of Law*.[23] Seeking to justify our obedience to the law, Hart proposes 'the minimum content of natural law' – the universal desire to survive. Such an idea, like Popper's consequentialism, seeks to re-create the universality and consensus essential for public discourse. But it cannot provide a basis for a full-blown political theory. Human beings are willing to die and to kill for political ends and ideals. Arguments such as Hart's – that no one would willingly belong to a 'suicide club' – become irrelevant in contexts of intense political idealism and strife. Similarly, with Popper's insistence that we seek to minimize pain, conflict of interpretation over pain and misery will require a much fuller account of 'positive goods' than Popper believes we should attempt.

Popper's moral consequentialism and modification of utilitarianism barely touch on the problems in these doctrines. Utilitarianism seemingly 'would allow us to ignore the problematic distinctions between different qualities of action or modes of life which play such a large part in our actual moral decisions, feelings of admiration, remorse, etc., but which are so hard to justify when others controvert them.'[24]

Utilitarianism proposed the simple, universally applicable demand that, in estimating the best course of action, the happiness of each agent count for one and only one. It thus held out hope of settling ethical and policy disputes without needing to assess a number of incommensurable languages – of moral virtue and vice, of admiration and contempt, of conditional and unconditional obligation, etc. And yet, as we all know, we continually need to make this sort of determination in considering the many qualitative contrasts that our moral life demands.

Popper's naturalism and formalism implicate his thought in exactly the same sort of problem, for he shares with utilitarianism the illusion 'that there is a single consistent domain of the "moral", that there is one set of considerations, or mode of calculation, which determines what we ought "morally" to do.'[25] I believe that the underlying explanation for this reductionist illusion is not hard to locate. Both utilitarianism and Popper's negative reformulation of it have sought to purge all subjective considerations from accounts of our moral life and to avoid the sorts of thorny disputes that more robust, subject-related approaches undoubtedly would involve.

Pursuit of character-ideals such as personal integrity, Christian charity or *agapê*, and human liberation may conflict with the realization of other ideals and goals. A full account of our moral life must accept this conflict within the colony of our selves, as well as the pluralism of the communities that give rise to it, as its raison d'être. To Popper, such languages of qualitative contrast must seem suspect, for they refer to nothing 'in reality.' Instead, they designate purely 'subjective' factors, according to his epistemology – the way we feel and/or are prepared to act, – not the way 'things' are.

Ironically, Popper's 'subjectivization' of values provides a rational basis for ethical scepticism and relativism, forcing us to believe that there is no rational procedure for adjudicating between alternative modes of conduct. I believe that this is the unhappy result of Popper's determination to avoid the excesses of constructivist and utopian ethics and to model our understanding of the moral world on the experimental method and rationality of natural science.

This type of model implies consistency and clairvoyance as to our goals and distance and objectivity toward our ethical goods – all highly unlikely in a world worth living in. In the absence of a more positive, pluralistic conception of the communal bases of the self in the 'open society,' Popper's critical pedagogy remains much like a sermon in search of its congregation – perhaps moving to the odd listener, but failing as a communion of like-minded individuals.

As we have also seen (in chapter 5), for Popper the role of theory in the social sciences is overwhelmingly negative: the primary task of the social sciences is to explain the unintended consequences of our social action. Social science should explain those things 'which nobody wants.' It should assume not only the consistency of the self as analysed above but also that the 'rationality principle' and method of marginal utility theory can be generalized to the other social sciences.

This methodological commitment obscures a substantive bias. Once we assume that 'sane persons act more or less rationally' (OS II 265), as marginal utility suggests, we preclude systematic understanding of those respects in which 'market forces' may structure the very preferences we have advanced as our criterion of rationality. We thus obscure potential sources of irrationality and immunize the individual as an object of inquiry from possessing irrational and/or conflicting preferences. Popper writes: 'When we speak of "rational behavior" or of "irrational behavior" then we mean behavior which is, or which is not, in accord with the logic of that situation' (OS II 97). As though the situation itself might not be irrational! Once again, Popper's commitment to formalizable and elegant method obscures as much about the world as it reveals.

How can Popper square his account of situational logic with his requirements for the cumulative growth of objective knowledge? For him, the superiority of one theory to another in the natural sciences is always a logical matter, the result of comparing the deductive consequences or predictions of two (or more) theories vis-à-vis a pre-existing and 'absolutely' objective field of natural phenomena.[26] We cast our predictions with regard to properties and relationships which occur even if not experienced by a particular subject. But in the social world, the 'situated' problems human beings confront prevent us from making any such comparison. Unless, of course, we elevate one particular mode of preference and type of rationality above all others, as Popper does, thenceforth employing it as an evaluative (as opposed to a descriptive) basis for our predictions.

As a scientific moralist, Popper thus commits the naturalistic fallacy. If we take seriously the situations in which individuals find themselves, and appreciate that they do not exclusively 'maximize returns' as an Austrian economist might, but sometimes manipulate and mould, 'play at' and dramatize their roles and identities as they define their situations for themselves, then Popper's deductively cumulative comparison of situations turns out to be more moralizing than a framework for empirical inquiry. To discover meaningful regularities in our social and political world, we must look at concrete and specific institutions – families, religious institutions, schools, political and economic institutions, and media of communication, to name only a few. Popper's thought seldom descends to this level of analysis.

Popper insists on our studying only the unintended consequences of our social action. Surely we need to understand that which we intend no less than that which we do not! As examples: we need to learn more about how we come to define problems in the way we do and about why we choose certain tools and methods to solve those problems. Similarly, we need to understand not only the problems 'that nobody wants' but also the ones that arise from chosen courses of action. And we surely need to understand corporations, bureaucracies, and legislatures as intended implements and vehicles of rationalization, whether or not we think of them as 'problematic' in Popper's sense; they play far too large a role in our daily lives to ignore them until something in their operation goes seriously wrong.

Popper's reluctance to study intended social action stems from his conviction that intentions are not amenable to rational analysis except by way of their products or objectified repercussions. So strong has Popper's reaction been against all varieties of psychological explanation that he simply refuses to entertain the thought that what we want and what we value can be the objects of empirical, systematic analysis. Given the stark contrast in his ontology between 'subjective dispositions' to act and the transcendentally 'real' nature of logical propositions and other objects of thought, this view is hardly surprising. But, if my preceding discussion is even approximately correct, this view guarantees that a large measure of our experience goes unexplained, predestined to remain in the realm of the irrational. I doubt that an advocate of Enlightenment such as Popper would be happy with this result, if he knew that it followed from his assumptions. Once one severs the products of one's intentions from the process by which they became objects of thought and action, there is no consistent way of ever bringing the world of objects under rational control.

Lurking beneath the surface of Popper's logical and methodological objections to a more positive conception of social science is a marked antipathy towards contemporary politics. Thus, in spite of his laudable and, to me, convincing defence of the 'autonomy' and potency of politics against Marxist (and other) forms of economic reductionism, in *The Open Society and Its Enemies* he repeatedly denigrates statesmen, the effect of nationalism and the nation-state on world affairs, and power politics, (*OS* II 49–60, 257, and 270). Small wonder, then, that he places his faith in social engineers or technocrats to revitalize the liberal democracies. *Their* requirements for knowledge of a certain kind – negative knowledge, which tells us what we should not do – ultimately inform Popper's proposals for the conservation of liberal societies. At no point in these proposals is there even a hint of politics as a field of creative activity or of a social science that might help expand such a sphere.

Popper has probably got the relation between democracy and social engineering and technology just the opposite of the reality. As a regrettably small group of thinkers has been trying to show since at least the time of Vico,[27] the more decisions are entrusted to 'expert' opinion, the more they are removed from the informed oversight, control, and possible understanding of the general public. Popper seems secure in his rationalist recommendation that we 'plan' for our freedom by relying increasingly on the technological approach of 'piecemeal engineers.' But there is every indication that a bureaucratic culture has emerged and taken a deep hold on the liberal polities of our time; this trend threatens whatever measure of democracy they hitherto may have attained.

In this, the age of Weber's Iron Cage, cases replace people, functions replace significant actions and social relations, means replace all ends as ultimate criteria of choice and evaluation, cost-effectiveness and strategic considerations replace ethics in public life, the needs of the system replace the needs of the people, administration replaces politics, management replaces leadership, and on and on.[28] Far from being the unintended repercussions of individuals' behaviour, bureaucracy and the ever-more sophisticated forms of technocratic administration are the direct consequence of the growth of rationality, as Popper typically uses the term. Consequently, his own proposals for lessening the strain of life in this increasingly abstract culture are more a symptom and diagnosis of, rather than a cure for, the difficulties that the 'open societies' of the West now face.

9

Conclusion

The ideals of liberalism and the Enlightenment have seldom found a more gifted and determined advocate than Karl Popper. While this study at times has been critical of certain features or implications of Popper's thought, I have tried to subordinate that aspect to the task of faithfully reconstructing the unity of his vision. Moreover, whenever possible I have employed here the tactic of 'immanent critique' (originally practised by Schleiermacher, Ranke, Dilthey, and their successors), in which criticism of a man or woman's thought is held to flow from his or her own assumptions and values. As I indicated in the preface, these features of this book stem largely from the current state of the discussion of Popper's work – an excessively specialized and polemical discussion in which the unity of his thought and its significance to our culture frequently get obscured.

As suggested in chapters 3 and 4, the unity of Popper's thought – the heat of his vision – is a morally inspired consequentialism, which originated in his creative elaboration of the metaphysical structure of Kant's philosophy – a metaphysics of orderly growth of mind and society alike. Throughout his long career, Popper has never tired of reminding us that, while science may 'annihilate the importance of man, considered as part of the physical universe,' a proper understanding of the Kantian self – as citizen and builder of its own world – can raise 'immeasurably his value as an intelligent and responsible being' (*SB* 3). Underlying virtually everything Popper has written is this determination to treat human beings as 'ends in themselves' and to insist on the corollary that the choice in selecting among competing ideas and theories is never 'simply an intellectual affair, or a matter of taste. It is a moral decision' (*OS* II 232). And at a time when most scholars find it increasingly difficult to master more than a subfield or two in their disciplines, Popper has deployed this metaphysics of orderly growth across a staggering range of subjects, defying the fragmentation and bureaucratization of learning that threatens creativity and our capacity to solve problems in their broader contexts of significance. For his principled example as a truly polymathic, integrative thinker, we owe Popper a great debt.

For a number of reasons discussed in chapter 7, Western political thought since the Second World War has been deeply disillusioned with its inherited traditions of discourse and foundations of optimism, a particularly disconcerting situation for liberalism, whose appeal resides largely in its meliorism and its faith in the cumulative power of reason to enlarge human freedom. With a sense of historic mission and moral intensity seldom encountered in our times, Popper proclaims that just as there is no reason to despair of the growth of knowledge and the progress of science, so there is no reason to forsake the essence of liberalism, provided that we learn from our mistakes in the manner that he suggests is possible. While history in and of itself 'has no meaning,' Popper insists that 'we can give it meaning' if we learn to live within the limits of how little we know about its ultimate structure and the frequently unpredictable consequences of our actions (OS II 169 and 278). Thus, unlike the often caricatured optimism of older liberal visions, Popper's political theory is decidedly cautious and conservative in tone, a sustained interrogation of liberalism's own utilitarian vocabulary of desiring and its underlying subjectivism and a reaffirmation of a sobered, combat-toughened conception of rationality and the 'ends' that are reasonable to pursue. He repeatedly reminds us that in social and political life 'nothing ever comes off exactly as intended' and that a social science worthy of an 'open society' – at once individualist and humanitarian – must 'explain those things which nobody wants' (CR 124–5). This is a tremendously important lesson for liberalism to learn during a century of escalating violence, unprecedented means of destruction, and shrill ideological combat.

Like Kant, but during far more tumultuous and sceptical times, Popper thus locates the rational grounds of hope and progress in our capacity to understand the orderly and methodical growth of knowledge: 'Our mind grows and transcends itself. If humanism is concerned with the growth of the human mind, what then is the tradition of humanism if not a tradition of criticism and reasonableness?' (CR 384). Popper's ability to renew our faith in such humanist ideals during a century known better for their denial is no small achievement; indeed, the very survival of civilization may depend upon their renewal. For the most compelling reality of contemporary history is the existence of weapons of such overwhelming destructive capability that their use would quite probably destroy civilization itself. There can be little doubt that the emphasis in Popper's thought on our ineradicable fallibility, on the morality (or lack thereof) of our beliefs and the theories we embrace, on the survival value of our ideas, and on the merits of criticism and reasonableness all tend to promote a more secure future. This study has shown why we owe these (and a host of other) insights to an appreciative survivor of an earlier, less fortunate age.

Notes

PREFACE

1 John Dunn, *The Political Thought of John Locke* (Cambridge: Cambridge University Press 1969) x. For an extended review of the secondary literature on Popper's thought, see my 'Masons, Evangelists, and Heretics in Popper's Cathedral,' *Queen's Quarterly* 91 (Autumn 1984) 679–92.
2 The most recent example of such an approach is David Stove, *Popper and After* (Oxford: Pergamon Press 1982).
3 For a treatment of Popper's thought along these lines, see T.E. Burke, *The Philosophy of Popper* (Manchester: Manchester University Press 1983).
4 Quentin Skinner, 'Meaning and Understanding in the History of Ideas,' *History and Theory* 8 (1969), and 'Some Problems in the Analysis of Political Thought and Action,' *Political Theory* 2 (1974) 279–85; John Dunn, 'The Identity of the History of Ideas,' *Philosophy* (April 1968) 85–104; and J.G.A. Pocock, *Politics, Language, and Time* (New York: Atheneum 1971)
5 Dunn, *The Political Thought of John Locke* ix
6 Skinner, 'Meaning and Understanding' 6
7 Walter Kaufmann, 'The Hegel Myth and Its Method,' *Philosophical Review* (Oct 1951), reprinted in his *Hegel's Political Philosophy* (New York: Atherton Press 1970) 138
8 On this aspect of Rawl's political theory, see Michael J. Sandel, *Liberalism and the Limits of Justice* (Cambridge: Cambridge University Press 1982).
9 For example, see R. Bambrough, ed, *Popper, Plato and Politics* (Cambridge and New York: Barnes and Noble 1967); Kaufman, 'The Hegel Myth'; and Ronald B. Levinson, *In Defense of Plato* (Cambridge, Mass: Harvard University Press 1953).

CHAPTER ONE: INTRODUCTION

1 Michael Oakeshott, Introduction to *Leviathan* by Thomas Hobbes (Oxford 1946) ix; and W.W. Bartley III, 'Theory of Language and Philosophy of Science as Instruments of Educational Reform: Wittgenstein and Popper as Austrian School-teachers,' in R.S. Cohen and M.W. Wartofsky, eds, *Boston Studies in the Philosophy of Science* 14 (1974) 307

2 Plato, *The Collected Dialogues* ed Edith Hamilton and Huntington Cairns (Princeton: Princeton University Press 1961) 1575 (Letter VII: 325e)

3 Sheldon S. Wolin, 'Paradigms and Political Theories,' in P. King and B.C. Parekh, eds, *Politics and Experience* (Cambridge: Cambridge University Press 1968) 147–8

4 Lionel Trilling, *Mind in the Modern World* (New York: n.p. 1973) 6

5 This notion is developed with great skill by Michael D. Biddiss, *The Age of the Masses: Ideas and Society in Europe since 1870* (Harmondsworth: Penguin Books 1977) chapter 2.

6 Friedrich Nietzsche, *The Will to Power* trans W. Kaufmann and R.J. Hollingdale (New York: Vintage Books 1968) section 65 (written Nov. 1887–March 1888) 43

7 Haultain is quoted in S.E.D. Shortt, *The Search for an Ideal: Six Canadian Intellectuals and Their Convictions in an Age of Transition 1890–1930* (Toronto: University of Toronto Press 1976) 3; and Biddiss, *The Age of the Masses* 142.

8 H. Stuart Hughes, *Consciousness and Society* (New York: Vintage Books 1958) 66, and Max Weber, 'Politics as a Vocation,' in H. Gerth and C.W. Mills, eds, *From Max Weber: Essays in Sociology* (New York: Oxford University Press 1946) 128

9 Hughes, *Consciousness* 430, and Thomas Carlyle, 'Sign of the Times,' in *Selected Writings* ed A. Shelston (Harmondsworth: Penguin Books 1971) 61–85

10 Hans Rosenberg, 'Political and Social Consequences of the Great Depression of 1873–1896 in Central Europe,' *Economic Historical Review* 13 (1943) 58–73; cf George Lichtheim, *Europe in the Twentieth Century* (New York: Praeger 1972) 3–42 and 99–164, and Reinhard Bendix, *Nation-Building and Citizenship* (New York: Anchor Books 1969) chapters 2, 3, and 6.

11 Biddiss, *The Age of the Masses* 143; cf Robert Nisbet, *History of the Idea of Progress* (New York: Basic Books 1980) chapter 9

12 Hughes, *Consciousness* 402. The effects of these events on intellectual activity in Germany and Austria (Popper's main cultural reference points

at the time) have been discussed by Fritz K. Ringer, *The Decline of the German Mandarins* (Cambridge, Mass: Harvard University Press 1969) 128–252, and William M. Johnston, *The Austrian Mind: An Intellectual and Social History 1848–1938* (Berkeley and Los Angeles: University of California Press 1972) 76–111, 323–34, and 365–79.

13 Gerard Radnitzky, *Contemporary Schools of Metascience* 3rd edition (three volumes in one) (Chicago: Henry Regnery 1973) 331; and John Kekes, 'Popper in Perspective,' *Metaphilosophy* 8 (1977), 36

14 For discussions of Popper's influence on contemporary biology, see Michael Ruse, 'Karl Popper's Philosophy of Biology,' *Philosophy of Science* 44 (1977) 638–61, and Melvin Cohn, 'Reflections on a Discussion with Karl Popper: The Molecular Biology of Expectation,' *All-India Institute of Medical Science Bulletin* 1 (1967) 6–16. For geography, see James H. Bird, 'Methodological Implications for Geography from the Philosophy of Karl R. Popper,' *Scottish Geographical Magazine* 91 (1975) 153–63.

15 Peter Medawar, BBC Radio 3 talk of 28 July 1972, John Eccles, *Facing Reality* (1970), and Hermann Bondi (no source given) are all quoted by Bryan Magee in his brief and excessively sympathetic *Popper* (London: Fontana 1973) 9–10.

16 Magee, *Popper* 10; cf his 'Karl Popper: The Useful Philosopher,' *Heritage* (1974) 52–7, and Edward Boyle, 'Karl Popper's Open Society: A Personal Appreciation,' in Paul A. Schilpp, ed, *The Philosophy of Karl Popper* (La Salle: Open Court 1974) II 843–58.

17 Incredibly, Popper's socio-political thought and methodology have yet to be the subject of a single published book. In comparison, during the last decade, there has been a flood of interpretations of members of the Frankfurt School, some of whom are among Popper's major targets in debates concerning the logic of the social sciences. In an otherwise helpful introduction to his thought, Robert Ackermann doubts that Popper has made any original contribution to 'theoretical debates about social theory,' *The Philosophy of Karl Popper* (Amherst: University of Massachusetts Press 1976) 157. In view of so many testimonials from social scientists to the contrary, it would seem that either Ackermann claims to know more about the 'theoretical dimension' of their work than they do or that he has a restrictive and erroneous concept of a thinker's originality. At least two unpublished PhD dissertations in English exist on Popper's thought: Charles R. Embry, 'A Critical Examination of the Thought of Karl Popper' (Duke University 1972), and Joel Kassiola, 'Fallibilism and Political Knowledge: A Non-Justificationist Epistemology and Its Implications for Norma-

tive Political Theory in Our Contemporary Age Destitute of Faith
(Princeton 1974). I do not share the assumptions of either of these
interesting works.

18 Isaiah Berlin, *Karl Marx, His Life and Environment* 3rd edition (London:
Oxford University Press 1963) 287. This also seems to have been Gilbert
Ryle's judgment; he reportedly said that, with the appearance of *The
Open Society*, 'Marxist exegesis would never be the same again.' Quoted in
George A. Feaver, 'Popper and Marxism,' *Studies in Comparative Commu-
nism* (July–Oct 1971) 21

19 Peter Laslett, Introduction to *Philosophy, Politics and Society* 1st series
(Oxford: Basil Blackwell 1956) xii

20 Quoted by Magee, *Popper* 13. The two studies of Popper's philosophy
of history referred to are Peter Skagestad, *Making Sense of History: The
Philosophies of Popper and Collingwood* (Oslo, Bergen, and Troms: Scandina-
vian Universities Press 1975), and Burleigh T. Wilkins, *Has History Any
Meaning? A Critique of Popper's Philosophy of History* (Hassocks, Sussex:
Harvester 1978).

21 To cite examples from each discipline mentioned, see T.W. Hutchison,
Knowledge and Ignorance in Economics (Chicago and Oxford: University of
Chicago Press 1977) chapters 3 and 4, and Mark Blaug, *The Methodology
of Economics* (Cambridge: Cambridge University Press 1980) chapters 1, 2,
and 15; Stephen Mennell, 'Sociology,' in C.B. Cox and A. E. Dyson,
eds. *The Twentieth Century Mind: History, Ideas and Literature in Britain* (Lon-
don: Oxford University Press 1972) 154–5 in particular; and John O'Neill,
'Scientism, Historicism and the Problem of Rationality,' in J. O'Neill, ed,
Modes of Individualism and Collectivism (London 1973) 3–26; David Ricci,
'Reading Thomas Kuhn in the Post-Behavioral Era,' *Western Political
Quarterly* 30 (March 1977) 8–11, in particular; Alan Ryan ' "Normal"
Science or Political Ideology?' in P. Laslett, W.G. Runciman, and Q. Skin-
ner, eds, *Philosophy, Politics and Society* 4th series (Oxford: Basil Blackwell
1972) 86–100; and I.C. Jarvie, *The Revolution in Anthropology* foreword by
Ernest Gellner (London: Routledge and Kegan Paul 1964) chapters
1 and 6.

22 John N. Gray, 'The Liberalism of Karl Popper,' *Government and Opposition*
11 (summer 1976) 354 and 339; cf, Anthony Quinton, 'Karl Popper:
Politics without Essences,' in A. de Crespigny and K. Minogue, eds, *Contemporary Political Philosophers* (New York: Dodd, Mead 1975) 167: 'Popper's
aim is directly continuous with Mill's, and the measure of his superiority
to Mill in this respect is that of the superiority of the *Logik der Forschung* to
Mill's *System of Logic*.'

23 Feaver, 'Popper and Marxism' 10
24 *Conjectures and Refutations: The Growth of Scientific Knowledge* 2nd edition (New York 1965) 228 (hereafter *CR*)
25 Dante Germino, 'Karl Popper's Open Society,' *The Political Science Reviewer* 8 (fall 1978) 60–1; cf, his 'Preliminary Reflections on the Open Society: Bergson, Popper, Voegelin,' in D. Germino and K. von Beyme, eds, *The Open Society in Theory and Practice* (The Hague: Martinus Nijhoff 1974) 12–20.
26 James Petras, 'Popperism: The Scarcity of Reason,' *Science and Society* 30 (1966) 1, and Norman Birnbaum, 'Social Constraints and Academic Freedom,' *Universities and Left Review* 5 (1958) 50
27 *Politics and Vision* (Boston 1960) 352
28 George W. Stocking, Jr, Editorial, 'On the Limits of "Presentism" and "Historicism" in the Historiography of the Behavioral Sciences,' *Journal of the History of the Behavioral Sciences* 1 (1965) 211–18
29 D.H. Mellor, 'The Popper Phenomenon,' *Philosophy* 52 (1977) 195
30 Kekes, 'Popper in Perspective' 37; cf Anthony M. Madiros, 'Karl Popper as a Social Philosopher,' *Canadian Journal of Philosophy* 5 (Sept 1975) 157, for a similar disappointment with 'the lack of critical bite' in the Schilpp essays.
31 Henry Veatch, 'A Neglected Avenue in Contemporary Religious Apologetics,' *Religious Studies* 13 (1977) 31

CHAPTER TWO: PORTRAIT OF A CRITICAL INDIVIDUALIST

1 Joseph Schumpeter, *Capitalism, Socialism and Democracy* (New York: Harper and Row 1962) 3rd Edition 148
2 Quoted in Stanley J. Kunitz, *Twentieth Century Authors, First Supplement: A Biographical Dictionary of Modern Literature* (New York: H.W. Wilson 1955) 783
3 Karl R. Popper, 'Intellectual Autobiography,' in Paul A. Schilpp, ed. *The Philosophy of Karl Popper* I 41–2 (hereafter IA)
4 Kunits, *Authors* 783
5 William M. Johnston points out that granting titles of nobility was a recurring Habsburg form of political co-optation and means of checking anti-traditionalist thought and institutional innovation: cf William M. Johnston, *The Austrian Mind: An Intellectual and Social History 1848–1938* (Berkeley and Los Angeles: University of California Press 1972) 39–44.
6 Peter Berger has underscored the convergence of Kraus and Musil on this point in 'The Problem of Multiple Realities: Alfred Schutz and Robert

Musil,' in Thomas Luckmann, ed, *Phenomenology and Sociology* (Harmondsworth: Penguin Books 1978) 344.

7 This was the apocalyptic title of one of Kraus's most important novels, *Die Letzten Tage der Menscheit* (1922). Several excellent commentaries on Kraus are now available in English; see in particular Erich Heller, 'Karl Kraus: The Last Days of Mankind,' in *The Disinherited Mind* (Cleveland and New York: Meridian 1959) 235–58; Frank Field, *The Last Days of Mankind: Karl Kraus and His Vienna* (London, Melbourne, and Toronto: Macmillan 1967); and Wilma Abeles Iggers, *Karl Kraus: A Viennese Critic of the Twentieth Century* (The Hague: Martinus Nijhoff 1967).

8 Carl E. Schorske, 'Politics in a New Key: An Austrian Triptych,' *Journal of Modern History* 39 (Dec 1967) 343

9 'Memories of Otto Neurath,' in *Empiricism and Sociology* ed Marie Neurath and R.S. Cohen (Holland and Boston: D.H. Reidel 1973) 52

10 Cf Henry Schnitzler, 'Gay Vienna – Myth and Reality,' *Journal of the History of Ideas* 15 (1954) 94–118; Carl E. Schorske, 'Politics and Psyche in *fin de siècle* Vienna: Schnitzler and Hoffmansthal,' *American Historical Review* 66 (1961) 930–46; and John Torrance, 'The Emergence of Sociology in Austria, 1885–1935,' *European Journal of Sociology* 17 (1976) 185–219.

11 A.J.P. Taylor, 'National Independence and the "Austrian Idea," ' *The Political Quarterly* 16 (1945) 234–46

12 'Memories of Otto Neurath' 53

13 Ibid 54

14 For example see Michael Lessnoff, 'Review Article: The Political Philosophy of Karl Popper,' *British Journal of Political Science* 10 (1980) 99–120.

15 The best-known proponent of this interpretation of Popper's political thought is Bryan Magee, *Popper* (London: Fontana 1973) 87.

16 Dante Germino, 'Karl Popper's Open Society,' *Political Science Reviewer* 8 (1978) 61

17 Karl R. Popper, 'On Reason and the Open Society,' *Encounter* 38 (May 1972) 13

18 Albert Einstein, *Relativity: Special and General Theory* (n.p. 1920; originally published in German in 1916), quoted in Popper, IA 29

19 W.W. Bartley III, 'Theory of Language and Philosophy of Science as Instruments of Educational Reform: Wittgeustein and Popper as Austrian School-teachers,' in R.S. Cohen and W.W. Wortofsky, eds, *Boston Studies in the Philosophy of Science* 14 (1974) 309

20 Torrance, 'Emergence of Sociology' 204. For an excellent introduction to Herbart's thought and its impact on Austrian philosophy, see Johnston, *The Austrian Mind* 281–6. Gottfried Wilhelm Leibniz (1644–1716), the

progenitor of Austrian philosophy referred to in the text, was a celebrated mathematician, physicist, historian, engineer, and philosopher. He was best known for his conciliatory and ecumenical spirit in an age when such an attitude was all too rare ('I have found that most sects are right in a good part of what they affirm, but not so much in what they deny,' he wrote, in a letter to Nicholas Resmond on 10 January 1714; quoted by Johnston, *The Austrian Mind* 453, note 1). His doctrines commanded progressively more support throughout most of the empire during the nineteenth century, most notably in the exposition of Bernard Bolzano (1781–1848) and in conscious opposition to Kant's critical idealism and Hegel's dialectic, both associated with speculative idealism, 'free-thinking' Protestantism, and anti-feudal developments in the North. For a penetrating exposition of Leibniz, see Lewis White Beck, *Early German Philosophy: Kant and His Predecessors* (Cambridge, Mass: Harvard University Press 1969) 196–240; also compare Johnston, *The Austrian Mind* chapter 19, and Frederick C. Copleston, *A History of Philosophy* IV (New York: Image Books 1963) 270–336.

21 Johnston, *The Austrian Mind* 284
22 Ibid 283
23 Karl Strack, *Geschicte des Deutschen Volksschuylwesens* (Gutersloh 1872) 327, quoted by Bartley, 'Theory of Language and Philosophy of Science' 309
24 Ibid
25 Johnston, *The Austrian Mind* 285
26 Heinrich Gomperz, 'Philosophy in Austria during the Last Sixty Years,' *The Personalist* (1936) 307–11
27 Bartley, 'Theory of Language' 309; cf 310–13 and Johnston, *The Austrian Mind* 282 and 285–6
28 'Die Gedachtnispflege unter dem Gesichtspunkt der Selbsttatigkeit,' *Die Quelle* 81 (1931) 607–9. Popper has repeated this expression often, though without reference to its origin or philosophical background in Glöckel's movement. See, for example, *The Open Society and Its Enemies* II 213–14, 260, and 361 and 'The Bucket and the Searchlight: Two Theories of Knowledge,' appendix to *Objective Knowledge* 341–61.

Die Quelle was one of the two major publications of Glöckel's school reformers, the other being *Schulreform*. In 1934, when the Dollfuss dictatorship brought all 'progressive' educational reform to an abrupt halt, *Die Quelle* and *Schulreform* were both permanently forced to stop publishing. As early as 1927, Christian Socialist and Roman Catholic pressure increasingly mounted against Glöckel's program (sometimes referred to as 'School Bolshevism' by its opponents), and censorship and persecution increased drastically even in Vienna, the last Social Democratic enclave in the empire. Both journals were periodically seized and locked up (*gessperrt*) in the National Library during this period, thereby rendering them inaccessible to the general public. Under Dollfuss, this became the permanent plight of educational reform: many of its leaders (including Glöckel) were arrested, its journal was totally and permanently silenced, and many of its younger associates, like Popper and Lazarsfeld, fled in fear of and disgusted by Austria's failure to prevent the rise of fascism.

29 Bartley, 'Theory of Language' 324
30 Bertrand Russell, 'The Philosophy of Logical Atomism,' *The Monist* (1918–19), quoted in ibid 314–15
31 Ibid 313
32 Ibid 311
33 Karl Bühler, *Die geistige Entwicklung des Kindes* (Jena 1918), English translation (London: n.p. 1930)
34 Herbert Feigl recalls Popper's relationship to the Circle as follows: 'There were two outstandingly brilliant minds in Vienna who, though close to us in philosophical orientation, never joined the Circle: Edgar Zilsel and Karl Popper. Both were convinced of their intellectual independence from us, and tried to preserve that independence by remaining outside the Circle. Indeed, I felt that both these men, each in his own way, were among our most valuable critics'; 'The Wiener Kreis in America,' in D. Fleming and B. Bailyn, eds, *The Intellectual Migration: Europe and America, 1930–1960* (Cambridge, Mass: Harvard University Press 1969) 641. Similarly, Carl Hempel notes: 'Though Popper carried on an intensive and fruitful exchange of ideas with various logical positivists, and although there were important affinities between his views and theirs, he has consistently represented himself as an outside critic of the movement, and he cannot, therefore, be reckoned among its proponents'; 'Logical Positivism and the Social Sciences,' in P. Achinstein and S.F. Barker, eds, *The Legacy of Logical Positivism* (Baltimore: Johns Hopkins University Press 1969) 164–5.

Nevertheless, the view that 'Popper did not share the beliefs of the Wiener Kreis' can be, and frequently has been, overstated. See M. Cranston, *Philosophy and Language* (Toronto: CBC 1969) 11. Victor Kraft rightly notes that although 'Popper never belonged to the Vienna Circle, never took part in its meetings, ... [he] cannot be thought of as outside of it' and that 'if Popper was called an "opponent" of the Vienna Circle, his opposition still rested on a common ground on which the dispute took place.'

See 'Popper and Vienna Circle,' in Paul A. Schlipp, ed. *The Philosophy of Karl Popper* I 185 and 187. The best discussion of the 'common ground' can be found in J.F. Malherbe, *La philosophie de Karl Popper et le positivisme logique* (Paris: Presses Universitaires de Namur et France 1976).

35 *The Logic of Scientific Discovery* rev edition (New York and Evanston: Harper and Row 1968) (hereafter *LSD*)

36 *The Poverty of Historicism* rev 3rd edition (New York and Evanston: Harper and Row 1964) and rev 5th edition (Princeton 1971) *The Open Society and Its Enemies* (hereafter *PH* and *OS*, I and II, respectively)

37 *Objective Knowledge* (Oxford: Oxford University Press 1972) (hereafter *OK*)

38 'Normal Science and Its Dangers,' in Imre Lakatos and Alan Musgrave, eds, *Criticism and the Growth of Knowledge* (Cambridge: Cambridge University Press 1970) 51–8 (hereafter NSD)

39 'The Logic of the Social Sciences,' in T.W. Adorno et al, *The Positivist Dispute in German Sociology* trans Glyn Adey and David Frisby (London: Heinemann Educational 1976; originally published in German in 1969) (hereafter LSS)

40 With Sir John Eccles, *The Self and Its Brain* (Berlin, Heidelberg, London, and New York: Springer Verlag International 1977) (hereafter *SB*)

41 *Postscript to the Logic of Scientific Discovery* 3 vols. (New Jersey and London: Rowman and Littlefield) (*Realism and the Aim of Science*; *The Open Universe: An Argument for Indeterminism*; and *Quantum Theory and the Schism in Physics*) (hereafter *P* I, *P* II, and *P* III respectively)

CHAPTER THREE: KANT, POPPER, AND THE CRISIS

1. Friedrich Nietzsche, *The Will to Power* section 610 (1884); and Bertolt Brecht, *The Life of Galileo*, quoted by William Leiss, *The Domination of Nature* (Boston: Beacon Press 1974) 3

2 Ernest Gellner, *Spectacles and Predicaments: Essays in Social Theory* (Cambridge: Cambridge University Press 1980) 3; cf, 'The Saltmines of Salzburg, or Wittgensteinianism Reconsidered in Historical Context,' Introduction to rev edition of *Words and Things* (London, Boston, and Henley: Routledge and Kegan Paul 1979) 2–13

3 Gellner, *Spectacles and Predicaments* 7

4 Ernst Cassirer, *The Myth of the State* (New Haven: Yale University Press 1946) chapter 10; Leo Strauss, *Thoughts on Machiavelli* (Glencoe: Free Press 1958); and Isaiah Berlin, 'The Originality of Machiavelli,' in his *Against the Current* (Harmondsworth: Penguin Books 1982) 25–79

5 Ernst Cassirer, *The Philosophy of the Enlightenment* (Boston: Beacon Press 1951) and Peter Gay, 'The Enlightenment in the History of Political Theory,' *Political Science Quarterly* (Sept. 1954) 374–89

6 *Physics* III in *The Basic Works of Aristotle* ed Richard McKeon (New York: Basic Books 1941) 254

7 A.C. Crombie, *Augustine to Galileo* I (Cambridge, Mass: Harvard University Press 1961) 6.

8 Alisdair MacIntyre, 'Epistemological Crises, Dramatic Narrative, and the Philosophy of Science,' *The Monist* 60 (1977) 460. The philosophical and methodological parameters of this dispute are nicely outlined by Norwood Russell Hanson, 'The Genetic Fallacy Revisited,' *American Philosophical Quarterly* 4 (1967) 101–13; Derek L. Phillips, 'Epistemology and the Sociology of Knowledge: The Contributions of Mannheim, Mills, and Merton,' *Theory and Society* 1 (1974) 59–88; and Harold I. Brown, *Perception, Theory and Commitment: The New Philosophy of Science* (Chicago and London: University of Chicago Press 1977) chapter 9.

9 Edgar Zilsel, 'The Sociological Roots of Science,' *American Journal of Sociology* 47 (1942) 555

10 Ibid 556

11 Ibid

12 Ibid 555

13 Alfred N. Whitehead, *Science and the Modern Mind* (New York: Macmillan 1948) 55 and 180

14 Francis Bacon, *The Great Instauration*, in *The Works of Francis Bacon* ed J. Spedding, R.L. Ellis, and D.D. Heath (New York: n.p. 1869) VIII 46

15 Cited in Paolo Rossi, *Francis Bacon: From Magic to Science* trans S. Rabinovitch (London: Routledge and Kegan Paul 1968) 141

16 This way of reading Bacon's fable was initially brought to my attention by Robert McRae, 'The Unity of the Sciences: Bacon, Descartes, and Leibniz,' *Journal of the History of Ideas* 18 (1967) 29–30. The passage is taken from Bacon's *De Augmentis Scientarium* book II chapter 13 in *Works* 456. Also see J. Weinberger, 'Science and Rule in Bacon's Utopia: An Introduction to the Reading of the *New Atlantis*,' *American Political Science Review* 65 (1976) 863–85.

17 Cited in Marjorie Grene, *The Knower and the Known* (Berkeley, Los Angeles, and London: University of California Press 1974) 65

18 *Rules for the Direction of the Mind*, rule III in *The Philosophical Works of Descartes* I trans and ed E.S. Haldane and G.R.T. Ross (Cambridge: Cambridge University Press 1931; New York 1955) 7

19 Ibid 1

20 Compare C.P. Snow, *The Two Cultures and a Second Look* (New York: Mentor 1964; originally published 1959), and Fred R. Dallmayr, 'Political Science and the "Two Cultures," ' *The Journal of General Education* 19 (1968) 269–95.

21 Cf Grene *The Knower and the Known* 96–7.

22 Lewis White Beck, *Studies in the Philosophy of Kant* (Indianapolis and New York: Library of Liberal Arts, Bobbs-Merrill 1965) 3

23 On this aspect of the Enlightenment, compare Cassirer, *The Philosophy of the Enlightenment* 3–133; Lucien Goldmann, *The Philosophy of the Enlightenment* (Cambridge, Mass.: MIT Press 1973); Judith Shklar, *After Utopia* (Princeton: Princeton University Press 1957) chapter 1; Norman Hampson, *The Enlightenment* (Harmondsworth: Penguin Books 1968) chapters 2–4; and Isaiah Berlin, *Against the Current* (Harmondsworth: Penguin Books 1982) 1–24 ('The Counter-Enlightenment').

24 Gellner, *Words and Things* 12

25 Beck, *Studies in Kant* 4

26 For an excellent account of reason's attempt to determine its own limits in the face of challenges from sceptics, see Giorgio Tonelli, 'The "Weakness" of Reason in the Age of the Enlightenment,' *Diderot Studies* 14 (1971) 217–44.

27 I have followed the standard practice of citing pagination from both the 1781 first edition as well as the 1787 second edition of *Critique of Pure Reason*, trans F.M. Muller in *The Essential Kant* ed Arnulf Zweig (New York and Toronto: New American Library 1970) 287 and 292–3.

28 Kant worked on the problems he felt he had finally resolved in the first *Critique* and other 'critical' writings (i.e. post–1781) for many, many years, and so any discussion of his philosophy as a unitary whole is somewhat misleading. Nevertheless, the three *Critiques* constitute Kant's definitive positions on the matters. Further, if Kant had had his way about the matter, his 'pre-critical' writings would never have seen the light of day, as his letter of 13 October 1797 to his editor, Tieftrunk, reveals: 'I assent with pleasure to your proposal for collecting and editing my minor writings. Only I wish you would not include writings earlier than 1770.' This letter is cited in Keith Ward's excellent *The Development of Kant's Ethics* (Oxford: Oxford University Press 1972) 51. On the earlier phase of Kant's thought, see Herman-J. de Vleeschauwer, *The Development of Kant's Thought* trans A.R.C. Duncan (Edinburgh, London, and Melbourne: University of Edinburgh Press 1962), and Lewis White Beck, *Early German Philosophy* (Cambridge, Mass: Harvard University Press 1969) 426–501.

29 *A Treatise of Human Nature* book I part I sections 1, 2, and 4, from the

Selby-Bigge edition (Oxford 1955) 4, 10, 10–11, cited by Grene, *The Knower and the Known* 99

30 *Treatise* book III part I section 1, cited by Sheldon S. Wolin, 'Hume and Conservatism,' *American Political Science Review* 48 (Dec 1954) 1001

31 *An Inquiry Concerning Human Understanding* section 5, cited by Wolin, 'Hume' 1001. On the relation between Hume's epistemology and his political theory, compare C.R. Morris, *Locke, Berkeley, and Hume* (Oxford: Oxford University Press 1931) 108–58; Arnold B. Levison, *Knowledge and Society* (Indianapolis and New York: Library of Liberal Arts, Bobbs-Merrill 1974) 12–44; and Shirley Robin Letwin, 'Hume: Inventor of a New Task for Philosophy,' *Political Theory* 3 (May 1975) 134–58. The relationship between Kant's and Hume's thought is very complex; compare E.W. Schipper, 'Kant's Answer to Hume's Problem,' *Kant-Studien* Band 53 (1961–1) 68–74, and D.R. Cousin, 'Kant on the Self,' ibid Band 49 (1957–8) 25–35.

32 *Kant's Theory of Knowledge* trans M. Holmes Hartshorne (New York: Harcourt, Brace and World 1967) 1–10

33 Grene, *The Knower and the Known* 102

34 Cf Aristotle, *Analytica Priora* book I , in *Works* 65–107.

35 Kant's more specific 'answer to Hume' is to be found in the transcendental analytic of the first Critique (cf *Pure Reason*, A 177–217 B 218–64 in *The Essential Kant* 157–82.

36 For an excellent discussion of Kant's relationship to Copernicus, see Norwood Russell Hanson, 'Copernicus' Role in Kant's Revolution,' *Journal of the History of Ideas* (1959) 274–81. Hanson demonstrates conclusively – *pace* Kemp-Smith, Ewing, and Paton – that Kant never spoke of the 'Copernican Revolution' or of 'a Copernican hypothesis.'

37 Zweig's *The Essential Kant* does not include the preface to the second edition of the Critique; the passages cited here from Norman Kemp-Smith's translation 2nd Edition (London: Macmillan 1933), were brought to my attention by Grene, *The Knower and the Known* 128–9, and Beck, *Early German Philosophy* 473–4.

38 Grene, *The Knower and the Known* 131

39 For Kant's discussion of each of these questions, Zweig, *The Essential Kant* 59–79, 88–197, and 197–294, respectively.

40 Excellent commentaries on this aspect of Kant's thought can be found in Robin Paul Wolff, ed, *Kant* (New York: Anchor Books 1967) 54–171; cf Michel Meyer, 'The Transcendental Deduction of the Categories: Its Impact on German Idealism and Neo-Positivism,' *Dialectica* 35 (1981) 7–20.

41 For more on the Kantian background to Wittgenstein's thought, see David

Pears, *Wittgenstein* (London: Fontana 1971) 17–41, and, more generally, K.T. Fann, *Wittgenstein's Conception of Philosophy* (Berkeley and Los Angeles: University of California Press 1969). In his posthumously published *Philosophical Investigations*, Wittgenstein's relationship to Kant's thought becomes even more intriguing with aphorisms such as 'There are things I know but cannot say.' For a complete rejection of the thesis that there are Kantian themes and influences in Wittgenstein, compare W.W. Bartley III, *Wittgenstein* (London: Quartet Books 1977) 116.

42 In *Philosophy of the Enlightenment* (120–33), Ernst Cassirer makes a persuasive case for regarding Leibniz as the central figure in the development of the German Enlightenment and argues that his *Essais nouveaux* anticipates Kant's *Critique of Pure Reason*.

43 Lewis White Beck, *A Commentary on Kant's Critique of Practical Reason* (Chicago: University of Chicago Press 1960) 23. For insight into Kant's notion of 'totality' see Lucien Goldmann, *Immanuel Kant* (London: New Left Books 1971) chapter 2 part 1 .

44 John Herman Randall, Jr, *The Career of Philosophy* II (New York and London: Columbia University Press 1965) 136

45 *Critique of Practical Reason* (1788), trans Lewis White Beck (New York and Indianapolis: Bobbs-Merrill 1956)

46 Cf Beck, *Commentary* 25 note.

47 *Studies in the Philosophy of Kant* 16

48 The demise of Kant's system into either of its dominant poles is discussed by Jürgen Habermas, *Knowledge and Human Interests* trans Jeremy J. Shapiro (Boston: Beacon Press 1971; originally published in German in 1968); cf Meyer, 'The Transcendental Deduction.'

49 The first of these passages come from *Practical Reason* 4: cf 98–9. The second is cited by Beck in *Commentary* 27, though Beck is uncharacteristically obscure as to its origin.

50 David Tarbet, 'The Fabric of Metaphor in Kant's Critique of Pure Reason,' *Journal of the History of Philosophy* 6 (1968) 258

51 Friedrich Nietzsche, *The Will to Power* section 469

52 In *Philosophy and the Mirror of Nature* (Princeton: Princeton University Press 1979), Richard Rorty writes (161–2): 'The difference between the "mainstream" German tradition in twentieth-century philosophy is the expression of two opposed stances toward Kant. The tradition which goes back to Russell dismissed Kant's problem about synthetic *a priori* truths as a misunderstanding of the nature of mathematics, and thus viewed epistemology as essentially a matter of updating Locke. In the course of this updating, epistemology was separated off from psychology by being

202 / Notes to pages 45–6

viewed as a study of the evidential relations between basic and nonbasic propositions, and these relations were viewed as a matter of "logic" rather than of empirical fact. In the German tradition, on the other hand, the defense of freedom and spirituality through the notion of "constitution" was retained as the distinctive mission of the philosopher. Logical empiricism and, later, analytic philosophy, were dismissed by most German (and many French) philosophers as not "transcendental" and therefore neither methodologically sound nor properly edifying.' For Kant's influence on contemporary social theory, see Thomas E. Willey, *Back to Kant: The Revival of Kantianism in German Social and Historical Thought* (Detroit: Wayne State University Press 1978); Jeffrey T. Bergner, *The Origins of Formalism in Social Science* (Chicago and London: University of Chicago Press 1981); and Garbis Kortian, *Metacritique: The Philosophical Argument of Jürgen Habermas* (Cambridge: Cambridge UniversityPress 1980).

53 Trilling, *Mind in the Modern World* 6

54 *Practical Reason* 153. For illuminating discussions of Kant's philosophy of history and moral theory, see Allan W. Wood, *Kant's Moral Religion* (Ithaca, NY: Cornell University Press 1970); Emil L. Fackenheim, 'Kant's Conception of History,' *Kant-Studien* Band 48 (1956–7), 381–98; Lewis White Beck, editor's introduction to *Kant on History* (New York and Indianapolis: Bobbs-Merrill 1963); and W.H. Walsh, *Philosophy of History* (New York and Evanston: Harper and Row 1967) 120–9.

55 Seneca's Epistle 107, II was a favourite of Kant's and appeared in several of his more important political and historical essays. See, for example, 'On the Common Saying: "This May be True in Theory, but it does not Apply in Practice" ' and 'Perpetual Peace: A Philosophical Sketch' in Hans S. Reiss, ed, *Kant's Political Writings* (Cambridge: Cambridge University Press 1970) 92 and 112 in particular.

56 *Lukács* (London 1970) 22

57 Richard J. Bernstein, 'Why Hegel Now?' *Review of Metaphysics* 30 (1977) 45. On historical precedents to this challenge to the ideals of the Enlightenment, see Tonelli, 'Weakness of Reason' and Shklar, *After Utopia*. But our own century's assault on the intellectual self-confidence and optimism of the philosophes and their followers has been especially acute and unprecedented and has affected intellectual discourse and perhaps practical politics; see Isaiah Berlin's magisterial 'Political Ideas in the Twentieth Century,' in *Four Essays on Liberty* (London, Oxford, and New York: Oxford University Press 1969), especially 7, 23–8, and 32–5; cf Michael Howard, *War and the Liberal Conscience* (Oxford, Toronto, and Melbourne: Oxford University Press 1981).

58 See Ralf Dahrendorf's discussion of the origin and contemporary relevance of Weber's notion in *Life Chances* (Chicago: University of Chicago Press 1979) chapters 2–3. I have discussed this aspect of Popper's thought in greater detail in 'Logic and Liberty: Notes on Popper's Institutional Theory of Progress and the Philosophy of Life Chances,' a paper presented to the American Political Science Association in Chicago, September 1983.

60 Paul Schilpp, editor of the Library of Living Philosophers, noted that the 'unusual size' of the two tomes of commentary (1,300-plus pages) was 'unprecedented' and 'calls for some explanation' (*The Philosophy of Karl Popper* I xv). Popper is the only living philosopher represented in the series The Arguments of the Philosophers under the editorship of Ted Honderich and has recently become the subject of a quarterly newsletter devoted completely to his thought. The newsletter announced formation of a 'worldwide network of Popperians' into the Open Society and Its Friends, which held its first convocation in November 1982, in New York. Popper indeed has become something of a 'phenomenon' among this generation of scholars, with all the benefits and costs that implies; cf D.H. Mellor, 'The Popper Phenomenon,' *Philosophy* 52 (1977) 195–207.

61 For a notable exception to the rule, see Paul Connerton, *The Tragedy of Enlightenment: An Essay on the Frankfurt School* (Cambridge: Cambridge University Press 1980) 116–17.

62 Ibid 116

63 Robert Musil, *The Man without Qualities* II trans Eithne Wilkins and Ernest Kaiser (London: Pan Books 1979; originally published in German in 1930–2 and in English in 1954) 286

CHAPTER FOUR: TRUTH AS CONSEQUENCES

1 C.S. Peirce, cited by Thomas A. Spragens, Jr, *The Dilemma of Contemporary Political Theory: Toward a Post-Behavioral Science of Politics* (New York: Dunellen 1973) 162

2 Jonathan Leiberson, 'Karl Popper,' *Social Research* 49 (spring 1982) 69

3 For Lakatos's distinction between '*Po, P1, P2*,' see his Appendix to 'Falsification and the Methodology of Scientific Research Programmes,' entitled 'Popper, Falsification, and the "Duhem-Quine Thesis",' in Imre Lakatos and Alan Musgrave, eds, *Criticism and the Growth of Knowledge* (Cambridge: Cambridge University Press, 1970) 180–9. According to Lakatos, *Po* represents 'the dogmatic falsification [of the 1920s] who never published a word: he was invented – and "criticized" – first by Ayer and then by many others.' Lakatos hopes his paper will 'finally kill this ghost' (181).

He argues that $P1$ and $P2$ represent the real Popper's intellectual odyssey from 'naive' to 'sophisticated' methodological falsificationism: 'The real Popper never abandoned his earlier (naive) falsification rules,' though he did realize the need to go beyond the simple requirement that genuine scientific theories be testable.

The occasion of Lakatos's discussion was the challenge posed to Popper's conception of scientific progress as the rational elimination of error by Thomas S. Kuhn's influential work on the history of scientific revolutions. Of particular concern was Kuhn's insistence on the fundamentally non-cumulative nature of scientific knowledge across different 'paradigms' and the at least partially 'irrational,' sociological and psychological reasoning that sustains andperiodically undermines so-called periods of 'normal' growth of 'puzzle-solving' activity. In the end, the issues at stake, particularly in Lakatos's attempt to rescue Popper's 'naive' and 'sophisticated' methodological falsificationism from Kuhn's (and others') objections, revolve around the role of individual propositions and theoretical formalizations in the evaluation of rival theories. I will be addressing these issues later in the text. The charge of 'whiggishness' in Lakatos's periodization of Popper's thought finds support in a note that Lakatos added to a tribute to Popper that he wrote before his untimely death in February 1974: 'Never in my life have I experienced more sharply pains of the historian than in this analysis.' After a careful collation of his own intellectual development with the 'three Poppers,' Lakatos candidly admitted to the 'grave suspicion that I might have missed some vital ingredient in the whole analysis.' See Imre Lakatos, 'Popper on Demarcation and Induction,' in P.A. Schilpp, ed, *The Philosophy of Karl Popper* I 244–5.

4 See the detailed comparison of Peirce and Popper by Eugene Freeman and Henryk Skolimowski, 'Peirce and Popper – Similarities and Differences' part III of 'The Search for Objectivity in Peirce and Popper,' in Schilpp, ed *Philosophy* 508–15.

Peirce coined the term 'pragmaticism' to distinguish the position from more common varieties of pragmatism and positivism. Peirce identified the meaning of a proposition with habits and conduct that are essentially conditional and general as opposed to a set of discrete experiments, observations, or facts. His 'Scholastic' (and, at times, Scotistic) realism differed from the nominalism of 'vulgar' pragmatism and positivism, both of which have (unsuccessfully) attempted to equate the meaning of a proposition with a determinate set of operational consequences or observations. For Peirce, realism and pragmatism entail each other. Thus, there are real laws, 'generals,' and habits (or 'Thirds'), which are irreducible to both unanalysed sense data (or 'Firsts') and to mere action or dyadic relations (or 'Seconds'), which hold among such data. For example, as Rorty notes, referring to a cat as a batch of sense data will 'miss the reference to a logical interpretant which makes the cat a cat. It will lose the same kind of thing that gets lost when we "reduce" giving to handing over and taking.' See Richard Rorty, 'Pragmatism, Categories, and Language,' *Philosophical Review* 70 (1971) 202–3. For useful introductions to Peirce's thought, see John Passmore, *A Hundred Years of Philosophy* (Harmondsworth: Penguin Books 1968) 102–10 and 136–44; R. Jackson Wilson, *In Quest of Community: Social Philosophy in the United States, 1860–1920* (London, Oxford, and New York: Oxford University Press 1970) chapter 2; and Richard Bernstein, *Praxis and Action* (Philadelphia: University of Pennsylvania Press 1971) 177–99.

5 Bernstein *Praxis and Action* 193
6 For excellent discussions of Kant's thought along these lines, see Bernstein, *Praxis and Action* 178, 209, 238–50, and 283; Richard Rorty, *Philosophy and the Mirror of Nature* (Princeton: Princeton University Press 1979), especially chapter 3; and Hans Reichenbach, *The Rise of Scientific Philosophy* (Berkeley and Los Angeles: University of California Press 1951) chapter 7. Popper's own admiration for Kant should be evident by now and will be expanded upon further in the text.
7 Herbert Feigl, 'The Wiener Kreis in America,' in D. Fleming and B. Bailyn, eds, *The Intellectual Migration: Europe and America, 1930–1960* (Cambridge, Mass: Harvard University Press 1969).
8 Ibid 651 and 637
9 'What Can Logic Do for Philosophy?' *Proceedings of the Aristotelian Society*, Supplementary Volume 22 (1948) 141. Hereafter LP
10 John Kekes, 'Popper in Perspective,' *Metaphilosophy* 8 (1977) 38
11 'Conversation with Karl Popper,' in Bryan Magee, ed. *Modern British Philosophy* (London: Paladin 1973) 91 (hereafter CKP)
12 Cf Harold I. Brown, *Perception, Theory and Commitment: The New Philosophy of Science* (Chicago and London: University of Chicago Press 1977) 21.
13 W.W. Bartley III 'Theory of Language and Philosophy as Instruments of Educational Reform: Wittgenstein and Popper as Austrian School-teachers,' in R.S. Cohen and W.W. Wartofsky, eds, *Boston Studies in the Philosophy of Science* 14 (1974) 313
14 Oswald Külpe, *Vorlesungen uber Logik* ed Otta Selz (Leipzig 1923), cited by Popper in IA 60 and note 92
15 Bühler's ideas also play a prominent, though radically different, role in the thought of Ernst Cassirer, particularly evident in *The Philosophy of Sym-*

206 / Notes to pages 58–60

bolic Forms trans Ralph Mannheim with intro by Charles W. Hendel
(New Haven: Yale University Press 1957; German original 1923, 1925,
and 1929) III especially chapter 1, part 2.

Systematic comparison of Popper's thought and Cassirer's 'phenomenology of knowledge' and philosophy of culture would illuminate the
development of strikingly different interpretations of the Renaissance and
Enlightenment, as well as of the nature of scientific knowledge and its
role in the future of liberal societies. For a helpful introduction to Cassirer's thought, see John J. Schrems, 'Ernest Cassirer and Political Thought,'
The Review of Politics 29 (1967) 180–203; an outstanding critique of the
formalism in Cassirer's (and a host of other Neo-Kantian thinkers') philosophies is Emil Oestereicher, 'Form and Praxis: A Contribution to the
Theory of Cultural Forms,' *Social Research* 49 (1982) 668–89.

16 More specifically, in his third *Critique*, Kant maintained that working solely
on the assumption of mechanical causality or Newtonian determinism
makes it impossible to explain the adaptability and self-organizing capacity
of living beings. Biologists must proceed 'as if' there were purposiveness
in organic development, hoping thereby to extend the mechanical ordering
of phenomena. Cf *Critique of Judgment* trans James C. Meredith in Arnulf
Zweig, ed, *The Essential Kant* (New York and Toronto: New American
Library 1970) sections 61, 83–4, and 87. Kant made the same point in his
writings on the philosophy of history. For example, he begins his 'Idea
for a Universal History' with the observation: 'If we assume a plan of nature, we have grounds for greater hopes. For such a plan opens up the
comforting prospect of a future in which we are shown from afar how the
human race eventually works its way upward to a situation in which all
the germs implanted by nature can be developed fully, and in which man's
destiny can be fulfilled here on earth. Such a justification here on earth
of nature – or rather perhaps providence – is no mean motive for adopting
a particular point of view in considering the whole.' In Hans Reiss, ed,
Kant's Political Writings (Cambridge: Cambridge University Press 1970)
52–3

17 Stephen Toulmin and Allan Janik, *Wittgenstein's Vienna* (New York: Simon
and Schuster 1973) 27

18 A typical example of dividing Popper's thought into early 'methodological'
and later 'metaphysical' phases is Henryk Skolimowski, 'Karl Popper and
the Objectivity of Scientific Knowledge,' in P.A. Schilpp, ed, *The Philosophy
of Karl Popper* I (La Salle: Open Court 1974) 483–508.

19 Jonathan Lieberson, 'The Romantic Rationalist,' *New York Review of Books*

(2 December 1982) 52, a review of *Postscript to the Logic of Scientific Discovery*
ed W.W. Bartley III (New Jersey and London: Hutchinson 1982), of
Anthony O'Hear, *Karl Popper* (London, Boston, and Henley: Routledge
and Kegan Paul 1980), and of Paul Levinson, *In Pursuit of Truth: Essays in
Honour of Karl Popper's 80th Birthday* (New Jersey and Sussex: Humanities
Press 1982).

20 There is scarcely a work of Dewey's that does not discuss experience along
the lines that Popper suggests here. Perhaps his most original insights
are in 'The Need for a Recovery of Philosophy,' where he lists five contrasts
between his conception and the 'orthodox' or 'traditional' view of experience. In the present context, the most important of these five contrasts are
the first three: (1) 'In the orthodox view, experience is regarded primarily
as a knowledge-affair. But to eyes not looking through ancient spectacles,
it assuredly appears as an affair of intercourse of a living being with its
physical and social environment.' (2) 'According to tradition experience is
(at least primarily) a physical thing, infected throughout by "subjectivity."
What experience suggests about itself is a genuinely objective world which
enters into the actions and sufferings of men and undergoes modifications
through their responses.' (3) 'So far as anything beyond a bare present
recognized by established doctrine, the past exclusively counts. Registration
of what has taken place, reference to precedent, is believed to be the
essence of experience. Empiricism is conceived of as tied up to what has
been, or is 'given.' But experience in its vital form is experimental, an
effort to change the given; it is characterized by projection, by reaching
forward into the unknown, connection with a future is its salient trait.'
Reprinted in *John Dewey: On Experience, Nature and Freedom*, ed Richard
Bernstein (New York: Liberal Arts Press 1960) 23. For a useful introduction to experience as the integrating concept in Dewey's political
thought, see Joseph G. Metz, 'Democracy and the Scientific Method in the
Philosophy of John Dewey,' *Review of Politics* 31 (1969) 242–62.

21 On the historical development of this movement, compare Richard Rorty's
introduction to *The Linguistic Turn* (Chicago and London: University of
Chicago Press 1967); Ian Hacking, *Why Does Language Matter to Philosophy?*
(Cambridge: Cambridge University Press 1975) chapters 6–13; Frederick
Jameson, *The Prison-House of Language* (Princeton: Princeton University
Press 1972) especially chapter 1; and Hanna Pitkin, *Wittgenstein and Justice*
(Berkeley, Los Angeles, and London: University of California Press 1972).

22 Passmore, *A Hundred Years* 148

23 Quoted in ibid 186

24 For a thoughtful discussion of Popper's thought as primarily an attempt to solve this problem, see Alan E. Musgrave, 'The Objectivism of Popper's Epistemology,' in Schilpp, ed, *The Philosophy of Karl Popper* I 560–96.

25 Passmore, *A Hundred Years* 186

26 On Lötze's critique of psychologism, see Nicola Abbagnano, 'Psychologism' trans Nino Languilli in *The Encyclopedia of Philosophy* VI ed Paul Edwards (New York and London: Collier-Macmillan 1967) 521.

27 Quoted in ibid

28 Gottlob Frege, quoted by Passmore, *A Hundred Years* 148. Passmore gives no specific citation to this passage; presumably it too comes from *Die Grundlagen der Arithmatik*, trans J.L. Austin as *Foundations of Arithematic* (Oxford: Clarendon Press 1950).

29 For examples of the charge that Popper's thought is ultimately irrationalist and/or a brand of radical scepticism, compare Anthony O'Hear, *Karl Popper* (London 1980) 207; D.H. Mellor, 'The Popper Phenomenon,' *Philosophy* 52 (1977) 196; and W.H. Newton-Smith, *The Rationality of Science* (London: Routledge and Kegan Paul 1981) 52.

30 Ingvar Johansson, *A Critique of Karl Popper's Methodology* (Stockholm: Scandinavian University Books 1975) chapters 2, 4–11, provides an exhaustive list of the other methodological rules proposed by Popper in *Logic of Scientific Discovery*.

31 Derek A. Kelly, 'Popper's Ontology: An Exposition and Critique,' *Southern Journal of Philosophy* (spring 1975) 71. I am also indebted to Kelly's article for the preceding reference to Santayana's *Realms of Being*.

32 J.W. Grove, 'Popper "Demystified": The Curious Ideas of Bloor (and Some Others) about World 3,' *Philosophy of the Social Sciences* 10 (1980) 172–180

33 A.H. Compton, *The Freedom of Man* 3rd edition (New Haven: Yale University Press, 1939) 51ff, cited in *Objective Knowledge* 229–30

34 Also see 'Indeterminism Is Not Enough,' *Encounter* 40 (April 1973) 20–6.

35 Alastair Hannay, 'Freedom and Plastic Control,' *Canadian Journal of Philosophy* 2 (1972) 180

36 Ibid

37 Ibid 282

38 Judith N. Shklar, 'Facing up to Intellectual Pluralism,' in David Spitz, ed, *Political Theory and Social Change* (New York: Atherton Press 1967) 278

39 Ernest Gellner, *Legitimation of Belief* (Cambridge: Cambridge University Press 1974) 185

40 Kenneth R. Minogue, *The Liberal Mind* (New York: Vintage Books 1968) 131

41 Ibid 133
42 *Realism and the Aim of Science* (London: Hutchinson 1982) 5
43 'The Rationality of Scientific Revolutions,' in R. Harré, ed, *Problems of Scientific Revolution* (Oxford: Oxford University Press 1975) 83 (hereafter RSR)
44 R.G. Collingwood, *An Essay on Philosophical Method* (Oxford 1933) 219
45 *On Human Conduct* (Oxford: Clarendon Press 1975) 87. I have explored this line of criticism further in 'Crisis and Renewal in the Social Sciences and the Colonies of Ourselves,' a paper presented at the joint International Political Science Association/Canadian Political Science Association/Société québécois science politique Roundtable, Crisis in Political Thought: In Search of New Directions, University of Ottawa, 2–4 October 1986, and forthcoming in the *International Political Science Review* (1989).
46 Hannah Arendt, *The Human Condition* (Chicago: University of Chicago Press 1958), and *Lectures on Kant's Political Philosophy* (Chicago: University of Chicago Press 1982) ed and intro by R.S. Beiner; Eric Voegelin, 'What Is Right by Nature?' in *Anamnesis* ed Gerhart Niemeyer (Notre Dame: University of Notre Dame Press 1978) 55–70; Michael Oakeshott, 'Learning and Teaching,' in R.S. Peters, ed, *The Concept of Education* (London: Routledge and Kegan Paul 1967) 156–76, and 'Political Education' in his *Rationalism in Politics* (London 1962); Hans Georg Gadamer, *Truth and Method* (New York: Seabury Press 1975); Jürgen Habermas, *Theory and Practice* trans John Viertel (Boston: Beacon Press 1974) introduction and chapters 6–7; and Ronald Beiner *Political Judgment* (London: Methuen 1983)
47 Anthony O'Hear, *Karl Popper* (London 1980); cf O'Hear, 'Rationality of Action and Theory-Testing in Popper,' *Mind* 84 (1975) 173–76; and John Krige, 'A Critique of Popper's Conception of the Relationship between Logic, Psychology, and a Critical Epistemology,' *Inquiry* 21 (1978) 313–35.
48 O'Hear, *Popper* 43
49 *The Uses of Argument* (Cambridge: Cambridge University Press 1958)
50 For example, see Karl Pribram's contribution to the volume in honour of Popper's 80th birthday, edited by Paul Levinson, *In Pursuit of Truth* (Atlantic Highlands, NJ: Humanities Press 1982), 'Scientist versus Philosopher on the Mind/Brain Issue and Induction,' or Peter Medawar's Jayne Lecture of 1968, *Induction and Intuition in Scientific Thought* (Philadelphia: American Philosophical Society 1969).
51 For a fuller defence of this conception of the growth of knowledge, see Stephen Toulmin, *The Uses of Argument, Human Understanding* I (Oxford: Oxford University Press 1972), and *The Philosophy of Science* (New York:

Harper and Row 1960); Thomas S. Kuhn, *The Essential Tension* (Chicago and London: University of Chicago Press 1977); and N.R. Hanson, *Observation and Explanation* (New York: Harper and Row 1971).

52 Toulmin, *The Uses of Argument* 184–5
53 I have explored this facet of Popper's thought in 'Logic and Liberty: Notes on Popper's Institutional Theory of Progress and the Philosophy of Life Chances,' presented before the Annual Meetings of the American Political Science Association in Chicago, 1–4 September 1983.
54 C.S. Peirce, 'How to Make Our Ideas Clear,' in *Essays in the Philosophy of Science* ed Vincent Tomas (Indianapolis and New York: Bobbs-Merrill 1957) 39
55 Oakeshott, *On Human Conduct* 236–7; cf, Victor Turner, *Dramas, Fields, and Metaphors* (Ithaca and London: Cornell University Press 1974); Erving Goffman, *Relations in Public* (New York: Basic Books 1971); and F.G. Bailey, *The Tactical Uses of Passion* (Ithaca and London: Cornell University Press 1983)

CHAPTER FIVE: CRITICAL RATIONALISM

1 Thomas Hobbes, *English Works* I ed W. Molesworth (London: 1839) 8; quoted by Sheldon S. Wolin, *Politics and Vision* (Boston: Little, Brown, and Co. 1961) 253
2 Karl R. Popper, 'Reason or Revolution?' *European Journal of Sociology* 11 (1970), 255–6 (hereafter RR)
3 For representative criticisms of Popper's 'decisionism,' see Jürgen Habermas, *Theory and Practice* trans John Viertel (Boston: Beacon Press 1973) 263 and 176–7; and Fred R. Dallmayr, 'Towards a Reconstruction of Ethics and Politics,' *Journal of Politics* 37 (1974) 937–8.
4 Max Weber, ' "Objectivity" in Social Science and Social Policy,' in *The Methodology of the Social Sciences* trans and ed E.A. Shils and Henry A. Finch (New York: Free Press 1949) 52
5 Anthony Giddens, *Studies in Social and Political Theory* (London: Hutchinson 1977) 89
6 Weber, 'Objectivity' 51–2
7 Ibid 57
8 *From Max Weber: Essays in Sociology* trans, ed, and intro by H.H. Gerth and C. Wright Mills (New York: Oxford University Press 1946) 120
9 Ibid
10 For possible connections between this variety of conventionalism and the non-rationalist thought of Hume and his fellow Scots Adam Smith and

Adam Ferguson, see F.A. Hayek, 'The Errors of Constructivism,' in his *New Studies in Philosophy, Politics, Economics and the History of Ideas* (Chicago: University of Chicago Press 1978) 11.

11 I.C. Jarvie, 'Popper on the Difference between the Natural and the Social Sciences,' in Paul Levinson, ed, *In Pursuit of Truth* (Atlantic Highlands, NJ: Humanities Press 1982) 83–4

12 Ibid 83

13 Cited in Dwight N. Lee and Robert N. Beck, 'The Meaning of "Historicism",' *American Historical Review* 59 (1954) 570. For an excellent introduction to Meinecke's thought and its place in the development of German historicism, see Georg G. Iggers, *The German Conception of History* (Middletown, Conn: Wesleyan University Press 1968).

14 See the excellent discussion of Dilthey's thought in the context of his theory of the Geisteswissenschaften by Rudolf A. Makreel, *Dilthey: Philosopher of the Human Studies* (Princeton: Princeton University Press 1975) especially part I. H.P. Rickman has made a number of Dilthey's most important writings available in English translation in two recent collections, both with useful introductions: *Pattern and Meaning in History: Thoughts on History and Society* (New York: Harper and Row 1962) and *Dilthey: Selected Writings* (Cambridge: Cambridge University Press 1976).

15 'On the Theory of the Objective Mind,' delivered in German to the 14th International Congress of Philosophy in Vienna, in September 1968, now chapter 4 of *Objective Knowledge*; see especially sections 11–12.

16 Jarvie, 'Difference' 84

17 Though I disagree with his interpretation of *The Poverty of Historicism*, I am indebted to I.C. Jarvie ('Difference' 85) for the idea of such a presentation.

18 Jarvie, 'Difference' 86

19 Ibid

20 Ibid

21 On the immense appeal of the marginalist revolution in Austrian economics for other liberal social scientists at the University of Vienna, see John Torrance, 'The Emergence of Sociology in Austria, 1885–1935,' *European Journal of Sociology* 17 (1976) 185–219, and William M. Johnston, *The Austrian Mind* (Berkeley: University of California Press, 1972) chapter 4.

22 For this illustration of the modus tollens I am indebted to Mark Blaug, *The Methodology of Economics* (Cambridge: Cambridge University Press 1980) 13.

23 Ibid 14

24 W.H. Dray, *Laws and Explanation in History* (Oxford 1957). Cf, Maurice

Mandlebaum, 'Historical Explanation: The Problem of "Covering Laws," '
History and Theory 1 (1961) 119–41; Carl G. Hempel, *Reasons and Covering
Laws in History: A Symposium* (New York: New York University Press
1963) 143–63; and Samuel H. Beer, 'Causal Explanation and Imaginative
Reenactment,' *History and Theory* 3 (1963) 6–29.

25 'Historical Explanation: The Popper-Hempel Theory Reconsidered,'
History and Theory 4 (1964) 3

26 'Popper's Examination of Historicism,' in P.A. Schilpp, ed, *The Philosophy
of Karl Popper* II (La Salle: Open Court, 1974) 909; Nicholas Tilley,
'Popper, Historicism, and Emergence,' *Philosophy of the Social Sciences* 12
(1982) 59–67

27 This also is a passage from H.A.L. Fisher's *A History of Europe*, cited by
W.H. Dray, *Philosophy of History* (Englewood Cliffs, NJ: Prentice Hall
1964) 62.

28 For helpful introductions and analyses of marginalism, see: James Bonar,
'The Austrian Economists and Their Theories of Value,' *Quarterly Journal
of Economics* 3 (1888–9) 1–31; Emil Kauder, 'Intellectual and Political
Roots of the Older Austrian,' *Zeitschrift fur Nationalokonomie* 17 (1957)
411–25; F.A. Hayek, 'Menger, Carl,' *International Encyclopedia of the Social
Sciences* x (1969) 124–7, and 'The Place of Menger's *Grundsätze* in the
History of Economic Thought' in Hayek, *New Studies* 270–82; George
Stigler, 'The Economics of Carl Menger,' *Journal of Political Economy*
45 (1937) 229–50; Phyllis Deane, *The Evolution of Economic Ideas* (Cam-
bridge: Cambridge University Press 1978) chapters 7–8; Eugen Bohm-
Bawerk, 'The Historical versus the Deductive Method in Political Economy,'
Annals of the American Academy of Political and Social Science 1 (1891), 244–
71, and 'The Austrian Economists,' ibid 361–84; and A.W. Coats, 'The
Historicists' Reaction in English Political Economy,' *Economica* (1954) 143–
53. Menger's *Grundsätze* is available in English as *Principles of Economics*
trans Dingwall and Hoselitz (Glencoe: Free Press 1950). Simultaneous with
Menger's formulation of marginalism were the writings of William S. Jevons and the French-born Swiss Leon Walras. Jevons first published
his views in *The Theory of Political Economy* (1871) and Walras in his *Elements
d'économie politique pure* (1874).

29 Torrance, 'Emergence of Sociology' 202

30 L.M. Lachmann, 'Methodological Individualism and the Market Economy,'
in E. Streissler, ed, *Roads to Freedom: Essays in Honour of F.A. Kayek* (London: Routledge and Kegan Paul 1969) 103

31 'Scientism and the Study of Society,' reprinted in J. O'Neill, ed, *Modes of
Individualism and Collectivism* (London: Heinemann 1973) 32

32 Torrance, 'Emergence of Sociology' 206

33 For useful introductions to this literature, see Robert Abrams, *Foundations of Political Analysis* (New York: Columbia University Press 1980); Brian Barry and Russell Hardin, eds, *Rational Man and Irrational Society?* (Beverly Hills: Sage 1982); Brian Barry, 'Methodology versus Ideology: The "Economic" Approach Revisited,' in E. Ostrom, ed, *Strategies of Political Inquiry* (Beverly Hills: Sage 1982) 123–47; Mark Sproule-Jones, 'Public Choice and Natural Resources,' *American Political Science Review* 76 (1982) 790–804; Michael Laver, *The Politics of Private Desires* (Harmondsworth: Penguin Books 1981); and D.C. Mueller, *Public Choice* (Cambridge: Cambridge University Press 1979).

34 W.H Walsh, ' "Meaning" in History,' in P. Gardiner, ed, *Theories of History* (Glencoe, NY: Free Press 1959); and Burleigh Taylor Wilkins, *Has History Any Meaning?* (Sussex: Harvester 1978) chapter 1

35 For an excellent example of the sort of sensitivity I have in mind, see W.H. Dray, 'Interpretive Frameworks in Historiography,' *Queen's Quarterly* 89 (winter 1982) 722–39.

36 *On the Study Methods of Our Time* trans Elio Gianturco (Indianapolis: Bobbs-Merrill 1965). Cf Isaiah Berlin, 'The Philosophical Ideas of Giambattista Vico,' in his *Vico and Herder* (New York: Viking Press 1976).

37 See Charles Taylor, 'Interpretation and the Sciences of Man,' in Paul Rabinow and William M. Sullivan, eds, *Interpretive Social Science: A Reader* (Los Angeles, Berkeley, and London: University of California Press 1979) 25–71; Paul Ricoeur, 'The Model of the Text: Meaningful Action Considered as a Text,' in Rabinow and Sullivan, *Interpretive Social Science* 73–101; and Zygmunt Bauman, *Hermeneutics and Social Science* (London: Heinemann 1979).

38 For an illuminating discussion, see William E. Connolly, 'Theoretical Self-Consciousness,' in his and Glen Gordon's edited volume, *Social Structure and Political Theory* (Lexington, Mass: D.C. Heath 1974) chapter 2.

39 Daniel Bell and Irving Kristol, eds, *The Crisis in Economic Theory* (New York: Harper and Row 1981); Blaug, *The Methodology of Economics* chapter 15; E.J. Mishan, *What Political Economy Is All About: An Exposition and Critique* (Cambridge: Cambridge University Press 1982) part v; and A. Gamble and P. Walton, *Capitalism in Crisis: Inflation and the State* (London: Macmillan 1976) chapter 2

40 'Rational Fools: A Critique of the Behavioural Foundations of Economic Theory,' in Martin Hollis and Frank Hahn, eds, *Philosophy and Economic Theory* (Oxford: Oxford University Press 1979) 102, originally published in *Philosophy and Public Affairs* 6 (1976–7) 317–44

41 Douglas Rae et al, *Equalities* (Cambridge, Mass, and London: Yale University Press 1981) 131

42 *Power and Civility* trans Edmund Jephcott (New York: Pantheon Books 1981) 241

43 Ibid 141–2

44 For a slightly different use of the notion of the 'colonies of our selves,' see the splendid development of the metaphor, ultimately derived from the great German sociologist Georg Simmel, by anthropologist F.G. Bailey in *The Tactical Uses of Passion* (Ithaca and London: Cornell University Press 1983) chapter 2.

45 For an extended discussion of this point, see Charles Taylor, 'The Diversity of Goods,' in A.K. Sen and Bernard Williams, eds, *Utilitarianism and Beyond* (Cambridge: Cambridge University Press 1982) 129–44; and 'Rationality' in Martin Hollis and Steven Lukes, eds, *Rationality and Relativism* (Oxford: Basil Blackwell 1982) 87–105.

46 Amaryta Sen, 'The Impossibility of a Paretian Liberal,' in Hollis and Hahn, eds, *Philosophy and Economic Theory* chapter 8, originally published in *Journal of Political Economy* 78 (1970) 152–7

47 'From Substantive to Procedural Rationality' in Hollis and Hahn, eds, *Philosophy and Economic Theory* 68, originally in S. Latsis, ed, *Method and Approach in Economics* (1976)

48 This way of stating the matter was suggested to me by Alan Ryan in his meditation on the implications of the late Erving Goffman's work, 'Maximising, Moralising and Dramatising,' in Christopher Hookway and Philip Petit, eds, *Action and Interpretation* (Cambridge: Cambridge University Press 1978) 65–82.

CHAPTER SIX: FALLIBILISM AND THE SOCIOLOGY OF KNOWLEDGE

1 Karl Mannheim, *Ideology and Utopia*, trans Louis Wirth and Edward Shils (New York: Harcourt, Brace, and World 1936) 264 (hereafter *IU*); cf Gustav Bergmann, 'Ideology,' *Ethics* (April 1951) 205–18; Talcott Parsons, review of Alexander von Schelting's *Mas Weber's Wissenschaftslehre* in *American Sociological Review* 7 (Aug 1936) 681; Hans Speir, review of *Ideology and Utopia* in *American Journal of Sociology* (July 1937) 160–1; and Richard Ashcraft, 'Political Theory and Political Action in Karl Mannheim's Thought: Reflections upon *Ideology and Utopia* and Its Critics,' *Comparative Studies of Society and History* 23 (1981) 23–50, for an illuminating discussion of Mannheim's many critics, but with little reference to Popper's frontal assault. Several other important responses to *Ideology and Utopia* have been

collected in Volker Meja and Nico Stehr, eds, *The Sociology of Knowledge Dispute* (London: Routledge and Kegan Paul 1987), an abridged translation of the two-volume *Der Streit und die Wissenssoziologie* (Frankfurt: Suhrkamp 1982), parts of which have also appeared in International Society for the Sociology of Knowledge, *Newsletter* 10 nos. 1 and 2 (May 1986).

2 John Curtis and James Petras, eds, *The Sociology of Knowledge: A Reader* (New York and Washington: Praeger 1970) 649–60

3 I.C. Jarvie, *Concepts and Society* (London and Boston: Routledge, Kegan and Paul 1972)

4 Compare Renford Bambrough, ed, *Plato, Popper and Politics* (Cambridge: Heffer 1967); Walter Kaufmann, 'The Hegel Myth and Its Method,' in his *Hegel's Political Philosophy* (New York: Atherton 1970) chapter 10; G.E.R. Lloyd, 'Popper versus Kirk: A Controversy in the Interpretation of Greek Science,' *British Journal for the History of Science* 18 (1967) 21–38; W.H. Walsh 'Plato and the Philosophy of History: History and Theory in *The Republic*,' *History and Theory* 2 (1962) 3–16; and Richard Kraut, 'Socrates and Democracy,' in G. Currie and A. Musgrave, eds, *Popper and the Human Sciences* (Dordrecht, Boston, and Lancaster 1985) chapter 12.

5. Evidence that Mannheim's thought and the sociology of knowledge are experiencing something of a renaissance can be found in my review of Colin Loader's recent study, *The Intellectual Development of Karl Mannheim* (Cambridge and London: Cambridge University Press 1985), in *Journal of the History of the Behavioral Sciences* 23 (Oct 1987) 395–8, note 1.

6 Derek L. Phillips, 'Epistemology and the Sociology of Knowledge: The Contributions of Mannheim, Mills, and Merton,' *Theory and Society* 1 (1975) 59–88

7 *Essays on Sociology and Social Psychology* trans and ed Paul Kecskemeti (London: Routledge and Kegan Paul 1953) 30

8 *Essays on the Sociology of Knowledge* trans and ed Paul Kecskemeti (London: Routledge and Kegan Paul 1952) 194

9 Ibid, translation modified by Kurt Wolff, editor's introduction to *From Karl Mannheim* (New York: Oxford University Press 1971) lii

10 This work brought to my attention by David Kettler's rich essay, 'Sociology of Knowledge and Moral Philosophy: The Place of Traditional Problems in the Formation of Mannheim's Thought,' *Political Science Quarterly* 82 (Sept 1967) 399–426, at 424; Mannheim's essay has been translated in its entirety as part I of *Structures of Thinking* ed and intro by David Kettler, Volker Meja, and Nico Stehr, trans J.J. Shapiro and S.W. Nicholsen (London, Boston, and Henley: Routledge and Kegan Paul 1982).

11 On the significance of the distinction between Seinsverbundenheit ('connectedness to existence') and Seinsgebundenheit (or 'existential boundedness') in Mannheim's sociology of knowledge, and of its omission altogether
from the English version of *Ideologie und Utopie*, see the translation of
Mannheim's *Habilitationsschrift* (Heidelberg 1925) in David Kettler, Volker
Meja, and Nico Stehr, *Conservatism* (London and New York: Routledge
and Kegan Paul 1986), 'Introduction: The Design of Conservatism,'
especially 12–13 and 25 note 31.

12 *Economy and Society* 1 trans and ed G. Roth and C. Wittich (New York:
Bedminster Press 1968) 4

13 See, for example, his Introduction to the *Critique de la raison dialectique:
Search for a Method*, trans Hazel Barnes (New York: Knopf 1967).

14 The work of Thelma Lavine and Arthur Child was a notable exception to
this rule. See, for example, Lavine's provocative essays, 'Naturalism and
the Sociological Analysis of Knowledge,' in Yervant Krikorian, ed, *Naturalism and the Human Spirit* (New York: Columbia University Press 1944);
'The Sociological Analysis of Cognitive Norms,' *Journal of Philosophy* 39
(1942) 342–56; and 'Karl Mannheim and Contemporary Functionalism,'
Philosophy and Phenomenological Research 25 (1965) 560–71. Two of Child's
more important contributions to this debate are his 'The Theoretical
Possibility of the Sociology of Knowledge,' *Ethics* 51 (1941 200–19), and
'On the Theory of the Categories,' *Philosophy and Phenomenological Research*
7 (1946) 316–35.

15 *Essays on the Sociology of Knowledge* 228–9

16 *From Max Weber* ed and trans H.H. Gerth and C. Wright Mills (New York:
Oxford 1957) 145. Cf Toby E. Huff, 'On the Methodology of the Social
Sciences: A Review Essay,' *Philosophy of the Social Sciences* 11 no. 4 (Dec
1981) and 12 no. 1 (March 1982) for a helpful survey of Weber's work and
the interpretive context from which it arose.

17 *Ideology and Utopia* 38, emphasis added. Cf the illuminating discussion
of this point by Ashcraft, 'Political Theory and Political Action' especially
26 and 44–5.

18 For more on his conception of a revised model of social rationality, see
part 1 of Mannheim's *Man and Society in an Age of Reconstruction* trans
Edward Shils (New York: Harcourt, Brace and World 1940).

19 Ibid 254; cf *Essay on Sociology and Social Psychology* 185–94.

20 Ashcraft, 'Political Theory and Political Action' 34

21 *Ideology and Utopia* 3, 28, and 43. For historical background see Peter

Steinberger, 'Hegel as a Social Scientist,' *American Political Science Review* 71 (1977) 95–110; and Ashcraft, 'Political Theory and Political Action.'

22 *Ideology and Utopia* 28 and 58–9; cf Kurt Wolff's 'Introduction: A Reading of Karl Mannheim,' *From Karl Mannheim* xxix and lxxxi.

23 German original of *Ideology and Utopia* trans Kurt Wolff, *From Karl Mannheim*, lxxxi

24 *Man and Society in an Age of Reconstruction* 381

25 The influence of Nietzsche and/or Heidegger may account for the latter thinkers' deeper scepticism, and at times hostility, toward the prospects of 'enlightenment.' See, for example, Michel Foucault, *Language, Counter-memory, Practice* ed with intro by Donald F. Bouchard (Ithaca: Cornell University Press 1977) 139–64; Hans George Gadamer, *Truth and Method* (New York: Crossroad 1984; originally published in German in 1960) especially 235–74, 413–48, and 460–598; and *Reason in the Age of Science* trans F.G. Lawrence (Cambridge, Mass: M.I.T. Press 1981); and more generally Zygmunt Bauman, *Hermeneutics and Social Sciences* (New York: Columbia University Press 1978); Fred R. Dallamyr, *Polis and Praxis* (Cambridge, Mass: M.I.T. Press 1984) chapters 3–4; and Richard J. Bernstein, *Beyond Objectivism and Relativism* (Philadelphia: University of Pennsylvania Press 1983) part 3 in particular.

26 *Ideology and Utopia* 5; cf *Man and Society* 27.

27 David Kettler, Volker Meja, and Nico Stehr, *Karl Mannheim* (Chichester, London, and New York 1984) 153; cf 62, 64–5, 78 note 19, and 87

28 Ibid, 154

29 *Knowledge and Human Interests* trans Jeremy Shapiro (Boston: Beacon Press 1971) 214

30 For further discussion of this aspect of Habermas's thought, see Thomas McCarthy, *The Critical Theory of Jurgen Habermas* (Cambridge, Mass: M.I.T. Press 1978) chapters 3 and 4; Raymond Geuss, *The Idea of a Critical Theory* (Cambridge: Cambridge University Press 1981); and Gabris Kortian, *Metacritique* (Cambridge: Cambridge University Press 1980).

31 *Knowledge and Human Interests* chapters 10–12

32 Anthony Giddens, *New Rules of Sociological Method* (London: Hutchinson 1976) 59

33 *Knowledge and Human Interests* 166

34 On the fluctuations in Mannheim's thought along these lines, see Kettler, Meja, and Stehr, *Mannheim* 29; and, more generally, Loader, *The Intellectual Development of Karl Mannheim*.

CHAPTER SEVEN: CONSERVING LIBERALISM

1 Lionel Trilling, *The Liberal Imagination* (New York: Scribner's 1976; originally published in 1950) x
2 Sheldon S. Wolin, *Politics and Vision* (Boston: Little, Brown and Co. 1961) 194
3 Judith Shklar, *After Utopia* (Princeton: Princeton University Press 1957) ix; cf, Isaiah Berlin, 'Political Ideas in the Twentieth Century,' in his *Four Essays on Liberty* (London and Oxford: Oxford University Press 1969) 1–40; Henry S. Kariel, *In Search of Authority: Twentieth Century Political Thought* (Glencoe, NY: Free Press 1964); D.J. Manning, *Liberalism* (London: J.M. Dent 1976) 94–118 in particular; and Rodney Barker, *Political Ideas in Modern Britain* (London: Methuen 1978).
4 Trilling, *Imagination* xiii
5 In 'Peter Gay and the Politics of Skeptical Liberalism,' *Politics and Society* 1 (1970) 133–49, Robert Booth Fowler notes a similar tendency in the thought of Isaiah Berlin, Bernard Crick, Reinhold Niebuhr, Judith Shklar, Thomas Thorson, and T.D. Weldon, as well as Peter Gay.
6 Isaiah Berlin, 'Does Political Theory Still Exist?' in his *Concepts and Categories* ed H. Hardy and intro by Bernard Williams (New York: Viking Press 1979) 149
7 Karl R. Popper, 'On Reason and the Open Society,' *Encounter* 38 (May 1972) 13
8 Interesting comparisons of Bergson's and Popper's 'open' and 'closed' societies can be found in Dante Germino, 'Preliminary Reflections on the Open Society: Bergson, Popper, and Voegelin,' *The Open Society in Theory and Practice*, which he co-edited with Klaus von Beyme (The Hague: Martinus Nijhoff 1974) 1–20; and Richard Vernon, 'The "Great Society" and the "Open Society": Liberalism in Hayek and Popper,' *Canadian Journal of Political Science* 9 (1976) 170–5.
9 In 2 volumes (Baton Rouge 1957), II: *The World of the Polis* 1 and 3
10 *Collected Papers of Charles Sanders Peirce* I, ed Charles Harshorne and Paul Weiss, paragraph 615, cited by Richard Bernstein, *Praxis and Action* (Philadelphia: University of Pennsylvania Press 1971) 196
11 Wolin *Politics and Vision* 395, 191–5, and 313–15
12 Kenneth R. Minogue, *The Liberal Mind* (New York: Vintage Books 1968) 69
13 Wolin, *Politics and Vision* 392
14 Perry Anderson, 'Components of the National Culture,' in *Student Power* ed Robin Blackburn (Harmondsworth: Penguin Books 1969) 231. Some of Popper's other radical critics include: A.C. Macintyre, 'Breaking the

Chains of Reason,' in *Out of Apathy* ed E.P. Thompson (London: Stevens 1960); Michael Freeman, 'Sociology and Utopia,' *British Journal of Sociology* 26 (1975) 220–35; James Petras, 'Popperism: The Scarcity of Reason,' *Science and Society* 30 (1966) 1–10; and Maurice Cornforth, *The Open Philosophy and the Open Society* (London: International Publishers 1968).

15 On Schumpeter's work in relation to American pluralism, see David Ricci, 'Democracy Attenuated: Schumpeter, The Process Theory and American Democratic Thought,' *Journal of Politics* 32 (1970) 239–67.

16 Some recent examples of such a relativization of democracy include C.B. Macpherson, *The Real World of Democracy* (Toronto: CBC 1965); Carl Cohen, *Democracy* (New York: Random House 1973); and John Plamenatz, *Democracy and Illusion* (London: Macmillan 1973).

17 Trilling, *Imagination* xiv

18 Ralf Dahrendorf, *Life Chances* (Chicago: University of Chicago, 1979). I have developed this connection between Popper, Weber, and Dahrendorf in 'Logic and Liberty: Notes on Popper's Institutional Theory of Progress and the Philosophy of Life Chances,' a paper presented to the Annual Meetings of the American Political Science Association in Chicago, Illinois, September 1983.

19 *Themes from the Lectures* trans John O'Neill (Evanston: Northwestern University Press 1970) 31

20 For helpful discussions of these problems in Kant's political theory, see Lucien Goldmann, *Immanuel Kant* (London: New Left Books 1971); Ronald Beiner, *Political Judgment* (London: Methuen 1983) chapter 3; and Michael J. Sandel, *Liberalism and the Limits of Justice* (Cambridge: Cambridge University Press 1982) especially introduction, chapter 4, and conclusion.

21 *The History of Manners* trans Edmund Jephcott (New York: Pantheon Books, 1978) 100

22 Goldmann, *Kant* 170

23 Ibid

24 Ibid

25 'Rational Conduct,' in his *Rationalism in Politics and Other Essays* 105

26 'Reflections on Social Theory and Political Practice,' the 1981 Wolfson College Lecture Series, in *Social Theory and Political Practice* ed Christopher Lloyd (Oxford: Oxford University Press 1983) 36

27 Ibid

28 For an exceptionally rich treatment of this dimension of contemporary political reality, see Crawford Young, *The Politics of Cultural Pluralism* (Madison and London: University of Wisconsin Press 1976).

CHAPTER EIGHT: THE LIMITS OF POPPER'S LIBERALISM

1 Max Weber, *Economy and Society: An Outline of Interpretive Sociology* 3 vols, ed Guenther Roth and Claus Wittich, trans E. Fischoff et al (New York: Bedminster Press 1968) 1393 and 992

2 R.M. MacIver, *The Rampants We Guard* (New York 1960) 57

3 Richard Hofstadter, *Social Darwinism in American Thought* (Boston: Beacon Press 1955) Introduction

4 For a critical survey of the most recent commentary on Popper's thought, see my essay, 'Masons, Evangelists, and Heretics in Popper's Cathedral,' *Queen's Quarterly* (winter 1984) 679–92; and my review of G. Currie and A. Musgrave, eds, *Popper and the Human Sciences* (Dordrecht, Boston, Lancaster: Martinus Nijhoff 1985), in *Ethics* 98 (1988).

5 Michael Ruse, 'Karl Popper's Philosophy of Biology,' *Philosophy of Science* 44 (1977) 639

6 For an extended analysis of these criticisms, see ibid.

7 This distinction reveals the criticisms of Popper by Ernest Gellner, in *The Legitimation of Belief* (Cambridge: Cambridge University Press 1974) 170–6, to be wide of the mark.

8 *The Sociology of Georg Simmel* ed and trans Kurt H. Wolff (Glencoe, NY: Free Press 1950) 312

9 F.G. Bailey, *The Tactical Uses of Passion* (Ithaca and London: Cornell University Press 1983) 24

10 Ibid 23

11 For an excellent discussion of this point see Charles Taylor, 'The Diversity of Goods,' in *Utilitarianism and Beyond* ed Amaryta Sen and Bernard Williams (Cambridge: Cambridge University Press 1982) 129–44.

12 Alistair Hannay, 'Freedom and Plastic Control,' *Canadian Journal of Philosophy* 2 (1972) 284

13 John Kekes, 'Popper in Perspective,' *Metaphilosophy* 3 (1977) 55–6

14 Ibid 56

15 Marjorie Grene, 'People and Other Animals,' *Philosophical Forum* 3 (winter 1972) 165

16 Quoted in ibid 170

17 For useful discussions of Plessner's thought, see ibid 169–70, and Peter Berger and Thomas Luckmann, *The Social Construction of Reality* (Garden City, NY: Anchor Doubleday 1967) 17 and chapter 2.

18 Susan Haack, 'Epistemology with a Knowing Subject,' *Review of Metaphysics* 33 (Dec 1979) 324–5

19 Philip Rieff, *The Triumph of the Therapeutic: Uses of Faith after Freud* (New York: Harper and Row 1968) chapter 2
20 Ibid 73
22 Charles Taylor, 'Interpretation and the Science of Man,' *Review of Metaphysics* 25 (Sept 1971) 3–51.
23 H.L.A. Hart, *The Concept of Law* (Oxford 1961) 189
24 Taylor, 'The Diversity of Goods' 130
25 Ibid 132
26 I borrow this use of 'absolute' explanations from Bernard Williams, *Descartes – The Project of Inquiry* (Harmondsworth: Penguin Books 1978).
27 *On the Study of Methods of Our Time* (1709) trans Elio Gianturco (Indianapolis: Bobbs-Merrill 1965); cf Jürgen Habermas, *Theory and Practice* trans John Viertel (Boston: Beacon Press 1973).
28 Ralph Hummel, *The Bureaucratic Experience* (New York: St. Martin's Press 1977), and Langdon Winner, *Autonomous Technology* (Cambridge, Mass: M.I.T. Press 1977)

Bibliography

WORKS BY POPPER

'Die Gedachtnispglege unter dem Gesichtspunkt der Selbsttatigkeit,' *Die Quelle* 81 (1931) 607–19

Logik der Forschung (Vienna: Julius Springer 1934)

The Open Society and Its Enemies I and II (London: Routledge and Kegan Paul 1945; revised edition, Princeton, NJ: Princeton University Press 1971)

'What Can Logic Do for Philosophy?' *Proceedings of the Aristotelian Society* supplementary volume, 22 (1948) 141–54

The Poverty of Historicism (London: Routledge and Kegan Paul 1957; revised edition, New York and Evanston: Harper and Row 1964)

'Philosophy of Science: A Personal Report,' in C.A. Mace, ed, *British Philosophy in the Mid-Century* (London: Allen and Unwin 1957)

The Logic of Scientific Discovery (London: Hutchinson 1959; revised edition, New York and Evanston: Harper and Row 1968)

Conjectures and Refutations (London: Routledge and Kegan Paul 1963; 2nd edition, New York and Evanston: Harper and Row 1968)

'Le rationalité et le statut de principe de rationalité,' in E.M. Claassen, ed, *Les fondements philosophiques des systèmes économiques* (Paris: Payot 1967) 142–50

'Remarks on the Problems of Demarcation and Rationality,' in Imre Lakatos and Alan Musgrave, eds, *Problems in the Philosophy of Science* (Amsterdam: North-Holland 1968) 88–102

'Normal Science and Its Dangers,' in Imre Lakatos and Alan Musgrave, eds, *Criticism and the Growth of Knowledge* (Cambridge: Cambridge University Press 1970) 51–8

'Reason or Revolution?' *European Journal of Sociology* 11 (1970) 13–18

Objective Knowledge: An Evolutionary Approach (Oxford: Oxford University Press 1972)

'On Reason and the Open Society,' *Encounter* 38 (May 1972) 12–18

'Conversation with Karl Popper,' in Bryan Magee, ed, *Modern British Philosophy* (London: Paladin 1973) 88–107

'Indeterminism Is Not Enough,' *Encounter* 40 (April 1973), 10–26

'Memories of Otto Neurath,' in Marie Neurath and R.S. Cohen, eds, *Empiricism and Sociology* (Holland and Boston: D.H. Reidel 1973) 51–6

'Intellectual Autobiography of Karl Popper,' in P.A. Schilpp, ed, *The Philosophy of Karl Popper* I (La Salle: Open Court 1974) 3–181

'Replies to My Critics,' in P.A. Schilpp, ed, *The Philosophy of Karl Popper* II (La Salle: Open Court, 1974) 961–1197

'How I See Philosophy,' in J. Bontempo and S.J. Odell, eds, *The Owl of Minerva* (New York: McGraw-Hill 1975) 41–55

'The Rationality of Scientific Revolutions,' in R. Harré, ed, *Problems of Scientific Revolution* (Oxford: Oxford University Press 1975) 72–101

'The Logic of the Social Sciences,' in T.W. Adorno et al, *The Positivist Dispute in German Sociology* trans Glen Adey and David Frisby (London: Heineman 1976) 87–104

The Self and Its Brain with John Eccles (Berlin: Springer Verlag 1977)

'Some Remarks on Panpsychism and Epiphenomenalism,' *Dialectica* 31 (1977) 177–86

'Three Worlds,' in S. McMurrin, ed, *The Tanner Lectures on Human Values* (Salt Lake City: University of Utah Press 1980)

Postscript to the Logic of Scientific Discovery: I: *Realism and the Aim of Science* II: *The Open Universe: An Argument for Indeterminism,* III: *Quantum Theory and the Schism in Physics,* ed W.W. Bartley, III (New Jersey: Rowman and Littlefield 1982)

WRITINGS ON POPPER

Ackermann, Robert *The Philosophy of Karl Popper* (Amherst: University of Massachusetts Press 1976)

Agassi, Joseph *Science in Flux* (Dordrecht: Reidel 1975)

— *Towards an Historiography of Science* (The Hague: Mouton 1963)

Albert, Hans *Treatise on Critical Reason* trans Mary Varney Rorty (Princeton: Princeton University Press 1985)

Bambrough, Renford, ed, *Popper, Plato and Politics* (Cambridge and New York: Barnes and Noble 1967) Bartley, W.W., III 'Theory of Language and Philosophy of Science as Instruments of Educational Reform: Wittgenstein and Popper,' in R.S. Cohen and M.W. Wartofsky, eds, *Boston Studies in the Philosophy of Science* 14 (1974) 307–37

Bunge, Mario, ed *The Critical Approach to Science and Philosophy* (Glencoe, NY: Free Press 1964)

Burke, T.E. *The Philosophy of Karl Popper* (Manchester: Manchester University Press 1983)

Cornforth, Maurice *The Open Philosophy and the Open Society* (New York: International Publishers 1968)

Currie, Gregory, and Alan Musgrave, eds *Popper and the Human Sciences* (Dordrecht: Martinus Nijhoff 1985)

Donagan, Alan 'Historical Explanation: The Popper-Hempel Theory Reconsidered,' *History and Theory* 4 (1964) 3–26

Freeman, Michael 'Sociology and Utopia: Some Reflections on the Social Philosophy of Karl Popper,' *British Journal of Sociology* 24 (1975) 220–35

Gray, John N. 'The Liberalism of Karl Popper,' *Government and Opposition* 11 (1976) 337–55

Grove, J.W. 'Popper "Demystified": The Curious Ideas of Bloor (and Some Others) about World 3,' *Philosophy of the Social Sciences* 10 (1980) 173–80

Hannay, Alistair 'Freedom and Plastic Control,' *Canadian Journal of Philosophy* 2 (1972) 177–96

Hutchison, T.W. *Knowledge and Ignorance in Economics* (Chicago: University of Chicago Press 1977)

Johansson, Ingvar *A Critique of Karl Popper's Methodology* (Stockholm: Akademiforlaget 1975)

Kekes, John 'Popper in Perspective,' *Metaphilosophy* 3 (1977) 36–61

Kelly, Derek A. 'Popper's Ontology: An Exposition and Critique,' *Southern Journal of Philosophy* (spring 1975) 71–82

Levinson, Paul, ed *In Pursuit of Truth: Essays in Honour of Karl Popper's 80th Birthday* (New Jersey: Humanities Press 1982)

Levinson, Ronald B. *In Defense of Plato* (Cambridge, Mass: Harvard University Press 1953)

Lieberson, Jonathan 'Karl Popper,' *Social Research* 49 (1982) 68–115

Magee, Bryan *Popper* (London: Fontana 1973)

Malherbe, J.-F. *La philosophie de Karl Popper et le positivisme logique* (Paris: Press Universitaires de Namur et France 1976)

Medawar, Peter *Induction and Intuition in Scientific Thought* (Philadelphia: American Philosophical Society 1969)

Mellor, D.H. 'The Popper Phenomenon,' *Philosophy* 52 (1977) 195–202

O'Hear, Anthony *Karl Popper* (London: Routledge and Kegan Paul 1980)

— 'Rationality of Action and Theory-Testing in Popper,' *Mind* 84 (1975) 173–6

Quinton, Anthony 'Karl Popper: Politics without Essences,' in A. de Crespigny and K. Minogue, eds, *Contemporary Political Philosophers* (New York: Dodd and Mead 1975) 147–67

Ruse, Michael 'Karl Popper's Philosophy of Biology,' *Philosophy of Science* 44 (1977) 638–61

Ryan, Alan ' "Normal Science" or Political Ideology?' in P. Laslett, W.G. Runciman, and Q. Skinner, eds, *Philosophy, Politics and Society* (Oxford: Basil Blackwell 1972) 86–100

Schilpp, Paul Arthur, ed *The Philosophy of Karl Popper* 2 vols. (La Salle, Ill.: Open Court, 1974)

Skagestad, Peter *Making Sense of History: The Philosophies of Popper and Collingwood* (Oslo: Scandinavian Universities Press 1975)

Stove, David *After Popper* (Oxford: Pergamon Press 1982)

Tilley, Nicolas 'Popper, Historicism, and Emergence,' *Philosophy of the Social Sciences* 12 (1982) 59–67

Vernon, Richard 'The "Great Society" and the "Open Society": Liberalism in Hayek and Popper,' *Canadian Journal of Political Science* 9 (1976) 261–76

Wilkins, Burleigh T. *Has History Any Meaning? A Critique of Popper's Philosophy of History* (Hassocks, Sussex: Harvester 1978)

Williams, Douglas E. 'Masons, Evangelists and Heretics in Karl Popper's Cathedral,' *Queen's Quarterly* 91 (autumn 1984) 679–92

Index

(Popper, Karl Raimund, *continued*)
his evolutionism, 111, 165–70; on
experimental research design, 97;
on facts and their confusion with
values, 90–2, 94; and fallibilism, 6,
15, 48, 54, 59, 76, 85, 99, 144;
on falsificationism, 65–6, 106; on
fascism, 96; on foundationalism,
76; on freedom, 15, 47, 50, 60, 70,
71, 86, 89, 136, 139, 144, 150,
152, 154–5; on Freud, 16–17; Geisteswissenschaften, the tradition of
the, 97, 108; on generalization in
science, 97; and Glöckel's Pedagogic Institute, 17, 56, 195–6 n28;
on the growth of knowledge, 19,
51, 61–2, 69, 99, 137, 143; on
happiness as a moral ideal, 149–50;
the 'heat' of his vision, 25, 60, 75;
on Hegel, ix, 86–7, 92, 129–30;
and Heiden, 87; and hermeneutics,
97; as a historian of ideas,
ix–x, 122, 126; on 'historical sciences,' 108; and historicism, 10, 24,
92, 96, 101, 104, 107, 111, 113–
14, 120, 130, 155; on history, 51,
113–14, 137; 'The History of Our
Times: An Optimist's View,' 137,
140, 142; on the history of science,
53; and holism (*also see* collectivism), 23, 104, 108–9; on hope and
progress, the grounds for belief
in, viii, 51, 141, 146; 'How I See
Philosophy,' xiii; on humanism, 51,
75; on hypothetico-deductive
explanations, 6, 106–8; and
idealism, 75; on ideas, the power
of, 50, 140; his ideas, the reception of, 4–8, 49; on imprinting
as learning theory, 61; on in-

determinism, 72; and individualism, 49, 139, 141, 145, 156,
162, 164, 178, 186; on induction,
55, 60, 101; on institutuions, 86,
88, 93, 102, 104, 147–9, 153–5;
'Intellectual Autobiography,' xiii;
on the intersubjectivity of scientific
method, 102; on intuitionism, 64–5,
86; on irrationalism, 47, 49, 85–7,
120, 122; on justice, 50; on justifi-
cationism, 100; on Kafka, 87; the
Kantian structure of his thought,
vii, 7, 8, 46–51, 54, 60, 86, 91,
100, 105, 114, 138, 146–7, 150;
on language, the functions
of, 57–62, 70, 95, 102; law, the
rule of, 50; on laws, historical, 97,
109; on laws, natural (or universal), 93, 97, 110; on laws, normative
(or social), 93, 95; and liberalism,
vii–viii, 7–9, 15–16, 46, 50, 53,
77, 92, 95, 136–7, 142, 151; on life,
the value of, 48; on the juridical
role and priority of logic, 48, 58,
76, 100; 'Logic and Philosophy,'
xiii; *The Logic of Scientific Discovery*,
xiii, 22, 66, 106; on the logic of
the situation, 111–15; 'The Logic
of the Social Sciences,' 99, 101–7; as
a logical pragmatist, 48, 53, 77;
Logik der Forschung, 22–3, 59, 69,
96–7, 100; on the maieutic art
of criticism, 85; on man, the dignity
of, 50, 63; on Mannheim, 25, 102,
108, 119, 120–35; on Marx, 104,
126, 153; on Marxism, 90, 96, 102,
110, 122, 143, 155; on metaphysical ideas, 56; his metaphysical pluralism, 67; and the metaphysics
of orderly growth, viii, x, 8, 27, 46–